武汉体育学院青年教师科研基金项目（2014QZ04） 资助

TIYU SANWEI ZHANSHI JISHU:
YI TAIJIQUAN JIAOHU PINGTAI WEILI

体育三维展示技术：
以太极拳交互平台为例

周彤 ◎ 著

中国地质大学出版社
ZHONGGUO DIZHI DAXUE CHUBANSHE

图书在版编目(CIP)数据

体育三维展示技术:以太极拳交互平台为例/周彤著. —武汉:中国地质大学出版社,2016.12
ISBN 978-7-5625-3851-6

Ⅰ.①体…
Ⅱ.①周…
Ⅲ.①三维动画软件-应用-武术-套路(武术)
Ⅳ.①TP391.41②G852.019-39

中国版本图书馆 CIP 数据核字(2016)第 284196 号

体育三维展示技术:以太极拳交互平台为例	周 彤 著
责任编辑:段连秀 彭钰会　　策划编辑:段连秀	责任校对:张咏梅

出版发行:中国地质大学出版社(武汉市洪山区鲁磨路388号)	邮政编码:430074
电　话:(027)67883511　　传真:67883580	E-mail:cbb@cug.edu.cn
经　销:全国新华书店	http://www.cugp.cug.edu.cn
开本:787毫米×1092毫米 1/16	字数:330千字　印张:13
版次:2016年12月第1版	印次:2016年12月第1次印刷
印刷:武汉教文印刷厂	印数:1—1000册
ISBN 978-7-5625-3851-6	定价:45.00元

如有印装质量问题请与印刷厂联系调换

我们处于一个信息表现形式多样化的时代,多媒体技术的创新正挑战着我们传统的信息传播方式。体育领域也需要新技术的渗入,如何利用多媒体技术辅助传统体育教学和训练,是众多体育组织和单位面临的共同问题。而这个问题的解决又依赖两方面的技术:一是对体育的专业技术要求,特别是对技术动作的表现方式和教学方法的运用;二是能将技术动作进行数字化处理,并能通过多种平台进行展示。因此,寻求一个合理可靠的体育多媒体展示解决方案是目前体育领域的热点与重点。

一、为什么要选择太极拳?

体育运动项目数量庞大,我们目前还没有能力将所有的体育项目技术动作进行数字化处理。鉴于以下原因,我们选择太极拳作为本课题的研究对象。

(1)太极拳是我国民族传统文化重要的组成部分,由于其起源和发展中融入了中国的文化内涵和哲学思想,成为最能体现中国传统思想文化的拳术。太极拳在国内有着广泛的群众基础,伴随中国改革开放的不断推进,太极拳在国外也已不断推广和普及,深受国内外武术爱好者的喜爱。

(2)太极拳运动对环境的要求不高,在面积不大的空间即可完成整套动作,这为数字化采集工作带来了极大的便利,同时由于技术动作的特点是"刚柔相济,快慢相间",也将大大提高动作捕捉的精度和准确度。

(3)科技的发展改变了人们认识事物的传统方式,人们更希望愉快地学习,动作捕捉技术的成熟与应用,使人们与计算机的交互有了新的选择,传统的教授和学习太极拳的方式已很难再满足人们的需求。

二、本书有什么内容？

本书试图介绍新的交互技术和方法，为体育技术动作的学习和研究提出新的思路和解决方案。全书共分5章。第一章是对太极拳的起源及发展的介绍，旨在说明太极拳数字化保护是目前太极拳发展的必然趋势；第二章是对人体模型建模技术、骨骼绑定技术和运动控制方法进行理论介绍，使读者对人体运动仿真技术的研究内容和方向有所认识；第三章是在经过大量文献资料查阅的基础上，综合各方观点对太极拳技术动作从影响关节和生物力学两个方面进行动作分析；第四章是对本研究成果之一的软件平台所需开发技术进行介绍，包括展示平台所需的主要开发引擎 Unity 3D、人体模型的搭建以及蒙皮绑定工具 3ds Max 和人机互动所需的 Kinect 设备及其开发技术等方面的介绍；第五章是对本课题设计平台的创建过程，以及模型创建和太极拳数字化采集过程进行详细说明，并将本平台核心程序代码进行了说明。

三、致谢

本书的研究工作得到了武汉体育学院青年教师科研基金的资助。在此笔者要感谢同仁们的帮助和支持；感谢中国地质大学出版社为本书出版付出的辛勤劳动。书中有部分内容参考了有关单位或个人的研究成果，均已在参考文献中列出，在此一并致谢。

由于本书追求的目标是介绍当前较新的技术和方法，这给撰写本书增加了难度，鉴于笔者水平有限，虽几经改稿，书中错误和不足之处在所难免，欢迎广大读者不吝赐教。

周 彤
2016 年 10 月

目录

第一章 太极拳教学发展现状 (1)

第一节 太极拳运动发展简史 (1)

第二节 太极拳运动特点 (2)

第三节 太极拳的发展瓶颈 (3)

第四节 展望未来 (3)

第二章 人体运动仿真技术现状 (6)

第一节 人体运动仿真的应用领域 (6)

第二节 计算机模拟人体运动的关键技术 (6)

一、人体模型构建技术 (6)

二、骨骼与皮肤绑定技术 (8)

三、运动控制方法 (10)

四、运动捕捉技术 (12)

第三章 太极拳动作分析 (13)

第一节 受影响关节分析 (13)

一、太极拳的基本动作 (13)

二、以二十四式太极拳作为代表性的研究对象 (14)

三、二十四式太极拳动作中各主要关节部位的活跃情况 (14)

第二节 生物力学角度分析 (17)

第四章 开发平台应用技术介绍 ……………………………………………（20）

第一节 Unity3D ………………………………………………………（20）
第二节 3ds Max 建模技术 ……………………………………………（20）
  一、基础建模 …………………………………………………………（20）
  二、高级建模 …………………………………………………………（21）
第三节 Kinect 开发技术 ………………………………………………（22）
  一、Kinect 设备硬件结构 ……………………………………………（22）
  二、Kinect for Windows SDK 简介 …………………………………（23）
  三、Kinect 骨骼追踪技术 ……………………………………………（24）

第五章 平台设计与实现 ………………………………………………（32）

第一节 平台设计 ………………………………………………………（32）
  一、设计思想 …………………………………………………………（32）
  二、设计目标与原则 …………………………………………………（32）
  三、系统的总体结构 …………………………………………………（32）
  四、技术路线 …………………………………………………………（34）
  五、接口设计 …………………………………………………………（34）
第二节 平台实现 ………………………………………………………（39）
  一、专业太极拳运动数据的采集 ……………………………………（39）
  二、人体模型的建立 …………………………………………………（41）
  三、脚本编写 …………………………………………………………（58）
  四、太极拳学习-反馈功能模块实现 ………………………………（192）

参考文献 …………………………………………………………………（200）

第一章　太极拳教学发展现状

第一节　太极拳运动发展简史

1. 起源

太极拳是我国优秀文化之一，是中华武术的一大瑰宝。"太极"二字是我国古代哲学的一个基本概念，是对事物生成发展的一种状态表达，在"太极"之前的状态即为"无极"，无极即混沌一气，太极即在"一气"的基础上发展出了"阴阳二气"，即事物的对立状态。众所周知，太极拳是一种刚柔并进、动静结合的拳术。长期以来，关于它的起源有很多版本，归纳起来有以下两种说法。

(1)"张三丰创太极拳说"。在李兆生的《中国太极拳统真大典卷一》中提出：太极功是武当派的张三丰创造的一种动功，按其风格分析，太极拳是属于武当派的内家拳。

(2)20世纪30年代初由唐豪提出的"陈王廷创太极拳说"。在程峰的《太极拳起源问题的再探讨》中，以河南博爱唐村千载寺的碑文资料和新近发现的康熙五十五年所修的唐村《李氏家谱》为依据，河南博爱唐村千载寺应为太极拳的发源地，唐十力和尚应为太极拳的鼻祖，李仲、李信和陈王廷同为太极拳的创始人。

第一种说法带有很强的主观色彩和历史背景；第二种说法是从技术角度分析太极拳技术动作而得出的结论，具有一定的学术价值，并且唐豪通过对太极拳研究发现，明代戚继光《纪效新书》中"拳经三十二势"拳法对明清陈家沟和赵堡等地拳法及太极拳技术产生与发展具有重要的影响。

不可否认的是，当前盛行的陈氏太极拳是结合"太极""阴阳""五行"等中国古代哲学理论，由河南温县陈家沟的陈氏家族第九世陈王廷总结自己多年"披坚执锐"的实践经验，并吸收和借鉴了明代戚继光和程冲斗等著名武术家创立的武术套路而形成，并在此基础上不断推陈出新、发扬光大。

2. 发展

自明末清初，陈氏第九世传人陈王廷创建太极拳后，18世纪20~60年代，为了适应不同学习对象和不同的保健需要，相继出现了陈有本在老架基础上编成的陈氏新架太极拳，陈有本的弟子陈青萍又在此基础上创编的赵堡架和忽雷架。随后，河南省陈家沟陈氏拳械的第一位外姓传人杨露禅删改陈氏老架，创编成架式宽舒、动作圆润的"绵拳"架，并于1881年由李亦编定为《太极拳谱》。

此后，由杨露禅编传的"绵拳架"，经其子杨健候和其孙杨澄甫修润定型为后世广为流传的杨式太极拳套路。河北省武清（今属天津）人李瑞东以从王兰亭学得的"杨式"搬拦锤、肘底锤、撇身锤、指裆锤、栽锤等五锤为基础，编成"太极五星椎"（今被称为李式太极拳）。民国初年，李亦之徒郝为真在北京传授武禹襄创编的武式太极拳。河北完县人孙禄堂得郝为真的传授，并在此基础上融会形意拳和八卦掌技法，创编成孙式太极拳。河北大兴人吴鉴泉将其父吴全佑的杨式拳架作了删难就简、突出轻柔的整理，创编成吴式太极拳。1928年，陈长兴的曾孙陈发科到北京传授陈式老架太极拳。当时，年近古稀的和兆元长孙和庆喜开门授徒，其弟子郑伯英和郑悟清迁居西安致力传拳，为"和式太极拳"在西北的传播打下基础。太极拳苑出现了分支迅速、流派繁衍的景象。

太极拳作为一种民族传统文化，具有一定的动态性和可变性，受到社会政治、经济、文化等各方面的影响。面对以市场经济为中心的改革大潮，武术同许多体育项目一样也遇到如何转型、如何适应、如何生存的问题。

竞技太极拳是太极拳发展的重要方向。改革开放以来，随着太极拳比赛在各种全国性的武术观摩交流评奖的竞赛活动中出现，在全国挖掘整理了许多太极拳流派，使之迅速得到了不同程度的普及和发展。又相继创编了陈氏、杨氏、吴氏、孙氏、武氏太极拳竞赛套路，为适应国际比赛又创编了四十二式太极拳和四十二式太极剑竞赛套路，还对太极推手进行研究整理，并出版了《太极推手竞赛规则》，极大地丰富了太极拳竞赛的内容，为太极拳的进一步普及、推广及竞赛创造了条件，太极拳竞赛随之兴盛起来。

太极拳是文化拳，它是凝聚着东方文化智慧的结晶，它融健身、防身、修身、养性、娱乐为一体，主张内外兼修，养性和健身并举。作为中国传统文化的杰出代表，在历经了三百余年的演变发展后，它已不是一项单纯意义上的体育运动。21世纪是人类注重自我保健的世纪，而自我保健，是心态健康和身体健康的统一。要想实现这两个健康的有机统一，首选的当属太极拳运动。为什么要首选它？这是由它的文化内涵和特殊的功能所决定的。

第二节　太极拳运动特点

1. 体松心静

体松心静是太极拳的重要特点之一。体松是指练拳时，在维持动作姿势的基础上，尽量使身体肌肉处于放松状态，要求动作自然舒展，不用僵力，腿部在运动时经常是半弯曲的，肌肉必须用力，但在两腿交替支撑体重时，负重腿仍然要放松。心静是指要排除一切杂念，注意力集中。

2. 缓慢柔和

缓慢柔和也是太极拳的重要特点之一。一套太极拳一般要求在5～10分钟内完成。缓慢还包含连贯，各拳式之间不得停顿，应做到连绵不断。缓慢的前提是放松，在此基础上使两臂动作姿势及运动路线都保持弧形。

3. 动作、呼吸和意念相配合

练太极拳到一定程度要把动作、呼吸和意念配合起来，这样才能表现出太极拳的特点，才能取得较好的锻炼效果。一方面是动作与呼吸的配合，太极拳的技术动作是由起落开合动作组成的,要求起(向上)的动作要吸气,落的动作要呼气;开(两臂张开)时为吸,合时为呼。无论哪种呼气方式都应求其自然。另一方面是动作与意念的配合,在练拳时首先要排除杂念,把注意力集中到动作的运动过程中,以意识引导动作,做到"意领身随"。

第三节 太极拳的发展瓶颈

1. 太极拳人才流失严重,拳师匮乏,资质参差不齐

在陈家沟被誉为"四大金刚"的拳师中,陈小旺定居澳大利亚,陈正雷工作在郑州,朱天才在新加坡,王西安在温县教拳。还有近千名拳师散布于国内外,各自为战,小打小闹,仅满足于养家糊口。特别是在国外教拳,每小时可收入100美元的学费,高收入诱惑着许多拳师把未来的发展定位于国外。即便是在世界各地授拳的拳师,也都各自为政;缘于门户间隔,互相之间缺乏协作。在目前普及的太极拳中,有很多的指导员或教练员,没有经过系统的专业训练和培训,使得太极拳练习者得不到正规的指导,动作不规范、技术不正确,等等,造成在练习过程中很多不应有的伤害屡屡发生。太极拳专业人才的匮乏和奇缺不仅影响其普及的质量、规模和速度,而且还严重影响了太极拳所蕴藏理论体系价值的发掘。

2. 基础设施建设相对落后,配套工程的规模较小、档次和起点较低

国家已经授予焦作"太极圣地""中华武术太极拳发源地"的称号,可以作为太极拳发展的核心圣地,但陈家沟以及太极拳相关场馆的规划开发与其"世界级品牌"的地位还不匹配,相当一部分太极拳学校的规模和档次无法满足太极拳产业快速发展的需要。部分太极拳商标、产品等还局限于少数太极大师家族式的经营,虽然有一定的号召力,但距离产业化相去甚远。

3. 太极拳产品品牌繁杂,相关产业没有集团化、规模化

现有的太极拳相关产品品牌分散、孤立,各个流派的太极拳馆和生产厂家各自为战,多是以个人名义出现,形不成规模,缺乏高知名度的国际化大品牌,无法满足世界范围内对太极文化和相关产品的需求。

4. 缺乏有组织的引导和管理,缺少权威认证,国际发展受限

尽管目前世界上已经有100多个国家成立了太极拳组织,但其自发性、随意性强,且相当一部分缺乏正规的引导和管理。在外国建立起陈氏太极拳组织后,能否在普及的基础上提高太极拳的运动水平,还缺少权威的太极拳协会或组织的认证和机制上的管理,在很大程度上限制了太极拳更快地国际化。

第四节 展望未来

太极拳同其他拳种一样,是融技击防卫、健身养生、艺术审美于一体的价值功能多元的统一体,而且由于太极拳在发展过程中结合导引术的内容,其健身养生效果可能优于其他任何一个拳种。

1. 太极拳分化发展之一:健身养生类太极拳

太极拳具有多种价值功能,人们既可以通过太极拳来增强防卫能力,又可以通过太极拳来健身养生,还可以用于表演,进行艺术审美。这是一个价值选择的问题,太极拳不会因为某些人仅仅选择其某方面功能而改变了其技击防卫之术的性质。太极拳与其他拳种相比,最明显的外在形式特点是具有以慢练为主的套路运动形式,而这种练习形式很适合普通大众特别是中老年人健身养生,所以,以老年群体为主的普通大众选择了太极拳的健身养生功能。太极拳技术体系中以慢练为特点的套路运动在 20 世纪武术的城市化发展进程中,在普通民众中得到了膨胀式发展。

如果说最初人们通过太极拳进行健身养生仅仅是价值选择问题,那时的太极拳套路还保持着原貌,仍然是太极拳技击防卫技术体系中的一个环节,那么当绝大多数习练者都以健身养生为目的,而对太极拳的技击不求甚解,并按其一知半解的理解再进行代代传授时,太极拳套路技术肯定会发生变化,其技术肯定会扭曲变形,特别是根据健身养生需要,对其进行有目的的改造以后。当太极拳套路已经发展成目前的老年拳时,就已由技击术领域跨入健身术领域。浙江大学教育学院王健教授、美国总统体质与竞技体育委员会科学顾问朱为模教授在他们的学术报告中都曾介绍:美国对太极拳健身的研究将超越中国,他们正以高度量化的实验数据,研究太极拳的哪些动作可以锻炼身体的哪些部位和哪种机能,从而更加科学合理地编排太极拳套路。这些经过有目的改造之后专门以健身养生标准编排的太极拳,已经与原生态的太极拳套路大相径庭,它们已经由技击术质变为健身术。

2. 太极拳分化发展之二:艺术表现类太极拳

对于一般大众而言,从艺术审美角度来看,除了以刚柔相济、快慢相间为特色的陈式太极拳套路以外,其他以一味的松、柔、慢为运动特点的太极拳套路存在先天性的外在审美不足。

以前的武术比赛,竞技武术套路裁判最头疼的就是太极拳比赛,即使安排两个运动员同时上场演练,也很累人,以致国际级武术裁判温力教授提出"太极拳不宜继续作为竞技武术比赛项目"的结论(崔周等,2012)。对于武术内行的裁判都如此,更何况对于一般大众。武术套路赛场上本来就少得可怜的观众在太极拳比赛时都纷纷离场,正说明了其审美严重不足的缺陷。究其原因,中国传统文化的主旨是以"刚健"为主导的刚柔相济。张岱年等总结了中国文化基本思想的四要素:刚健有为、和与中、崇德利用、天人协调,并指出这些以刚健有为的思想为纲(王若冰等,2014)。李泽厚在《美的历程》中也提到儒家美学列在首位的是"阳刚"之美,一味松、柔、慢显然不符合中国人的审美观。如果从提高整体协调能力、形成完整劲力或从健身养生角度出发,进行松柔练习确实是很好的途径,但是,从外在的艺术审美的角度来看,长拳太快,南拳太刚,杨式太极拳套路太慢、太柔,只有"如长江大海,滔滔不绝",以"快慢相间,刚柔相济"见长的初始形态的太极拳,最能体现中国文化特色,最符合中国人的审美要求。

为改变以往太极拳竞赛出现的不良局面,21 世纪的太极拳套路竞赛进行了深化改革。目前的竞技太极拳套路大多以陈式太极拳为蓝本进行艺术创作,并植入了腾空飞脚、外摆莲、旋风脚等速度快的腾空动作,或融入了形意、八卦等拳种的内容,从而使现在的太极拳竞赛套路发展成为一种刚柔相济、快慢相间的运动。这类新内容放在体育领域是难美表现型项目,放在艺术领域就是人体运动艺术。因此,这种改革符合了人们的审美需要,既得到了广大观众的认可,也得到了武术界专家的肯定。2007 年春晚节目《行云流水》演播后,很多体育专业同事感叹:"太极拳原来这么美呀!"在他们印象中大学里武术普修课学的二十四式太极拳是所有体育运动中最枯燥无味的内容,而《行云流水》所展示的太极拳与之形成鲜明对比,感叹由此而发。对这种新生太极拳的赞美绝非个例,在本课题调研过程中还有大批太极拳健身的习练者对此赞不绝口,认为这是太极拳表演的最高境界。郭志禹教授甚至将其称为"太极拳的新文化现象",并将其发明创造因素提炼总结为:"跳跃难度古不见,直落直起稳如钉;运劲刚柔快且匀,难落缓起势又承;诸动肘靠多攻防,各式荟萃融一炉;音配拳套势谐韵,陈式风格适少年"四方面(朱晓东等,2009),这是从专业角度很有战略眼光和深邃思想见地的陈述。

以21世纪新生竞技太极拳套路的形成为起点,一个新的太极拳分支已经初步形成。如果说这类太极拳仍属于技击术范畴,显然不合适,因为人们已经根据艺术审美的需要对其进行了有目的的改造,而且这类太极拳基本上失去了技击防卫的功能。经过一个从量变到质变的发展过程,这类太极拳迟早将跨入艺术范畴,成为人体运动艺术的新奇葩。

3. 太极拳分化发展之三:技击防卫类太极拳

曾有学者产生疑问:原生态的太极拳就属于技击防卫之术,还何谈现代化分化?之所以提出技击防卫类太极拳的现代化分化,是因为原生态的太极拳已经不适合当今大多数习武者对太极拳技击防卫的实际需求。原生态的太极拳虽然具有"以静制动,以柔克刚,以弱胜强,以小搏大,以老搏壮"等逆向思维特点的高级技击思想,但是,"太极十年磨一剑""太极十年不出功"的特点又令很多习武者望而却步。源于西方的现代文化是一种"快餐式"文化,本来快节奏的现代生活已经使当代人整日为生活疲于奔波,承受着巨大的精神压力,在这种状况下,有多少意欲学习技击防卫者还有时间去"十年磨一剑"?韩国的跆拳道在对外推广过程中正是摒弃了很多陈旧内容,形成了由几种简洁腿法组成的"快餐式"技术,才逐渐风靡世界,并占领了中国市场,将中国武术"踢"出都市时尚。太极拳技击要想满足绝大多数现代人的需求,也必须精简内容,从丰富多彩的技法中提炼出最核心的技术,形成一个简洁明了的现代太极拳技击防卫技术体系,唯此,才能得到大面积推广普及。

现代太极推手比赛的运动员很多没有练习太极拳套路的基础,虽然其技法难以上升到更高的层次,但是这种省略了很多内容的"快餐式"技法,却是太极拳技击现代化发展的一个新尝试,如果将其推广开来,也许能满足大多数习武者对太极拳技击的实际需求。太极推手已经开始了现代化发展的尝试,太极散手呢?传统的太极拳技术体系中不乏对付拳腿等击打型进攻技法的技术,只有这类技法才更能真正体现太极拳"以柔克刚"的特点,应该将这些典型的技法挖掘提炼出来,形成一个适应现代人需要的简洁明了的太极拳技击防卫技术体系,从而形成太极拳现代化发展的另一个新分支。

第二章 人体运动仿真技术现状

人体运动仿真是计算机科学、生物力学和机器人学等学科交叉研究领域,其目的是在计算机中建立人体模型并模拟真实自然条件下的人体运动。本章首先介绍人体运动仿真的起源与典型应用,之后着重介绍计算机模拟人体运动所需的关键技术。

第一节 人体运动仿真的应用领域

在生物力学领域,科学家通过对人体运动的量化分析,使建立人体仿真模型成为可能。科学家们利用基于惯性和光学的运动捕捉设备对人体动作进行较为精准的定量分析。

在机器人领域,科学家在生物力学领域的研究基础上设计物理控制器,并将物理控制器的运动行为和稳定性同真实人体运动进行比较分析,设计出高效、稳定的类人机器人控制系统。

在计算机科学领域,科学家们以人体运动生物力学、机器人学的已有研究成果为基础,研究通过计算机在虚拟环境中模拟逼真人体各个部位的运动。

第二节 计算机模拟人体运动的关键技术

一、人体模型构建技术

人体是一个极为复杂的生物体,因此在人体运动仿真研究中需要将人体作某种程度的抽象。这种抽象既要尽可能反映人体的真实情况,又要易于实现。三维人体的建模方法很多,有实体建模、曲面建模、线框建模和基于物理建模。

1. 实体建模

实体建模可对三维人体的实心部分进行表达,从而使得三维人体得到无二义性描述,并且实体建模方法提供了人体几乎所有的几何和拓扑信息。

实体造型是采用实体建模的方法对人体建模。目前,实体建模系统中对人体的表达方式主要有 3 种。

(1)基于体素分解的表达方法。该方法能描述模型内部属性,如密度、材料等。体素化(Voxelization)是将物体的表面几何形式表示转换成最接近该物体的体素表示形式,产生体素数据集(Volume Datasets),其不仅包含模型的表面信息,而且能描述模型内部属性。体素(Voxel)可以理解为二维像素在三维空间的推广,它们是一组分布在正交网格中心的立方体单元。体素表达法可将复杂的人体层层分解,分解后的复杂人体可表示成一棵八叉树。

该方法简单易行,但对人体的表达只是近似,因而很难反映出人体的宏观几何特征,并且由于体素间的集合运算涉及大量面与面之间的交贯运算,难免出现奇异的情况,有时由于计算精度有限而带来的几何数据误差,还会造成体素之间拓扑关系的紊乱,从而使运算不能进行下去。因此在实际应用中会受到很大的限制。

(2)构造实体几何。它是以立方体、球体、圆柱体、椎体、楔形体等基本体为基本元素,通过交、并、差等布尔运算表达复杂人体外形,该表达方法可以用一棵二叉树描述。这些几何形体具有完整的几何信息,是真实而且唯一的三维实体。

构造几何表达方法可以清晰地表达复杂人体的构造过程,直观地描述人体的宏观几何特点。但是该表达方法存在着多种构造人体的表达方案,表示的人体模型也不够逼真,很难表示人体的动态特性。同样,由于存在集合运算,因此其计算量大,计算稳定性差。

(3)多面体建模。它是从构造多面体开始,对多面体的任意一个面、棱边、顶点进行局部修改,从而构造一个与实体外形相似的多面体(即基本立体),然后通过类似于磨光的处理,自动产生自由曲面的控制顶点,并拼接成所需的形状。它是一种根据设计者的构思来进行局部处理并生成人体模型的方法。用多面体建模可以灵活地进行人体形状设计。

2. 曲面建模

点曲线以及点曲面是曲面建模法中的基础元素,通过它们来构建物体的主要或大部分曲面,经过过渡、链接断裂、切分等修改变形方式,最终建立出所需的对象模型。

NURBS 建模的曲线并不依靠表面光滑的手段。该方法可以通过参数赋值或者手工绘制获得建模对象的边缘曲线,所以模型曲面曲率以及弧度等各方面在很大程度上可以保障其精确性。并且,由于使用曲面来进行建模,有效地减少了模型的固有面数,使得计算得到了精简,同时也达到了模型在建立后优化程度就很高的目的。

1971 年法国 Rneuat 汽车公司的 Bezier 正式发表了一种通过控制多边形来定义曲线的方法,这种方法使设计人员只需移动控制顶点就可以方便地修改曲线的形状,而且形状的变化完全在预料之中,因而得到了广泛的应用,最初的三维人体模型就采用了 Bezier 曲面模型,但是 Bezier 方法不具有局部特性,在设计复杂的人体曲面的过程中,存在着拼接方面的困难。为了解决 Bezier 方法局部修改的问题,Gordon 和 Riesenfeld 对 Bezier 方法进行了改进,用 B 样条函数代替 Bernstein 基函数,B 样条方法不但继承了 Bezier 方法的优点,而且还具有独特的局部特性,使得设计者能方便地对 B 样条曲线曲面进行修改。

使用曲面模型的方法对人体建模时,曲面模型能提供三维人体的表面信息,并进行隐藏线消除和真实感三维人体模型显示。但曲面模型方法也存在着缺陷,由于没有明确定义三维人体的实心部分,因此曲面建模方法不能进行剖面操作。

3. 线框建模

客观物可以被看作是三维空间中线段的集合,而三维物体的形状可以用其轮廓边来进行描述。对于平面立体,可由轮廓边直接构成;对于曲面立体,则可用一些线框围成。线框建模是采用点、直线、圆弧、样条曲线等构造三维物体的图形表示技术。它是计算机图形学 CADC/MA 领域中最早用来表示形体的模型,并且至今仍在广泛应用。线框建模只用点、线的信息表示一个形体,数据量少,定义过程简单,符合人们打样的习惯。很多复杂的形体设计往往先用样条勾画出基本轮廓,然后逐步细化。线框建模的数据存储量少,对其编辑、修改非常快。使用线框建模的方法对人体建模时，它是将人体轮廓用线框图形和关节表示，由于包含的信息有限，因此该建模方法在对人体建模时不能够无二义性地表达三维人体，也无法实现三维人体模型的自动消隐及真实感人体模型显示，与曲面建模方法一样无法进行剖面操作。

4. 基于物理的建模技术

由于人体模型庞大的自由度与复杂的运动链结构，人体模型的运动控制技术与机器人系统相比难度要高得多。基于物理的建模技术是考虑物体的物理属性如质量、弹性以及摩擦力，当物体与环境发生接触或受到外力作用时，综合利用运动学、动力学、机器人学、物理学和生物力学等前沿学科技术，基于物理的人体运动建模与仿真技术能逼真模拟各种物理现象。通过物理的建模技术建立的人体模型能处理各种复杂运动学模型，能生成逼真自然的人体运动，这是传统的人体运动建模与仿真技术所无法比拟的。

二、骨骼与皮肤绑定技术

骨骼与皮肤绑定技术主要解决的问题是使用运动数据驱动人体模型，得到骨骼动画。由于模型变形不当会产生失真，提高模型变形真实感和动画实时性就是绑定技术的目标，而骨骼与皮肤绑定技术的核心就是蒙皮算法。

蒙皮算法按大类可分为刚性绑定算法和柔性绑定算法，其中刚性绑定算法是最早出现的骨骼皮肤绑定算法，刚性绑定算法的计算和绑定比较简单，皮肤和顶点分别是一对一控制的，但缺点就是因为模型的整个皮肤网格由许多个分段的皮肤网格构成，由于各个皮肤网格之间缺乏自然的连接，皮肤变形时关节的连接处会不平滑，产生穿透和断裂等问题，使模型运动时真实感不强，为了解决这一问题，引入了柔性绑定思想，即由多个关节位置来确定最终的皮肤点的位置。

1. 刚性绑定算法

动画数据中不再像顶点动画中由每帧的皮肤点数据组成，而是由骨骼、分段皮肤网格和骨骼运动数据组成。由于用骨骼承载运动，对动画的控制不再是皮肤点信息，而是转化为对底层的骨骼数据、骨骼皮肤关系及绑定算法的控制，控制层次得到提高。

刚性绑定的公式为：

$$V' = \boldsymbol{M}_i \boldsymbol{L}_i V$$

其中，V 表示顶点变换前世界坐标系下的坐标。V 经过矩阵 $\boldsymbol{L}_i$ 转换成从皮肤顶点初始位置到相关联的那个关节初始位置的位移矢量，再经过骨骼的绝对转换矩阵 $\boldsymbol{M}_i$，得到世界坐标系下皮肤顶点的新位置 V'。

2. 线性混合蒙皮算法

线性混合蒙皮算法的主要内容是将皮肤顶点进行线性混合计算，得到新顶点的位置。该算法简单易实现，对硬件要求不高，是目前应用最多的蒙皮算法。不过由于该算法是简单的线性计算，未充分考虑现实情况下皮下脂肪对人体的影响，因而无法很好地保持皮肤的体积，在关节旋转较大的地方容易出现皮肤塌陷和"裹糖纸"现象。由于线性混合蒙皮算法的广泛应用，有许多研究集中于如何改进或克服该算法中的皮肤失真现象。

3. 点绑定算法

为了解决刚性绑定在关节处的失真问题，就产生了点绑定（Vertxe Blending）算法。从直觉的角度也可以发现这个算法比刚性绑定更符合实际。

点绑定算法虽然有很多的优点,但还存在如下缺陷:①弯曲时关节部位皮肤塌陷;②自转时关节部位的皮肤打结。这两个问题主要是因为点绑定过程中没有考虑到皮肤点本身的拓扑关系,也没有在算法中保持皮肤的体积造成的。

4. 添加骨骼链绑定算法

为了对点绑定算法的缺点进行改进,提高点绑定动画效果的真实感,骨骼链绑定算法对点绑定算法进行了改进,在此算法的基础上发现皮肤变形失真的直接原因在于关节运动角度过大(超过 60°)。

为了减小关节旋转角度可以增加一段骨骼,由骨骼链本身的拓扑结构决定:每个关节变化角度将减半,如果添加一条骨骼链(由几段骨骼组成),则可以更好地平滑角度。所以在超过 60°安全角度(安全角度即点绑定算法不易失真的角度)的关节处增加骨骼链,可以将所有关节角度控制在安全范围内,在运动幅度大的关节处将获得比点绑定更好的效果。

添加骨骼链绑定算法的缺点主要有:①添加骨骼链的过程会破坏原始骨骼的拓扑结构,骨骼链添加完成后需要重新绑定皮肤;②绑定算法复杂化,由于骨骼数量(骨骼的运动数据)与添加关节链后的骨骼数量不一致,需要进行运动重定向操作;③骨骼添加的数量和位置均由操作者人为指定,绑定过程复杂化,操作难度增大。

5. 骨粒串绑定算法

通过对骨骼链绑定算法进行拓展,将骨骼链的数量提高,当使得皮肤对单个骨粒的绑定可以退化为刚性绑定时,就得到了骨粒串绑定算法。骨粒串算法延续了添加骨骼链算法的思想,但通过拓展,使得关节旋转角度被 N 等分(N 为关节处的骨骼粒数目),皮肤变形效果理论上可以得到最好的改善,因为骨骼关节处的变形角度足够小;而且由于骨骼数量足够多,所有的皮肤与骨骼之间的绑定都退化为刚性绑定,算法也简单了。

但是,因为骨粒串算法是对添加骨骼链算法的扩展,所以它也将添加骨骼链算法的缺点进行了扩展:①对 N 个骨粒进行控制比骨骼链算法操作更加繁琐,也增加了其他绑定过程的复杂度;②由于不可能一步到位地得到骨粒的运动数据,所以不论在何种情况下都需要进行运动重定向操作;③由于在绑定之前不易确定骨粒的数量,上面使用的 N 值本身也不容易得到。

6. 骨骼绑定算法

通过对骨骼皮肤绑定过程的深入分析,将绑定中插值计算提前,即对变换矩阵进行插值,由于关节链结构中的变换为旋转变换,所以骨骼绑定算法对旋转进行插值操作。这样得到的算法就是骨骼绑定算法,它是骨骼皮肤动画发展中一个新的起点(类似于光照模型中的 Phong 模型对法向量进行插值计算)。

骨骼绑定算法的本质在于关节的旋转角度不再进行等分操作(骨骼链算法的手段),而是根据皮肤点与关节的关联权值计算皮肤点对应的旋转角度(旋转变换),然后利用这个角度计算得到皮肤点的真实位置。由于不再对结果点的位置进行插值,将保持皮肤的体积,解决点绑定中皮肤塌陷和打结的缺点,极大地改进了绑定效果。

骨骼绑定算法的不足不再是绑定效果方面,而是由于进行旋转插值方面,使用四元数进行插值操作的时间复杂度很高、实时性差成为影响该算法广泛应用的原因。

7. 加速的骨骼绑定算法

针对骨骼绑定算法中四元数插值时间复杂度高的缺点，Kvana 提出了一个改进的算法，用四元数线性插值代替四元数球面线性插值（使用 QLERP 代替 SLE 对），这种方法的思想即使用替代算法，但引入了计算误差。

8. 其他绑定算法

在骨骼皮肤绑定算法发展的过程中，产生了很多不同的绑定思想和对原有算法的改进策略，主要包括对 Vertxe Blending 算法效果的改进、对绑定关系设置方法的改进两个方面。另外还有很多算法打破了过去的流程，从皮肤模型反算对应关系、反算绑定权值直到反算整个骨骼结构，再使用运动数据驱动皮肤模型得到骨骼皮肤动画，在这个过程中骨骼的实际意义也越来越少了。

三、运动控制方法

作为虚拟环境中重要特征之一的虚拟人动画，目前国内外主要的运动控制方法包括：关键帧法、正逆向运动学法、动力学约束法、过程控制法、基于运动捕获数据法等。

1. 关键帧法

最早研究虚拟人运动控制的方法——关键帧法，源于早期迪士尼公司制作的卡通动画。它的制作思路是首先由高级动画师手工设置人体运动序列中的关键姿态画面（即关键帧），由助理动画师运用一些常规的插值方法（比如三次样条插值）进行中间帧画面的设置，从而得到一个运动的序列。早期的关键帧技术仅仅用于图形间的插值，后来该技术发展成一切影响画面的参数都可以作为关键帧插值的对象，因此也叫作参数关键帧。它是一种三维的生成虚拟人体运动的方法，区别于传统的二维画面关键帧设计法，其依据的原理是根据两个关键帧之间的时间差值进行中间帧插值计算，获得相对应时间的虚拟人动画数据，这是计算机三维卡通动画中最基础的且应用最广泛的方法。但是其占用内存空间大、费时费力，且插值计算时容易发生扭曲变形。

2. 正逆向运动学法（Kinematics）

运动学控制方法是通过计算运动学约束生成动画的方法，主要分为正向运动学和逆向运动学，由于人体骨骼结构可以被看作是层级的关节链模型，故虚拟人体的运动可以运用正向或逆向运动学技术来控制，其中正向运动学主要是通过设定人体各个关节的旋转角来获得人体在特定时刻的位置和转角，从而生成动画的技术。以图 2-1 为例，假设向量：

$$q = (q_1, q_2, \cdots, q_n)$$

它表明了人体全部关节的自由度，根据此向量关系 $x = f(q)$ 就可以唯一确定出该末端效应器的位置 X。但是在求解与确定一切运动关节点的运动位置时，往往需要一一求解关节链上的关节点，工作量很大，且运动的效果也难以保证。

逆向运动学控制方法则与正向的求解思维恰恰相反，它的基本原理是用户根据末端效应器的位置运用 Badler 等提出的逆向运动学求解算法求解出关节链中每个关节点的位置和方向。它在一定程度上减少了正向存在的繁琐问题，大大减轻了用户的工作量，它在人体动画的交互式设计和自动生成算法中获得了广泛应用。以图 2-1 为例，指定末端效应器的位置 X，

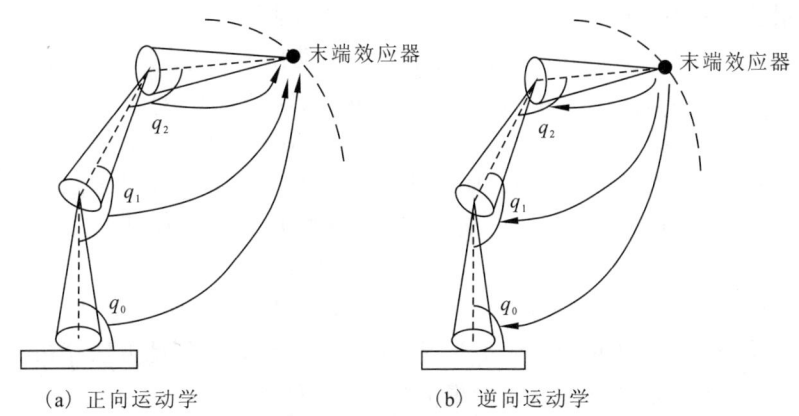

(a) 正向运动学 (b) 逆向运动学

图 2-1 运动控制方法

通过 $q=f^{-1}(x)$ 反向求解得到所有关节的自由度 q。对于自由度数超过 6 个的人体关节链,仅仅靠指定关节链末端效应器的位置与方向无法求解出整个关节链的信息,需要添加其他的约束条件来得到唯一解。最终运动效果的真实性,往往取决于所选择的约束条件,并且随着关节复杂度的增加,逆向运动学的复杂度与求解代价也会随之急剧增加。

3. 动力学约束法

人体的运动在一定程度上遵循某些物理定律,动力学方法的思想就是以物理学中的力为中心,主要研究人体各部分所承受的力与力矩,运用牛顿三大定律计算出它们的运动速度和加速度,从而得到它们运动的轨迹,就可以确定人体在下一个时刻的运动姿态。

比起运动学方法,采用动力学的方法控制人体的运动可以体现出运动的真实性,且符合人体运动的物理规律,但是由于人体骨骼和骨骼上肌肉组织的运动比较复杂,使得模型的计算也就非常复杂,需要进行大量的计算,这就使得其控制起来相当的复杂。

4. 过程控制法

过程动画是指用一个过程对动画中物体的形变或运动进行描述。以柔性物体动画来说,物体的形状是可以任意改变的,动画师可以对其进行任意的调控,而且动画中物体的形变都是建立在一定的数学模型或物理规律基础之上的。比如,雨水降落、雪花随风飘动就是用数学模型控制的比较简单的过程动画,较之复杂的动画就不仅仅是包含物体的形变,还包括动力学、碰撞检测等。此方法的优点是能够根据人体的特征和运动特征确定出人体的运动,逼真性很好,而且易于控制,可以生成实时的运动。除此之外,过程动画还能产生粒子与群体动画。在一些迪士尼的动画片中,过程动画技术被应用在大多数的群体场景中。但是,它也有一定的局限性,例如,它只在某些特定类型运动中适用,由于它自动生成的本质决定了角色动画缺乏独特性。

5. 基于运动捕获数据法

运动捕获(Motion Capture)技术目前在商业产品中是一种比较常用的动画技术,是目前具有较好效果的运动捕获数据的主要来源。它通过传感器跟踪设备直接记录运动实体关键点在三维空间的运动数据,并对其进行处理,得到不同时间、不同标志点在计量单位上的空间坐标,从而生成计算机动画,它为使用运动捕获数据生成动画提供了丰富的样本。运用这种方法,首先要使用设备捕捉演员的真实表演动作,随之将运动捕获数据映射到计算机生成的三维虚拟人体中,包括演员的各种动作与表情,每个演员的动作和表情记录成一组运动数据,然后在三维动画软件(Maya,3ds Max 等)中用这些运动捕获数据去驱动计算机中的三维虚拟人体模型,这样演员的动作和表情就可以在三维虚拟人体模型上体现出来,最终生成所需要的三维动画。它的优势在于记录的是真实的人体运动数据,包含有丰富的细节信息,因此产生的动画效果就会更好。但是,对于有些复杂的运动,需要对原始的运动捕获数据进行重新编辑与定向。

上述 5 种方法各有优缺点,相对而言,采用运动捕获的方法生成的运动不仅逼真而且生成效率高,采用运动编辑算法还可以实时地生成新的运动。但是采用此方法存在的主要问题有:①需要昂贵的运动捕获设备;②数据的采集主要是以人的动作为基础的,对应的也就只能应用在人体动画上。

四、运动捕捉技术

动作捕捉(Motion Capture,简称 Mocap)技术涉及尺寸测量、物理空间里物体的定位及方位测定等方面,其数据可以由计算机直接理解处理。在运动物体的关键部位设置跟踪器,由 Motion Capture 系统捕捉跟踪器位置,再经过计算机处理后得到三维空间坐标的数据。当数据被计算机识别后,可以应用在动画制作、步态分析、生物力学、人机工程等领域。

常用的运动捕捉技术从原理上可分为惯性式、光学式、声学式、电磁式。不同原理的设备各有其优缺点,一般可从以下几个方面进行评价:定位精度、实时性、使用方便程度、可捕捉运动范围大小、抗干扰性、多目标捕捉能力、与相应领域专业分析软件连接程度。

(1)惯性式:主要工作原理是在人体的主要关键点绑定惯性陀螺仪,分析陀螺仪的位移变差来判定人的动作幅度和距离。

(2)光学式:光学式运动捕捉是通过对目标上特定光点的监视和跟踪来完成运动捕捉的任务。目前常见的光学式运动捕捉大多基于计算机视觉原理。从理论上说,对于空间中的一个点,只要它能同时为两部相机所见,则根据同一时刻两部相机所拍摄的图像和相机参数,可以确定这一时刻该点在空间中的位置。当相机以足够高的速率连续拍摄时,从图像序列中就可以得到该点的运动轨迹。

(3)声学式:常用的声学式运动捕捉装置由发送器、接收器和处理单元组成。发送器是一个固定的超声波发生器,接收器一般由呈三角形排列的 3 个超声波探头组成。通过测量声波从发送器到接收器的时间或者相位差,系统可以计算并确定接收器的位置和方向。Logitech、SAC 等公司都生产超声波运动捕捉设备。

(4)电磁式:电磁式运动捕捉系统是目前比较常用的运动捕捉设备。一般由发射源、接收传感器和数据处理单元组成。发射源在空间产生按一定时空规律分布的电磁场,接收传感器(通常有 10~20 个)安置在表演者身体的关键位置,随着表演者的动作在电磁场中运动,通过电缆或无线方式与数据处理单元相连。

第三章 太极拳动作分析

在查阅大量文献资料之后,我们从影响关节和生物力学两个方面对太极拳动作进行了分析。

第一节 受影响关节分析

一、太极拳的基本动作

于涛(2013)在《基于动作捕捉的太极拳数字化保护研究》一文中指出,太极拳发展至今已经形成了诸多流派,但是不同流派的太极拳依然有着许多相通的地方。这些相通的部分也正是太极拳最基本、最核心的内容。

在太极拳中有着"十三势"的说法,即太极拳便是以"掤、捋、挤、按、采、挒、肘、靠"8种上肢动作以及"进、退、顾、盼、定"5种下肢步法为一体的武术拳法。这"十三势"也是太极拳在武术技击当中的基本动作。上肢的8种动作一般被称为"推手八法"。

1. 掤(péng,朋音)

它是一个太极拳专用字,意指向上向外之力。如对抗的双方搭手相贴,一方想要进攻,用手向前推进,而防守方则用劲力而将对方的力向上向外的引导,使得对方的劲力既不能向前直达自己的身体,又不能使其下降。总的来说,掤就是遇敌时以坚韧的劲力,采用捧托、架格、弹抖等技法使对方不能过于近身。

2. 捋(又作"履""挵"等)

捋是指先用双手以刚劲粘住对方进攻的手臂,放缓其进攻的速度,然后又以柔劲顺着对方原先进攻的劲势来回带、外拉。使对方原本集中的劲力偏散,进攻落空,进而导致对方立身不稳,下盘松动。

3. 挤

挤是用柔劲压住对方,贴住对方用于进攻的手脚,使得对方在发力的过程中始终受到挤压,无法施展开来。同时自己身体贴紧对方的重要部位,使其不能正常滑动,再猛然以刚强的劲力将对方击出。

4. 按

按是用手部动作,以纯柔之劲力压住对方的肩、肘、腕等关节部位,并随势而动,回转揉按,抑制阻断其劲路,最终使对方进攻失败的手法。

5. 采

采是用柔劲以抓、拿、掏、粘带等抓取方式来打击对方进攻的部位,使其进攻削弱,动作偏离。

6. 挒

在太极拳中,引导转移对方劲力还施其身,称之为挒。应用挒时,先是以刚劲承受架住对方的攻击,然后以柔劲通过划圆弧的方式改变劲力的方向,最后发还给对方。挒讲究的是先从人,后从己。

7. 肘

以肘击人成为肘,是指被敌抓拿或限制住时,以强刚之劲用肘贴住对方,用肘尖沉带对方将其击出的反制技法。

8. 靠

靠是肩、背或上臂向斜处发力,重心前倾地贴住对方的身体。在贴住的瞬间突然发力将对方轰出同时恢复自身重心的稳定。

"推手八法"结合八卦之理又可分成"四正"(掤、捋、挤、按)和"四隅"(采、挒、肘、靠)。下肢的5种步法又可称为五行,分属5个方位,太极术语的描述为"进为水,退为火,左顾木,右盼金,定之方中,土也。"

太极"十三势"很好地总结描述了太极拳的动作特点,其中也蕴含了中国传统五行八卦之说的深刻内涵。

二、以二十四式太极拳作为代表性的研究对象

二十四式太极拳是一种太极拳简易套路,也是一种健身拳术。1956年国家体委组织部分专家,在传统杨式太极拳的基础上,按由简入繁、循序渐进、易学易记的原则,去其繁难和重复动作,选取了二十四式,编成《简化太极拳》,即大家所熟知的二十四式太极拳。整个套路动作大约需要5分钟完成,非常适合日常练习。其中,主要动作有野马分鬃、搂膝拗步、倒卷肱、掤、捋、挤、按、单鞭、云手、左右蹬脚、独立、穿梭、海底针、闪通臂、搬拦锤等。

尽管只有24个动作,但相比传统的太极拳套路来讲,其内容更显精练,动作更显规范,并且也能充分体现太极拳的运动特点。二十四式太极拳动作鲜明,保留了传统太极拳中许多具有代表性的动作。其内容适中,手法步法完善,不包含难以理解和学习演练的太极拳高级动作。因此,具有典型代表性和一般普适性。

三、二十四式太极拳动作中各主要关节部位的活跃情况

人体的运动,从外形上看,大部分表现为人体关节的运动。为了将二十四式太极拳的动作清楚准确地复制到电脑中,必须清楚地知道哪些骨骼参与到运动中来。

本书将人体的主要关节部位分成以下9组(图3-1):

(1)头部——用于衡量头颈的活动强度。
(2)肩部——包含胸锁关节、肩锁关节和肩关节,用于衡量上肢躯干连接处的活动强度。
(3)肘部——肘关节手肘部位。
(4)腕部——双手手腕,包含桡腕关节、腕骨间关节、部分腕掌关节。
(5)手部——手掌手指,包括掌指关节、指骨间关节。
(6)腰部——腰身的动作,体现在脊柱的弯曲上。
(7)髋部——包括骶髂关节、髋关节。

图 3-1 人体的主要关节部位

(8)膝部——膝关节部分。

(9)足部——包括两脚踝关节以及两脚掌。

对于分组后的每个关节部位采用从 1～5 的 5 种程度来衡量其动作的活跃程度:1 表示没有活动;2 表示轻微的活动;3 表示有比较容易察觉的活动;4 表示有明显的活动;5 表示有剧烈快速的活动。

判断考虑一个分组的活动强度需要考虑该部位本身的最大活动范围以及该部位活动所包含信息的复杂程度。

经过学习太极拳与实际演练,得到如下关节部位活动情况评分表(表 3-1)。

表 3-1 关节部位活动情况评分表

动作编号	名称	头部	肩部	肘部	腕部	手部	腰部	髋部	膝部	足部
0	预备势	1	1	1	1	1	1	1	1	1
1	起势	1	3.75	3	2	2.25	2	2.75	3	2.25
2	左右野马分鬃	3	4	2.25	3	3	3	3	3.25	3.75
3	白鹤亮翅	2	4	2	2.5	2	3	2.25	4	3.5
4	左右搂膝拗步	2.75	4	3.25	3.75	3	3.25	3	3.75	3.25
5	手挥琵琶	2	3.75	3	3	4	2	2	4	3.75
6	左右倒卷肱	2.75	4.25	3.75	4.25	2.5	3.5	3	3	3
7	左揽雀尾	3	4	4	3.25	3	3.75	3.25	3	3

续表 3-1

动作编号	名称	头部	肩部	肘部	腕部	手部	腰部	髋部	膝部	足部
8	右揽雀尾	3	4	4	3.5	3	3.75	3.25	3	3
9	单鞭	2.75	3.5	3.5	4	4	2.75	3	2.75	3
10	云手	3	4	4	4.25	2	4	3	2.75	2.75
11	单鞭	3	4	3.5	4	4	3	3	2.75	3
12	高探马	2.75	3.75	3	3.75	4	3	3	3	2
13	右蹬脚	2	4	4.25	4	3.25	3.5	5	4.5	3.75
14	双峰贯耳	2.5	4.25	4	4	4.75	3	4	4	3
15	转身左蹬脚	2	4	3.75	4.25	3	3.25	4.75	4.5	3.75
16	左下势独立	3	4	3	4.75	4.75	3.75	4.75	4.25	3.5
17	右下势独立	3	4	3	4.75	4.75	4	4.75	4.25	3.5
18	左右穿梭	3.25	4	3.5	3.25	3	3.75	3	3	3
19	海底针	3	3.5	3	4	4	4	3.5	2.75	
20	闪通臂	2.75	3.5	3.25	2.25	2.25	3	3	3	2.25
21	转身搬拦捶	3	3.75	3	3	5	3.75	3	3.25	3
22	如封似闭	2	4	4	4.25	4	3	3	2.75	2.75
23	十字手	2.75	4	3	4	3	3	3	3	2
24	收势	1	3	2	2.5	2.75	2	2	2	2.5
统计	平均值	2.49	3.76	3.2	3.45	3.29	3.12	3.19	3.25	2.92
	大于4动作数	0	16	6	11	10	3	6	7	0
	大于3动作数	10	24	21	20	18	20	20	19	16

从图 3-1、表 3-1 中可以明确二十四式太极拳涉及到全身各个重要关节,中上肢部分明显表现活跃,特别是肩部,一直处于较高的活动状态中。整套动作中活动快速剧烈的关节部位很少,这与二十四式太极拳是一门动作相对舒缓、以健身和养身为目的的武术健身运动的事实符合。

第二节　生物力学角度分析

胡雁宾(2003)在《优秀太极拳运动员二十四式太极拳主要动作的生物力学分析》一文中，应用瑞典产QUALISYS MCU500红外线远射测试系统(16个镜头)对普及面最广而且保留着传统杨式大架太极拳风格特点的二十四式太极拳的主要动作做了生物力学的研究分析。研究对象为3名太极拳冠军，将一套二十四式动作分为定式动作和行进间动作。其中定式动作一类主要按步型分类；行进间动作按主要步法分类，主要包括进步类、退步类和侧行步类。对行进间动作左右膝角、肘角的变化趋势，重心变化趋势以及胸椎弯曲度的变化趋势进行统计和分析，研究结果如下。

(1)研究者以尾椎的垂直方向也就是z轴的坐标来反映重心的变化趋势，通过对"野马分鬃""倒卷肱""云手"3个动作的重心的变化进行监测得出结论：在太极拳的运动过程中，重心的运动不是一成不变，而是在一定幅度之间，随着动作的变化而有规律地变化。收脚时重心有小幅度上升，出脚时重心有小幅度的下降。

(2)太极拳中"屈膝坐腿"的姿势是区别于其他武术动作的，膝关节角度是研究"屈膝坐腿"动作的一个重要指标。通过对"野马分鬃"动作膝关节的角度变化进行检测得出：左右膝角的变化在交替进行，而且角度的变化幅度在70°~170°之间，并且后坐幅度较大，但是重心又没有完全移到后腿。通过对"倒卷肱"动作膝关节的角度变化进行检测得出：两膝关节角度在有规律地交替变化，变化幅度在30°~170°之间。在做退步转腰托掌的动作时，膝关节角度基本保持不变。通过对"云手"动作膝关节的角度变化进行检测得出：两膝关节角度在有规律地交替变化，变化幅度在70°~170°之间，并且两腿交替运动的速度不均匀。

(3)太极拳动作速度缓慢、均匀且连贯性好，是太极拳的主要特点之一。研究者对受试者的"野马分鬃"动作中头后、第七颈椎、第九胸椎、第五腰椎、左肩和右手6个关节点的速度进行监测得出结论：太极拳速度并不是一成不变的，而是由慢到快再到慢的变化，它是遵循动作从启动到完成再到结束，速度由慢到快再到慢的变化规律；动作与动作之间几乎没有停顿，说明太极拳节节贯串；各个关节点的速度几乎相同，充分体现了太极拳"上下相随"的特点。

(4)"含胸拔背"是太极拳最基本的身型要求之一。研究者通过受试者胸椎曲率的变化来研究在太极拳运动中含胸动作的具体变化规律。研究者将"野马分鬃"动作共分为3个阶段，即抱球出脚阶段、弓步分掌阶段和后移转身阶段。通过对"抱球出脚"胸椎曲率变化进行检测得出：此阶段胸椎的弯曲度加大，靠近腰弯和颈弯的弯曲度较大；第九和第六胸椎弯曲度的变化幅度大于第十二和第三胸椎，胸椎两头的弯曲度变化较小，而中间的弯曲度较大，这一现象充分体现了做"野马分鬃"的"抱球出脚"时，胸部始终保持内含。这也与太极拳"含胸"的拳理相吻合。通过对"弓步分掌"胸椎曲率变化进行检测得出："弓步分掌"定式时，胸椎弯曲度达到最大。由此说明在整个动作中胸椎的弯曲度并不是一成不变的，而是随着重心的前移有一个由屈到伸的变化过程；第九和第六胸椎弯曲度的变化幅度大于第十二和第三胸椎，胸椎两头的弯曲度变化较小，而中间的弯曲度较大，这一现象充分体现了做"野马分鬃"的"弓步分掌"时，胸部始终保持内含。对"后移转身"胸椎曲率变化进行检测得出：胸椎的弯曲度由大变小再变大，胸部的变化由含到展再到含。后移时含脚，转身时展胸，准备前移重心时含胸；第九和第六胸椎弯曲度的变化幅度大于第十二和第三胸椎。胸椎两头的弯曲度变化较小，而中间的弯曲度变化较大，这一现象充分体现了在做"野马分鬃"的"后移转身"时，也始终保持含胸姿势。

郅正（2005）在《二十四式简化太极拳典型动作对人体脊柱和足底压力影响的初探》一文中，应用 Footscan Insole System 足底压力分布测试系统、Qualisys 红外光点自动识别系统和非线性曲线拟合的方法，对两名专业运动员在练习二十四式太极拳中"野马分鬃""倒卷肱""单鞭""云手"和"右蹬脚"5 个动作时进行了三维运动学测试和足底压力动力学测试。得出以下结论。

（1）在做"野马分鬃"动作时，足一侧先着地，再逐渐过渡到全脚支撑。整个动作过程中足部各区都没有形成完全支撑。

（2）在做"倒卷肱"动作过程中，练习者仅仅右足有少量前足完全支撑时间，并且没有后跟完全支撑，这能较好地说明退步步法的特点。

（3）"单鞭"与"野马分鬃"动作有相同的现象，后足、前足没有完全支撑时间，这可以进一步说明太极拳练习者在丁步、弓步步型和上步步法上是有整体上的相似性。

（4）在脊柱方面指出，在运动过程中脊柱倾斜角、速度、起伏变化幅度都较小，能反映太极柔缓的特点，在整个演练过程中躯干纵轴与地面近似垂直，但并不垂直，这种倾斜角度可以有效增加身体前后的稳定，腰椎的变化要大于胸椎的变化幅度。

谷枫（2004）在《杨式太极拳练习者搂膝拗步下肢动作的生物力学分析》一文中，使用 QUALISYS MCU500 红外远射测试系统和 Footscan 足底压力测试系统，运用运动生物力学原理和方法对两组不同水平的杨式太极拳演练者的"搂膝拗步"下肢动作进行测试与分析，试图揭示这一动作技术的运动学特征和原理，从动力学上给以验证。研究者认为，太极拳的技术动作中最基本而又呈周期性变化的就是下肢步法的变化，下肢髋、膝、踝三大关节能否自如地活动和负重对正常的太极拳动作的完成具有重要意义，是衡量一个运动员完成太极拳动作的重要指标。因此，研究者通过对髋、膝、踝等方面进行监测和分析得出以下结论。

（1）通过对左、右髋关节的角度变化情况分析发现，完成"搂膝拗步"动作的过程中需松腰、松髋，髋松而不散，以腰为轴进行转动从而达到灵活变换步法的目的，在"搂膝拗步"动作转变方向时有一个缩胯降低重心的蓄势阶段。在"搂膝拗步"上右腿阶段右髋关节角度是一个变大的过程，而支撑腿的左髋关节角度是缩小的。

（2）通过"搂膝拗步"动作中左膝关节角度变化情况分析发现，"搂膝拗步"动作的蹬伸前有一个较大的屈曲拉伸腿部肌肉的过程，使腿部肌肉在蹬伸前得到充分的拉伸以储备较多的机械能，为的是在转向期和蹬离期蹬伸时产生较大的推进力和转动力。太极拳的左右"搂膝拗步"动作中承重腿膝关节角度的平均值在 120°左右，非承重腿的膝关节角度的平均值在 170°左右。这个角度值是膝关节蹬伸发力的最佳角度，使整个下肢支撑比较稳固。在"搂膝拗步"的摆动期内支撑腿的膝关节角度的平均值分别为 135.9°和 137.3°，因此摆动期是身体在转动换势的时期，是过渡性动作。在摆动期身体的重心完全落在支撑腿上，左腿的膝关节角度平均值为 135.9°左右，右腿的膝关节角度平均值为 137.3°左右，这个角度可以使太极拳练习者更好地利用转动惯性顺势运动，便于动作之间的衔接。

（3）通过对"搂膝拗步"动作中踝关节角度变化的分析发现，在太极拳的弓步中蹬伸腿的最佳踝关节角度值为 48°±2.9°。在摆动期间踝关节角度是先增大再变小的过程。

（4）通过对身体躯干姿态（倾斜角度）的分析，身体躯干绕纵轴基本在 80°～90°之间变化，躯干纵轴与地面近似垂直,却并不完全垂直。太极拳在演练过程中,身体躯干的倾斜角度并不是完全不变的,而是随着下肢动作各时相的变化而做相应的补偿性变化。

(5)通过对"搂膝拗步"动作中身体重心变化的分析,太极拳在演练过程中要求全身各个关节放松,各个环节重量下沉,特别是利用气沉丹田、膈肌下降使腹部充实,相对降低重心,从而追求人体稳定。

顾杰等(2015)在《太极拳中膝关节弯曲的力学》一文中,认为练习太极拳要根据自身实际情况而定,他将练习太极拳分为两种情况,即以养生为主要目的与以技击和养生兼顾为目的,其中以养生为主要目的的太极拳习练者应采用高拳架,有利于膝关节的保护;以技击和养生兼顾为要求的太极拳习练者可采用中架,也可先从高架练起,待膝关节功能增强后再适当放低拳架。

两条腿中承重多于一半的腿为实腿,另一条腿为虚腿。虚腿与实腿应做到四点同面(图3-2)。在做中架动作时,以前腿为实腿,应做到膝尖不过脚尖。但按照太极拳技术动作要求,后腿为实腿时,不能做到膝尖不过脚尖。后实腿膝关节的弯曲度跟架子的高低成反比,架子越低,膝关节弯曲度越高,越容易损伤膝关节。为了减少膝关节的工作量,要把功架放高;为了增加功架的发劲量,要把架子放低。为兼顾技击和养生的习练者,可练习中架,或者先练习高架,随着膝关节功能的增加,逐渐放低架子。

图3-2 四点同面示意图

经过研究后得出以下结论:①为兼顾技击和养身两方面的优势,定式时的前实腿要"膝尖齐涌泉",即小腿微量前倾,膝尖应在涌泉穴上方,膝尖不必平脚踝(即小腿不必垂直于地面),膝尖更不能过脚尖。②后腿为实腿和为迈步或撤步时,支撑单腿之膝关节的弯曲程度主要取决于拳架的高度,除了很高的拳架,一般膝尖应超过脚尖。③膝关节折曲是造成膝关节损伤的一个原因。避免膝关节折曲的重要方法是"四点一面",即髋关节、膝关节、脚尖、脚跟能够始终保持在同一个平面内。④膝关节的工作量随关节的弯曲度(几何度量)及弯矩(内力度量)的增加而增加。⑤中架杨式太极拳是兼顾养生和技击习练的最佳拳架。

第四章　开发平台应用技术介绍

本章节将对开发本平台所需的三维展示引擎 Unity3D、建立人物模型和蒙皮绑定的主要工具 3ds Max、人机互动的主要设备 Kinect 作相关介绍。

第一节　Unity3D

Unity3D 是一款横跨多个平台的增强现实开发软件，是当下主流的开发引擎之一。

Unity3D 的设计定位在于方便快捷的编辑模式，同时对 IOS、安卓、PC、网页、PS3、XBOX 等平台实现同步发布。作为业内主流应用之一，Unity3D 自身拥有非常强大的三维物理引擎。包括面向多个平台的同步发布、资源整合编辑器、脚本编辑、物理模拟等优质特性。

Unity3D 在对虚拟现实表现以及三维可视化交互等方面有着极强的表现力，无论是移动端，还是 PC 端都有出色的表现，并且通过 Unity Web Player 对网页虚拟现实进行最大力度的支持，为增强现实的具象表现提供完美优质的解决方案，使多平台的开发变得更自如愉悦。同时也使用户的选择更具多样化与选择性，提升了用户切实体验，最大限度地方便用户的使用。通过 Unity3D 的制作与整合，使增强现实的制作变得更加自如，让制作者可以更好地还原真实与事物的严肃性，同时让用户的体验更具直观，切实感受到虚拟现实所带来的真实感，提高用户体验和参与度。

第二节　3ds Max 建模技术

一、基础建模

基础建模包括内置模型建模、二维形体建模、车削建模、挤压建模、复合物体建模和放样建模六方面内容。

1. 内置模型建模

内置模型建模是建模技术中最基础的建模方法，是属于自带的一些模型，是把系统提供的扩展几何体跟标准几何体搭配一起，将其组合成为三维模型，然后对其进行编辑处理，以制作出较为复杂的模型。快捷简单是内置模型建模的优点，一般使用基本几何形体和扩展几何形体来建模只需调节参数和摆放位置，就能够轻松地完成模型的创建。但是这种建模方法只适合制作一些精度较低且结构较为规则的物体模型。

2. 二维形体建模

二维形体建模是利用样条曲线等图形，通过在 3ds Max 中进行旋转、拉伸等修改器操作，将二维图形转换为三维模型。

3. 车削建模

车削建模是二维图形转变为三维模型的重要方法，利用旋转轴向与旋转角度的控制，进行中心轴旋转，以此来生成三维模型。车削建模的具体建模思路是先有一个可以轴对称物体的横截面，然后绘制一半的横截面，进而对横截面进行修改或选择布尔运算，最后设置旋转角度及轴向，沿着中心轴旋转即可。

4. 挤压建模

挤压建模则是对截面曲线进行模型绘制，然后使用编辑器对图形修改处理，通过一定的方向挤压，生成三维形体模型。挤压建模技术的原理是以二维的平面形体为轮廓，可以制作出厚度可调整且横截面相同的三维模型。一般来说，有二维或三维物体的横截面就可以使用挤压建模技术来制作。

5. 复合物体建模

复合物体建模是将两个或者多个简单对象模型组合成一个新的对象模型。复合物体生成的方法有连接、变形、布尔、形体合并、包裹、地形、离散、水滴网格等。

6. 放样建模

放样建模也是将二维图形转变为三维模型的一种操作方法，但是它的应用范围比上述几种基础建模都要广，通过改变截面与路径，然后才能生成较为复杂的模型。放样建模是把两个或多个二维图形组合成一个三维物体，是通过制作一个路径然后对各个截面进行组合而创建出三维模型。放样至少需要两个或两个以上的二维曲线：一个是用于放样的路径，用来定义放样的物体高度；另一个是用于放样的截面，用来定义放样的物体形状。路径可以是各种各样的图形，但必须只有一个线段，截面也可以是各种各样的曲线，它在数量上就没有任何数量限制。

二、高级建模

高级建模的主要内容有多边形建模、面片建模、NURBS 建模。

多边形建模的主要命令有 Editable Mesh（支持编辑网络）与 Editable Poly（支持编辑多边形），在这两个命令的协调作用下，建模能够实现多边形曲面建模和网格方式建模等多种类型建模。在多边形建模的原料划分中，能够将多边形分为三角面，采用网格编辑的方式，进行大量的点、线、面编辑操作，多用于复杂的建模。

由多边形建模而发展出了面片建模，对于多边形表面不容易进行弹性编辑的问题能够得到很好的解决。此方法所使用的顶点不多，最适合用在生物模型的创建上。

NURBS 建模的原理是数学公式，是一种非常特殊的样条曲线，适合对有机曲面的描述，主要是对飞机等具有流畅线型的表面物体进行建模。

1. 多边形建模

多边形建模技术一般都是用于对规则形状的创建和对无曲面的对象的模型制作。这个建模技术可以用来创建基本集合。在多边形建模技术的基础上可使用修改编辑器对物体进行不同要求的标准修改,也可以通过放样或者布尔运算等操作将基本集合组合成物体对象。操作简单是多边形建模技术的最大特点。难度较大的操作,比如处理光滑的表面或曲面,建议使用多边形建模技术创造的物体对象,一般使用了多边形建模技术创造的物体对象可以很容易地通过对建模参数的调整获得不同分辨率的模型,能方便满足用户对不同虚拟场景显示的要求。

2. 面片建模

面片建模是在多边形建模的基础上发展而来的,但它是一种独立的模型类型,面片建模解决了多边形表面不易被弹性编辑的难题,可以使用类似于编辑 Bezier 曲线的方法去编辑曲面。面片与样条曲线的原理是相同的,同属 Bezier 方式,而且可通过调整表面的控制句柄去改变面片的曲率。面片与样条曲线的不同在于:面片是三维的,所以控制句柄有 X、Y、Z 3 个方向。编辑的顶点较少是面片建模的优点,可用较少的细节来做出模型上很光滑的表面或者有褶皱的表面。

3. NURBS 建模

NURBS 建模技术又叫非均匀性曲线建模,是属于图形理论中的数学概念。它是三维模型制作中主要的建模方式之一,适用于制作各种复杂的光滑模型、曲面模型。一般创建细节上较逼真的模型都是选用 NURBS 建模技术,其他建模技术跟它在这点上差距较大,因此该建模技术被应用的空间较为广泛。但因为制作的模型比较复杂,一般是在建立基本建模单元时就需要应用曲面片,这样做需要增加控制点,随着控制点的增加将会导致整体制作难于控制。为了方便后期模型的调整,还需要利用复杂的拓扑结构。

第三节 Kinect 开发技术

一、Kinect 设备硬件结构

Kinect 设备外观如图 4-1 所示,基座和感应器之间有一个电动的马达,可通过程序调整俯仰角度,具体内部结构如图 4-2 所示,从左往右依次是红外光源、LED 指示灯、彩色摄像头和红外摄像头,其中彩色摄像头用来收集 RGB 数据,红外摄像头用来采集景深数据。彩色摄像头最大支持 1280×960 分辨率成像,红外摄像头最大支持 640×480 成像。

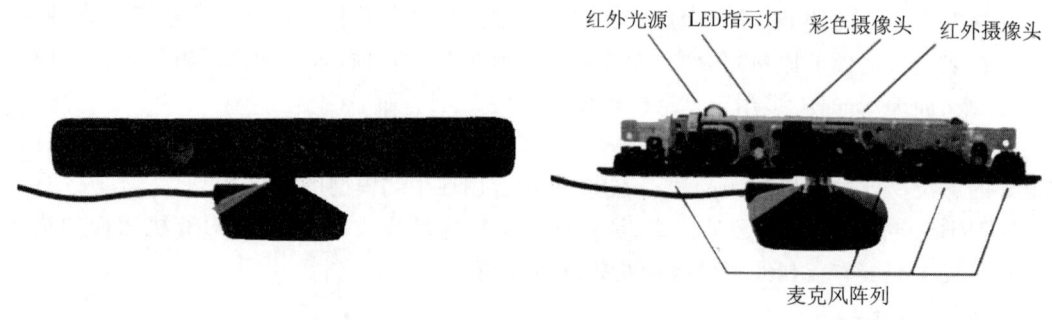

图 4-1 Kinect 设备外观　　图 4-2 Kinect 设备内部结构

在感应器的下方是麦克风阵列,包括 4 个不同的麦克风(1 个在左边的红外发射器下面,另外 3 个在右边景深摄像头下面)。

二、Kinect for Windows SDK 简介

Kinect for Windows SDK 是一系列的类库,可将 Kinect 作为输入设备开发各种应用程序。就像其名字所显示的那样,Kinect for Windows SDK 只能运行在 32 位或者 64 位的 Windows 7 及以上版本的操作系统上。

1. 发现和连接 Kinect 设备

KinectObject 对象没有公共的构造器,应用程序不能直接创建它。相反,该对象是 SDK 在探测到有连接的 Kinect 设备时创建的。当有 Kinect 设备连接到计算机上时,应用程序应该得到通知或者提醒。KinectSeneor 对象有一个静态的属性 KinectSensors,该属性是一个 KinectSensorCollection 集合,该集合继承自 ReadOnlyCollection,ReadOnlyCollection 集合很简单,只有一个索引器和一个称之为 StatusChanged 的事件。

使用集合中的索引器来获取 KinectSensor 对象。集合中元素的个数就是 Kinect 设备的个数。也就是说,一台电脑上可以连接多个 Kinect 设备,以便从不同的方向获取数据。应用程序可以使用多个 Kinect 设备来获取多方面的数据,Kinect 个数的限制只受电脑配置的限制。由于每个 Kinect 是通过 USB 来进行数据传输的,所以每一个 Kinect 设备需要一条 USB 线与电脑相连。此外,更多的 Kinect 设备需要更多的 CPU 和内存消耗。

查找 Kinect 设备可以通过简单的遍历集合找到。但是 KinectSensor 集合中的设备不是都能直接使用的,所以 KinectSensor 对象有一个 Status 属性,它是一个枚举类型,标识了当前 Kinect 设备的状态。表 4-1 中列出了传感器的状态及其含义。

表 4-1 Kinect 传感器状态及其含义

状 态	含 义
Undefined	设备的状态不能够确定
Connected	设备已经连接到电脑上,并能够提供数据
Device Not Genuine	连接的设备不是授权的 Kinect 设备
Disconnected	Kinect 与电脑的连接已经断开
Error	与 Kinect 通信产生了错误
Initializing	设备连接到了电脑上,正在进行连接中
Insufficient Bandwidth Kinect	不能够初始化,因为连接 Kinect 与电脑的 USB 数据线没有足够的带宽来操作设备
Not Powered	Kinect 供电不足,需要额外的电源
Not Ready	Kinect 设备已经连接到电脑上,但是还没有进入 Connected 状态

只有设备在 Connected 状态下，KinectSensor 对象才能初始化。在应用的整个生命周期中，传感器的状态可能会发生变化。应用程序不应该假定在一开始时 Kinect 设备就处于可用状态，也不应该假定在整个程序运行的过程中，Kinect 设备会一直与电脑连接。

2. 打开传感器

一旦发现了传感器，在应用程序能够使用传感器之前必须对其进行初始化。传感器的初始化包括 3 个步骤。

(1)应用程序必须设置需要使用的数据流，并将其状态设为可用。每一种类型的数据流都有一个 Enable 方法，该方法可以初始化数据流。每一种数据流都完全不同，在使用之前需要进行一系列的设置。主要工作包括初始化 ColorImageStream 数据流、初始化 DepthImageStream 数据流和 SkeletonStream 数据流。

(2)初始化之后就要确定应用程序如何使用产生的数据流。最常用的方式是使用 Kinect 对象的一系列事件，其中 ColorImageStream 对应 ColorFrameReady 事件，DepthImageStream 对应 DepthFrameReady 事件，SkeletonStream 对象对应 SkeletonFrameReady 事件以及 AllFramesReady 事件。各自对应的事件只有在对应的数据流 Enabled 后才能使用，AllFramesReady 事件在任何一个数据流状态 Enabled 时就能使用。

(3)应用程序调用 KinectSensor 对象的 Start 方法后，FrameReady 事件就会触发从而产生数据。

3. 停止传感器

一旦传感器打开后，可以使用 KinectSensor 对象的 Stop 方法停止。这样所有的数据产生都会停止，因此在监听 FrameReady 事件时要先检查传感器是否不为零。

KinectSensor 对象以及数据流都会使用系统资源，应用程序在不需要使用 KinectSensor 对象时必须能够合理地释放这些资源。在这种情况下，程序不仅要停止传感器，还要注销 FrameReady 事件。应用程序必须重启或者将 Kinect 重新拔出然后插入才能再次获得并使用对象。

三、Kinect 骨骼追踪技术

Kinect 产生的景深数据作用有限，要利用 Kinect 创建真正意义上交互，还需要除深度数据之外的其他数据。这就是骨骼追踪技术的初衷，骨骼追踪技术通过处理景深数据来建立人体各个关节的坐标，骨骼追踪能够确定人体的各个部分。骨骼追踪产生 X、Y、Z 数据来确定这些骨骼点。

骨骼数据来自 SkeletonStream。访问骨骼数据与访问彩色影像数据、景深数据一样，也有事件模式和"拉"模式两种方式。

Kinect SDK 中骨骼追踪有一些和其他对象不一样的对象结构和枚举。图 4-3 展示了骨骼追踪系统中涉及到的一些主要的对象模型。有 4 个最主要的对象，分别是 SkeletonStream、SkeletonFrame、Skeleton 和 Joint。下面将详细介绍这 4 个对象。

(一)SkeletonStream 对象

SkeletonStream 对象产生 SkeletonFrame。从 SkeletonStream 获取骨骼帧数据和从

ColorStream 及 DepthStream 中获取数据类似。可以注册 SkeletonFrameReady 事件或者 AllFramesReady 事件,通过事件模型来获取数据,或者是使用 OpenNextFrame 方法通过"拉"模型来获取数据。不能对同一个 SkeletonStream 同时使用这两种模式,如果注册了 SkeletonFrameReady 事件然后又调用 OpenNextFrame 方法将会返回一个 InvalidOperationException 异常。

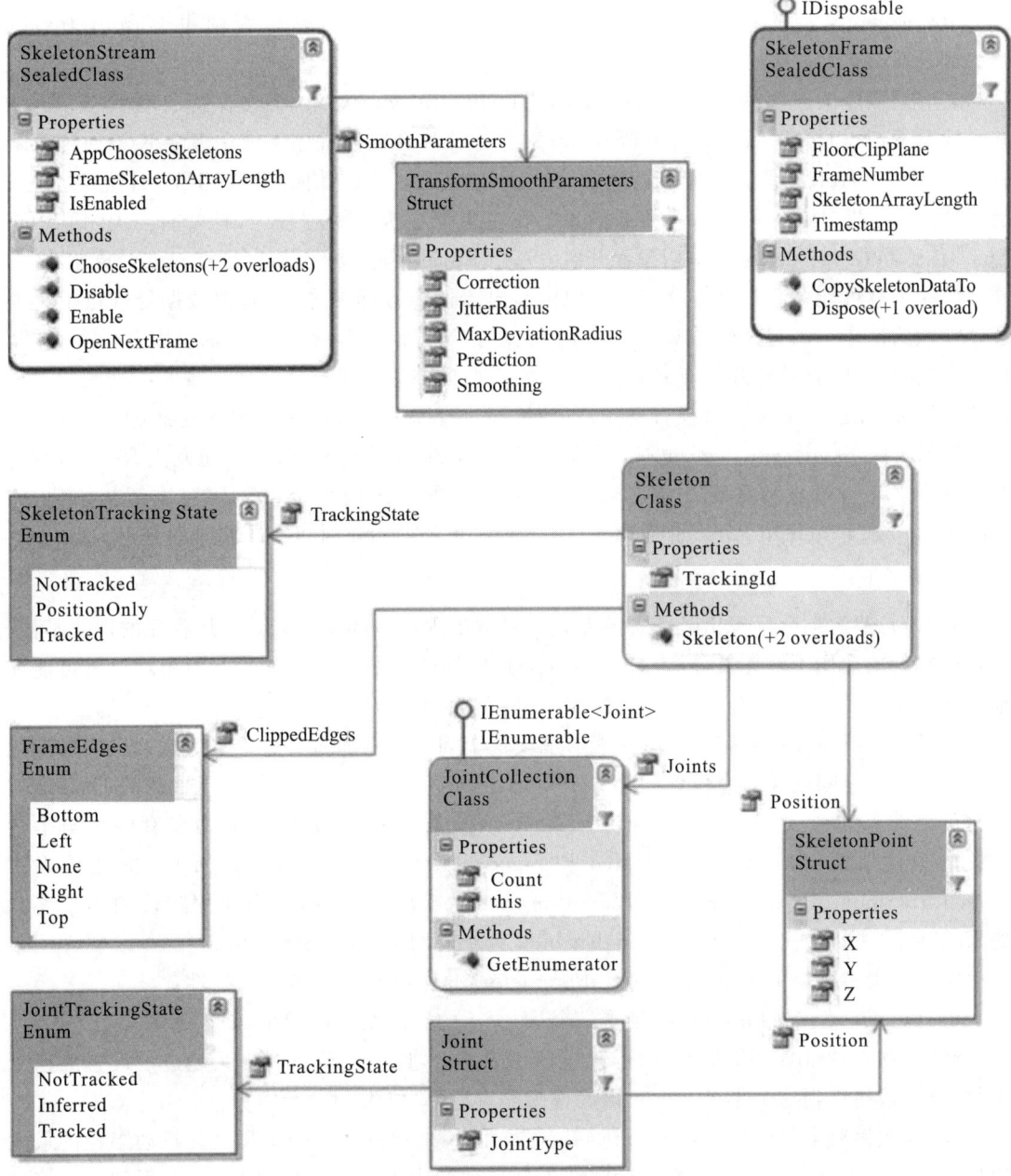

图 4-3 骨骼追踪系统中主要的对象模型示意图

1. SkeletonStream 的启动和关闭

除非启动了 SkeletonStream 对象,否则,不会产生任何数据,默认情况下,SkeletonStream 对象是关闭的。要使 SkeletonStream 产生数据,必须调用对象的 Enabled 方法。相反,调用 Disable 方法能够使 SkeletonStream 对象暂停产生数据。SkeletonStream 有一个 IsEnabled 方法来描述当前 SkeletonStream 对象的状态。只有 SkeletonStream 对象启动了,Kinect Sensor 对象的 SkeletonFrameReady 事件才能被激活。如果要使用"拉"模式来获取数据 SkeletonStream,也必须启动后才能调用 OpenNextFrame 方法。否则也会抛出 InvalidOperationException 异常。

在应用程序的声明周期中,一旦启动了 SkeletonStream 对象,将会保持启动状态。但在有些情况下,我们希望关闭 SkeletonStream 对象。比如在应用程序中使用多个 Kinect 传感器时。只有一个 Kinect 传感器能够产生骨骼数据,这也意味着,即使使用多个 Kinect 传感器,也只能同时追踪到两个游戏者的骨骼数据信息。在应用程序执行的过程中,有可能会关闭某一个 Kinect 传感器的 SkeletonStream 对象而开启另一个 Kinect 传感器的 SkeletonStream 对象。

另一个有可能关闭骨骼数据产生的原因是出于性能方面的考虑,骨骼数据处理是很耗费计算性能的操作。当打开骨骼追踪时可以观察到 CPU 的占用率明显增加。因此,当不需要骨骼数据时,关闭骨骼追踪很有必要。例如,在有些游戏场景中可能需要展现一些动画效果或者播放视频,在这个动画效果或者视频播放时,停止骨骼追踪可能使得游戏更加流畅。

当然关闭 SkeletonStream 也有一些副作用。当 SkeletonStream 的状态发生改变时,所有的数据产生都会停止和重新开始。SkeletonStream 的状态改变会使传感器重新初始化,将 TimeStamp 和 FrameNumber 重置为 0。在传感器重新初始化时也有几毫秒的延迟。

2. 平滑化

有时,骨骼运动会呈现出跳跃式的变化。导致出现这一问题可能是应用程序的性能不佳,或者游戏者的动作不够连贯,或者是 Kinect 硬件的性能问题。骨骼关节点的相对位置可能在帧与帧之间变动很大,这会对应用程序产生一些负面的影响。

SkeletonStream 对象有一种方法能够解决这个问题。它通过将骨骼关节点的坐标标准化来减少帧与帧之间的关节点位置差异。当初始化 SkeletonStream 对象调用重载的 Enable 方法时可以传入一个 TransformSmoothParameters 参数。SkeletonStream 对象有两个与平滑有关的只读属性:IsSmoothingEnabled 和 SmoothParameters。当调用 Enable 方法传入了 TransformSmoothParameters 时,IsSmoothingEnabled 返回 True,而当使用默认的不带参数的 Enable 方法初始化时,IsSmoothingEnabled 对象返回 False。SmoothParameters 属性用来存储定义平滑参数。TransformSmoothParameters 这个结构定义了一些属性:

(1)修正值(Correction)属性,接受一个从 0~1 的浮点型。值越小,修正越多。

(2)抖动半径(JitterRadius)属性,设置修正的半径,如果关节点"抖动"超过了设置的这个半径,将会被纠正到这个半径之内。该属性为浮点型,单位为 m。

(3)最大偏离半径(MaxDeviationRadius)属性,用来和抖动半径一起设置抖动半径的最大边界。任何超过这一半径的点都不会被认为是抖动产生的,而会被认定为一个新的点。该属性为浮点型,单位为 m。

(4)预测帧大小(Prediction)属性,返回用来进行平滑需要的骨骼帧的数目。

(5)平滑值(Smoothing)属性,设置处理骨骼数据帧时的平滑量,接受一个 0~1 的浮点值,值越大,平滑得越多。0 表示不进行平滑。

对骨骼关节点进行平滑处理会增加性能消耗。平滑处理得越多,性能消耗越大。设置平滑参数没有经验可循。需要不断地测试和调试,以达到最好的性能和效果。在程序运行的不同阶段,可能需要设置不同的平滑参数。

3.骨骼追踪对象选择

在默认情况下,骨骼追踪引擎会对视野内所有活动的游戏者进行追踪。但只会选择两个可能的游戏者产生骨骼数据,在大多数情况下,这个选择过程不确定。如果要选择特定的追踪对象,需要使用 AppChoosesSkeletons 属性和 ChooseSkeletons 方法,需要将 AppChoosesSkeletons 设置为 True,并调用 ChooseSkeletons 方法,传入 TrackingIDs 表明需要追踪的那个对象。在默认情况下,AppChoosesSkeletons 属性为 False。ChooseSkeletons 方法接受一个、两个或者 0 个 TrackingIDs,当 ChooseSkeletons 方法传入 0 个参数时,引擎停止追踪骨骼信息。

(二)SkeletonFrame 对象

SkeletonStream 产生 SkeletonFrame 对象。可以使用事件模型从事件参数中调用 OpenSkeletonFrame 方法来获取 SkeletonFrame 对象,或者采用"拉"模型调用 SkeletonStream 的 OpenNextFrame 来获取 SkeletonFrame 对象。SkeletonFrame 对象会存储骨骼数据一段时间,同时通过调用 SkeletonFrame 对象的 CopySkeletonDataTo 方法将其保存的数据拷贝到骨骼对象数组中。SkeletonFrame 对象有一个 SkeletonArrayLength 的属性,这个属性表示追踪到的骨骼信息的个数。

1.时间标记字段

SkeletonFrame 的 FrameNumber 和 Timestamp 字段表示当前记录中的帧序列信息。FrameNumber 是景深数据帧中用来产生骨骼数据帧的帧编号。帧编号通常是不连续的,但是之后的帧编号一定比之前的要大。骨骼追踪引擎在追踪过程中可能会忽略某一帧深度数据,这与应用程序的性能和每秒产生的帧数有关。例如,在基于事件获取骨骼帧信息中,如果事件中处理帧数据的时间过长,就会导致这一帧数据还没有处理完就产生了新的数据,那么这些新的数据就有可能被忽略了。如果采用"拉"模型获取帧数据,那么取决于应用程序设置的骨骼引擎产生数据的频率,即取决于深度影像数据产生骨骼数据的频率。

Timestap 字段记录 Kinect 传感器初始化以来经过的累计毫秒时间(FrameNumber 或者 Timestamp 字段不会超出上限)。FrameNumber 是一个 32 位的整型,Timestamp 是 64 位整型。如果应用程序以每秒 30 帧的速度产生数据,应用程序需要运行 2.25 年才会达到 FrameNumber 的上限,此时 Timestamp 离上限还很远。另外在 Kinect 传感器每一次初始化时,这两个字段都会初始化为 0。可以认为 FrameNumber 和 Timestamp 这两个值是唯一的。这两个字段在分析处理帧序列数据时很重要,比如进行关节点值的平滑、手势识别操作等。在多数情况下,我们通常会处理帧时间序列数据,这两个字段就显得很有用。目前 SDK 中并没有包含手势识别引擎。在未来 SDK 中加入手势引擎之前,我们需要自己编写算法来对帧时间序列进行处理以进行手势识别,这样就会大量依赖这两个字段。

2. 帧描述信息

FloorClipPlane 字段是一个有 4 个元素的元组：Tuple<int, int, int, int>，每一个都是 $Ax+By+Cz+D=0$ 地面平面（Floor Plane）表达式里面的系数项。元组中第一个元素表示 A，即 x 前面的系数，依次类推，最后一个表示常数项，通常为负数，是 Kinect 距离地面的高度。在可能的情况下，SDK 会利用图像处理技术来确定这些系数。但是有时这些系数不能确定下来，可能需要预估。当距地面高度不能确定时，FloorClipPlane 中的所有元素均为 0。

（三）Skeleton 对象

Skeleton 类定义了一系列字段来描述骨骼信息，包括描述骨骼的位置以及骨骼中关节可能的位置信息。骨骼数据可以通过调用 SkeletonFrame 对象的 CopySkeletonDataTo 方法获得 Skeleton 数组。CopySkeletonDataTo 方法有一些不可预料的行为，可能会影响内存使用和其引用的骨骼数组对象。产生的每一个骨骼数组对象都是唯一的。以下面代码为例：

Skeleton[ ]skeletonA=new Skeleton[frame.SkeletonArrayLength];
Skeleton[ ]skeletonB=new Skeleton[frame.SkeletonArrayLength];

frame.CopySkeletonDataTo(skeletonA);
frame.CopySkeletonDataTo(skeletonB);

Boolean resultA=skeletonA[0]==skeletonB[0];//false
Boolean resultB=skeletonA[0].TrackingId==skeletonB[0].TrackingId;//true

从上面的代码可以看出，使用 CopySkeletonDataTo 会产生两个不同的 Skeleton 数组对象。

1. TrackingId

骨骼追踪引擎对于每一个追踪到的游戏者的骨骼信息都有一个唯一编号。这个值是整型，它会随着追踪到的新游戏者的产生添加增长。与之前帧序号一样，这个值并不是连续增长的，但是能保证的是后面追踪到的对象的编号要比之前编号大。另外，这个编号的产生是不确定的。如果骨骼追踪引擎失去了对游戏者的追踪，比如被捕捉者离开了 Kinect 的视野，那么这个对应的唯一编号就会过期。当 Kinect 追踪到了一个对象，Kinect 会为其分配一个新的唯一编号，编号值为 0，表示这个骨骼信息不是被捕捉到的，其在集合中仅仅是一个占位符。应用程序使用 TrackingId 来指定需要骨骼追踪引擎进行追踪的信息。调用 SkeletonStream 对象的 ChooseSkeleton 能以初始化对指定游戏者进行追踪。

2. TrackingState

该字段表示当前的骨骼数据的状态。表 4-2 展示了 SkeletonTrackingState 枚举的可能值及其含义。

3. Position

Position 是一个 SkeletonPoint 类型的字段，代表所有骨骼的中间点。身体的中间点与脊柱关节的位置相当。该字段提供了一个最快且最简单的所有视野范围内的被捕捉者位置的信息，而不管其是否在追踪状态中。在一些应用中，如果不用关心骨骼中具体关节点的位置信息，那么该字段对于确定被捕捉者的位置状态已经足够。

表 4-2 SkeletonTrackingState 枚举的可能值及其含义

枚举值	含 义
NotTracked	不是正在追踪的游戏者的骨骼对象，在这个状态下，骨骼数据的 Position 字段以及相关的关节点数组中的每一个位置点值都是 0(SkeletonPoint 中的 X、Y、Z 值均为 0)
PositionOnly	探测到了骨骼对象，但是追踪没有被激活，骨骼数据的 Position 数据有值，但是相关的关节点数组的位置点值都是 0
Tracked	游戏者的骨骼信息正在被追踪，骨骼数据的 Position 信息和相关的关节点数组的位置点信息都非 0

4. ClippedEdges

ClippedEdges 字段用来描述追踪者的身体哪部分位于 Kinect 的视野范围外。它提供了一个追踪者的位置信息。使用这一属性可以通过程序调整 Kinect 摄像头的俯仰角或者提示被捕捉者让其返回到视野中来。该字段类型为 FrameEdges，它是一个枚举并且有 Flags Atribute 自定义属性修饰。这意味着 ClippedEdges 字段可以有一个或者多个 FrameEdges 值。表 4-3 列出了 FrameEdges 的所有可能的值。

表 4-3 FrameEdges 的所有枚举值及其含义

枚举值	含 义
Bottom	游戏者身体的一个或者多个部位超出了 Kinect 视场的下边界
Left	游戏者身体的一个或者多个部位超出了 Kinect 视场的左边界
Right	游戏者身体的一个或者多个部位超出了 Kinect 视场的右边界
Top	游戏者身体的一个或者多个部位超出了 Kinect 视场的上边界
None	游戏者完全位于 Kinect 视场中

当被捕捉者身体的某一部分超出 Kinect 视场范围时，就需要对骨骼追踪产生的数据进行某些改进，因为某些部位的数据可能追踪不到或者不准确。最简单的解决办法就是提示游戏者身体超出了 Kinect 的某一边界范围，让被捕捉者回到视场中来。另一个解决办法是调整 Kinect 设备的物理位置。Kinect 底座上面有一个小的马达能够调整 Kinect 的俯仰角度。俯仰角度可以通过更改 KinectSensor 对象的 ElevationAngle 属性来进行调整。如果应用程序对于游戏者脚部动作比较关注，那么通过程序调整 Kinect 的俯仰角就能够解决脚部超出视场下界的情况。

ElevationAnagle 以度为单位。KinectSensor 的 MaxElevationAngle 和 MinElevationAngle 确定了可以调整角度的上下界。任何将 ElevationAngle 设置超出上下界的操作将会导致 ArgumentOutOfRangeException 异常。微软建议不要过于频繁重复地调整俯仰角，以免损坏马达。为了使得开发者少犯错误和保护马达，SDK 限制了每秒能调整的俯仰角的值。SDK 限制了在连续 15 次调整之后要暂停 20 秒。

5. Joints

每一个骨骼对象都有一个 Joints 字段。该字段是一个 JointsCollection 类型，它存储了一些列的 Joint 结构来描述骨骼中可追踪的关节点（如 Head，Hands，Elbow 等）。应用程序使用 JointsCollection 索引获取特定的关节点，并通过节点的 JointType 枚举来过滤指定的关节点，即使 Kinect 视场中没有游戏者，Joints 对象也会被填充。

（四）Joint 对象

骨骼追踪引擎能够跟踪和获取每个用户的近 20 个点或者关节点信息。追踪的数据以关节点数据展现，它有 3 个属性。JointType 属性是一个枚举类型。图 4-4 描述了可追踪的所有关节点。

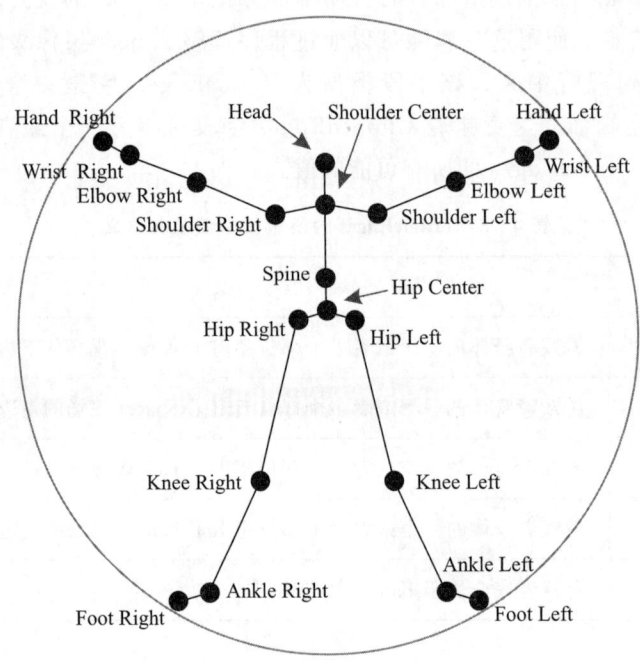

图 4-4 骨骼追踪引擎所能追踪的所有关节点

每一个关节点都有类型为 SkeletonPoint 的 Position 属性，它通过 X、Y、Z 3 个值来描述关节点的控件位置。X、Y 值是相对于骨骼平面空间的位置，与深度影像、彩色影像的空间坐标系不一样。KinectSnesor 对象有一系列的坐标转换方法，可以将骨骼坐标点转换到对应的深度数据影像中去。最后每一个 Skeleton 对象还有一个 JointTrackingState 属性，描述了该关节点的跟踪状态及方式，表 4-4 列出了所有的可能值。

在大多数情况下，原始的坐标数据是不能直接使用的。骨骼点数据和深度数据或者彩色影像数据的测量方法不同。每一类数据（深度数据、影像数据、骨骼数据）都是在特定的集合坐标或空间内定义的。深度数据或者影像数据用像素来表示，X、Y 位置从左上角以 0 开始，深度数据的 Z 方位数据以毫米为单位。与此不同的是,骨骼空间是以米为单位来描述的,以深度传感器为中心,其 X、Y 值为 0。骨骼空间坐标系是右手坐标系,X 正方向朝右,Y 正方向朝上,X 轴数据范围为-2.2~2.2m,总范围为 4.2m,Y 轴范围为-1.6~1.6m,Z 轴范围为 0~4m。图 4-5 描述了 Skeleton 数据流的空间坐标系。

表 4-4 JointTrackingState 属性所有的可能值及其含义

JointTrackingState	含 义
Inferred	骨骼追踪引擎在深度影像数据帧中看不到对应的关节点像素,但是通过计算能够确定关节点的位置
NotTracked	关节点的位置不能确定,关节点的 Position 值为 0
Tracked	关节点被探测到,且处于追踪状态

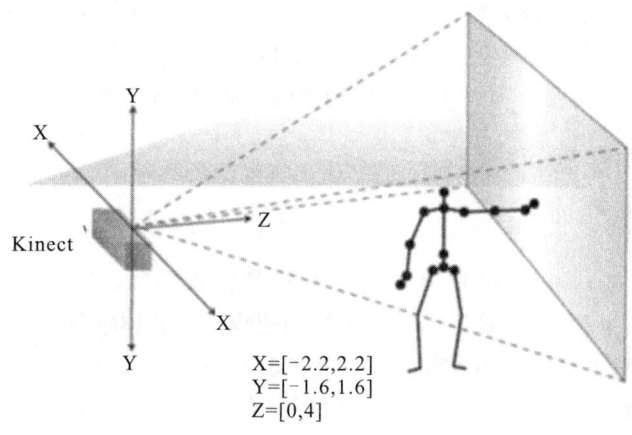

图 4-5 Skeleton 数据流的空间坐标系

(五)空间变换

SDK 提供了一系列方法来帮助我们进行骨骼数据空间和深度数据空间坐标系的转换。KinectSensor 对象有一个称之为 MapSkeletonPointToDepth 的方法能够将骨骼点数据转换到 UI 空间中去。SDK 中也提供了一个相反的 MapDepthToSkeletonPoint 方法。MapSkeletonPointToDepth 方法接受一个 SkeletonPoint 点和一个 DepthImageFormat 作为参数。骨骼点数据来自 Skeleton 对象或者 Joint 对象的 Position 属性。目标空间并不需要 Kinect 深度影像。事实上,DepthStream 不必初始化,可以通过 DepthImageFormat 来确定如何变化。一旦骨骼点数据被映射到深度空间中去了之后,它能够缩放到任意的纬度。

第五章 平台设计与实现

第一节 平台设计

一、设计思想

本课题所研究的二十四式太极拳三维互动展示平台是采用交互型模式,方便学习者自学并掌握二十四式太极拳的技术要点,为体育运动项目教学和训练提出一种全新的方式,开发本方法的目的是构建一个集教学和娱乐为一体的准确性高、操作性快、交互性强的综合平台。

二、设计目标与原则

1. 设计目标

通过本平台的研制,探索太极教学、娱乐三维视景仿真平台的研发和集成思路,借鉴市场上最新的软件技术成果和经验,采用当下较流行的建模技术和体感技术,综合运用三维视景仿真技术和原理,实现对太极教学场景和娱乐互动体验环节的三维虚拟化仿真演示,构建具有标准接口、准确性高、操作性快、交互性强的综合平台。

2. 设计原则

(1)一体化原则。平台设计要将角色动作数据准备、三维模型构建、三维仿真演示和用户体感互动等软件模块进行一体化设计,使它们之间接口清晰、功能明确。同时考虑到一体化教学演示的多样性和用户需求的多变性,系统在设计时需要将教学设计、情景设计、三维教学目标和用户体验等各种情况进行通盘考虑,要针对不同年龄段、不同类型的用户需求、不同应用情况进行一体化设计,使平台能够通过不同方式展示的模块定制、场景和难度的变换实现对不同情况的支持。

(2)实用性原则。平台设计要满足不同用户的需求,并能够适应用户灵活多变的需求;操作简单,界面显示符合学习者和太极爱好者的习惯,易学易用;系统使用主流的开发平台和软件,采用最通用的文件格式、界面风格和操作规范。

(3)标准化原则。在平台设计和实现时,采用了二十四式太极拳的标准动作和核心原则,贯彻落实太极禅的核心意义。该系统具有良好的兼容性和互联互通性。

三、系统的总体结构

本系统采用C#为主的系统开发语言,三维引擎以Unity3D为主,在体系架构上采用了

"框架+构件"的集成思路,通过统一的集成框架,能够方便地加入新的场景——新的软件模块;在开发技术上,采用面向对象、面向组件和面向接口的开发技术,使得系统的可扩展性、可维护性和灵活性等有所提高(图5-1)。

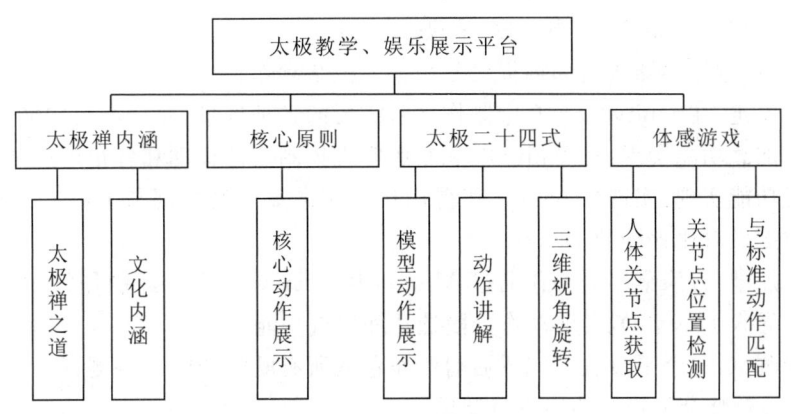

图5-1 系统主体结构图

太极教学、娱乐展示平台各个模块的主要功能如下。

1. 太极禅内涵

太极禅内涵主要是诠释太极的禅道意义和文化内涵,方便学习者更全面、深入地掌握太极拳的文化知识。

(1)太极禅之道。它主要从禅道的属性、礼仪和核心3个方面来诠释太极禅道,强调静心疗愈的律动属性,使用户更全面、具体地学习太极禅道的文化知识。

(2)文化内涵。它介绍了太极拳的基本骨架,即太极十三式的基本内容,是太极拳的最基本动作元素。将太极与阴阳、八卦、五行相关联起来,生动诠释了太极中的道,有益于用户理解"无极而太极"这一理念。

2. 核心原则

它主要是太极十三式中几个基本动作元素的三维模型展示和讲解,包括快进、回看、360°旋转观看等功能。

3. 太极二十四式

它包括太极二十四式的整套动作讲解和三维模型的标准动作展示,还有视角的360°随意旋转,动作的快进、回看,语音讲解和背景音乐的播放、关闭等功能。标准动作的获取是通过光学动作捕捉设备来获取录制的。

4. 体感游戏

体感游戏部分通过Kinect摄像头采集用户的身体关节点的空间坐标,与标准数据的对比,从而实现与标准动作的对比来打分的功能;还包括人体关节点坐标的获取、关节点位置检测和与标准动作的匹配等功能。

四、技术路线

技术路线如图 5-2 所示。

三维模型搭建：在 3ds Max 中建模、贴图。

角色模型蒙皮：在 3ds Max 中蒙皮、渲染。

动作采集：通过传感器式运动捕捉设备采集太极拳动作。

引擎环境设定：在 Unity3D 5.0 中制作平台需要的各种场景，实现灵活转换。

角色模型加载功能实现：在 Unity3D 5.0 中实现控制角色移动和各角度旋转的 Demo。

平台交互功能实现：实现从 Kinect 获得用户动作采集点的数据与 Unity3D 融合，然后与标准动作的数据做对比评分的 Demo。

三维动画加载：将采集到的动作通过 Motion Builder 导入到已经制作好的模型中。将带有动画的模型导入 Unity3D，实现动作分段选择和播放功能。

角色功能测试：整个平台制作完成后对于角色的所有既定功能进行测试。

平台测试：对整个平台的功能进行测试。

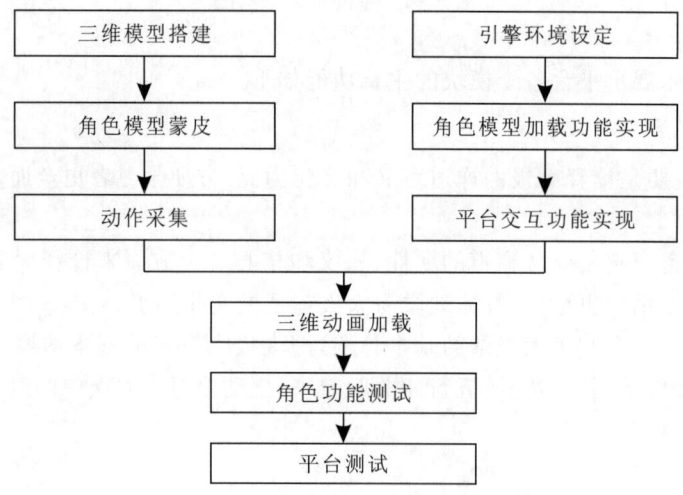

图 5-2 平台的制作流程概述

五、接口设计

1. 采集深度传感器接口

```
public interface DepthSensorInterface
{
    //功能:通过这个接口来初始化库和资源
    //参数:bNeedRestart:是否初始化标签
    //返回:true 初始化成功,false 失败
    bool InitSensorInterface(ref bool bNeedRestart);
```

//功能:通过这个接口来释放资源与库
//参数:无
//返回:无
void FreeSensorInterface();

//功能:获取当前可用的传感器数量
//参数:无
//返回:当前可用传感器的数量
int GetSensorsCount();

//功能:打开默认传感器和初始化需要的资源
//参数:dwFlags:帧标签
sensorAngle:传感器的当前角度
bUseMultiSource:数据资源使用情况
//返回:sensor-data 对象
KinectInterop.SensorData OpenDefaultSensor(KinectInterop.FrameSource dwFlags,
    float sensorAngle, bool bUseMultiSource);

//功能:关闭传感器并且释放正在使用的资源
//参数:sensorData:传感器获取到的数据
//返回:无
void CloseSensor(KinectInterop.SensorData sensorData);

//功能:实时获取传感器数据
//参数:sensorData:传感器获取到的数据
//返回:true 数据更新成功,false 数据更新失败
bool UpdateSensorData(KinectInterop.SensorData sensorData);

//gets next multi source frame, if one is available
//returns true if there is a new multi-source frame, false otherwise
//获取下一个多源帧,通过返回值判断是否有下一个多源帧

//功能:获取下一个数据帧
//参数:sensorData:传感器获取到的数据
//返回:true 获取数据成功,false 获取数据失败
bool GetMultiSourceFrame(KinectInterop.SensorData sensorData);

//功能:释放正在使用的数据帧
//参数:sensorData:传感器获取到的数据

//返回:无
void FreeMultiSourceFrame(KinectInterop.SensorData sensorData);

//功能:获取人体动态数据帧
//参数:sensorData:传感器获取到的数据
bodyFrame:人体数据帧
kinectToWorld:世界坐标
//返回:true 获取数据帧成功,false 获取失败
Bool PollBodyFrame(KinectInterop.SensorData sensorData, ref KinectInterop.
    BodyFrameData bodyFrame, ref Matrix4x4 kinectToWorld);

//功能:获取彩色帧数据
//参数:sensorData:传感器获取到的数据
//返回:true 获取到的彩色数据帧是可用的,false 获取失败
bool PollColorFrame(KinectInterop.SensorData sensorData);
//polls for new depth and body index frame data
//returns true if new depth or body index frame is available, false otherwise

//功能:获取深度帧数据
//参数:sensorData:传感器获取到的数据
//返回:true 获取到的深度数据帧是可用的,false 获取失败
bool PollDepthFrame(KinectInterop.SensorData sensorData);

//功能:获取红外帧数据
//参数:sensorData:传感器获取到的数据
//返回:true 获取到的红外数据帧是可用的,false 获取失败
bool PollInfraredFrame(KinectInterop.SensorData sensorData);

//功能:修改骨骼点的位置和旋转信息
//参数:sensorData:传感器获取到的数据
bodyData:人体数据
//返回:无
    void FixJointOrientations (KinectInterop. SensorData sensorData, ref KinectInterop.
            BodyData bodyData);

//功能:将 3D 空间坐标转为深度坐标
//参数:sensorData:传感器获取到的数据
spacePos:空间坐标值
//返回:深度坐标值

Vector2 MapSpacePointToDepthCoords(KinectInterop.SensorData sensorData,
　　Vector3 spacePos);

//功能:将深度坐标转为 Kinect 的 3D 坐标
//参数:sensorData:传感器获取到的数据
depthPos:深度坐标值
depthVal:深度值
//返回:Kinect 三维坐标值
Vector3 MapDepthPointToSpaceCoords(KinectInterop.SensorData sensorData,
　　Vector2 depthPos, ushort depthVal);

//功能:将深度坐标转为彩色坐标
//参数:sensorData:传感器获取到的数据
depthPos:深度坐标值
depthVal:深度值
//返回:彩色坐标值
Vector2 MapDepthPointToColorCoords(KinectInterop.SensorData sensorData,
　　Vector2 depthPos, ushort depthVal);

//功能:将当前深度帧转为彩色坐标
//参数:sensorData:传感器获取到的数据
vColorCoords:彩色坐标值
//返回:true 深度帧转为彩色坐标成功,false 转换失败
bool MapDepthFrameToColorCoords(KinectInterop.SensorData sensorData,
　　ref Vector2[] vColorCoords);

//功能:将骨骼点名称转为骨骼点索引值
//参数:joint:给定骨骼点对象
//返回:骨骼点的索引值
int GetJointIndex(KinectInterop.JointType joint);

//功能:通过索引值获取骨骼点名称
//参数:index:骨骼点的索引值
//返回:骨骼点数据
KinectInterop.JointType GetJointAtIndex(int index);

//功能:获取给定骨骼点的父级骨骼点,也就是上一个骨骼点
//参数:joint:给定骨骼点对象
//返回:骨骼点数据

```
        KinectInterop.JointType GetParentJoint(KinectInterop.JointType joint);

        //功能:获取同一级的下一个骨骼点
        //参数:joint:给定骨骼点对象
        //返回:骨骼点数据
        KinectInterop.JointType GetNextJoint(KinectInterop.JointType joint);
}
```
2. 动作识别接口
```
public interface GestureListenerInterface
{
        //功能:用户检测跟踪
        //参数:userId:用户 Id
        userIndex:用户索引
        //返回:无
        void UserDetected(long userId, int userIndex);


        //功能:用户跟踪丢失处理
        //参数:userId:用户 Id
        userIndex:用户索引
        //返回:无
        void UserLost(long userId, int userIndex);


        //功能:用户检测跟踪
        //参数:userId:用户 Id
        userIndex:用户索引
        gesture:人体姿势
        progress
        joint:骨骼点
        screenPos:屏幕坐标
        //返回:无
        void GestureInProgress(long userId, int userIndex, Gestures gesture, float progress,
                KinectInterop.JointType joint, Vector3 screenPos);


        //功能:判断人体姿势动作是否完整
        //参数:userId:用户 Id
        userIndex:用户索引
        gesture:人体姿势
        joint:骨骼点
        screenPos:屏幕坐标
```

//返回:true 姿势动作完成,false 姿势动作未完成
　　bool GestureCompleted (long userId, int userIndex, Gestures gesture, KinectInterop.
　　　　　　JointType joint, Vector3 screenPos);

//功能:判断是否取消当前动作
//参数:userId:用户 Id
userIndex:用户索引
gesture:人体姿势
joint:骨骼点
//返回:true 重新开始新动作,false 动作取消失败
　　bool GestureCancelled (long userId, int userIndex, Gestures gesture, KinectInterop.
　　　　　　JointType joint);

第二节　平台实现

　　本应用是基于 Unity3D 开发的,整套教学系统最为关键的部分是抓住教学要点,首先教学系统必须要得到用户的关注,因此需要向用户展现出一套生动逼真的太极拳影像,同时更需要抓住太极拳的精髓,更加方便用户的学习,提高用户的学习兴趣。

一、专业太极拳运动数据的采集

　　太极拳 3D 虚拟仿真教学系统实现的第一步是通过 Fab 光学运动捕捉系统采集运动数据。光学式运动捕捉大多数是基于计算机视觉原理。从理论上说,对于空间中的一个点,只要它能同时为两部相机所见,则根据同一时刻两部相机所拍摄的图像和相机参数,可以确定这一时刻该点在空间中的位置。当相机以足够高的速率连续拍摄时,从图像序列中就可以得到该点的运动轨迹。

　　典型的光学式运动捕捉系统通常使用 6~8 个相机环绕表演场地排列,这些相机的视野重叠区域就是表演者的动作范围。为了便于处理,通常要求表演者穿上单色的服装,在身体的关键部位,如关节、髋部、肘、腕等位置贴上一些特制的标志或发光点,称为"Marker",视觉系统将识别和处理这些标志。系统定标后,相机连续拍摄表演者的动作,并将图像序列保存下来,然后再进行分析和处理,识别其中的标志点,并计算其在每一瞬间的空间位置,进而得到其运动轨迹。为了得到准确的运动轨迹,相机应有较高的拍摄速率,一般要达到每秒 60 帧以上。

　　为了体现太极拳演示的标准性,本平台太极拳数据选用专业的武术运动员来充当数据采集样本。

　　本次采集所使用的传感器的装配没有严格的定位,但是装配传感器需要遵循以下规律(图 5-3):

　　(1)骨盆传感器(Pelvic sensor)装配在 L5~S1 之间。

　　(2)躯干传感器(Trunk sensor)装配在 T10~T11 之间,大约在胸腔底部。

　　(3)头部传感器(Head sensor)装配在枕骨部位。

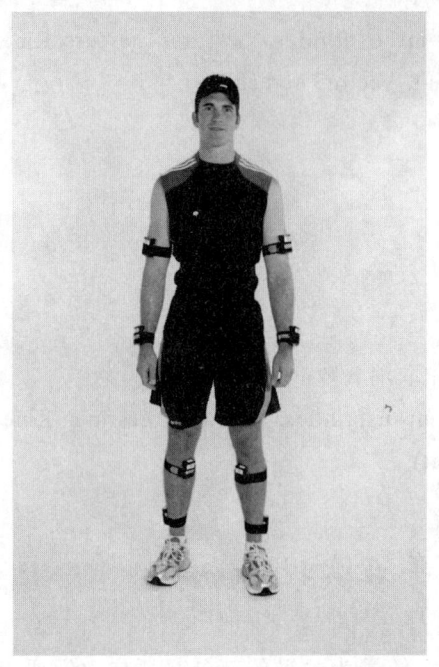
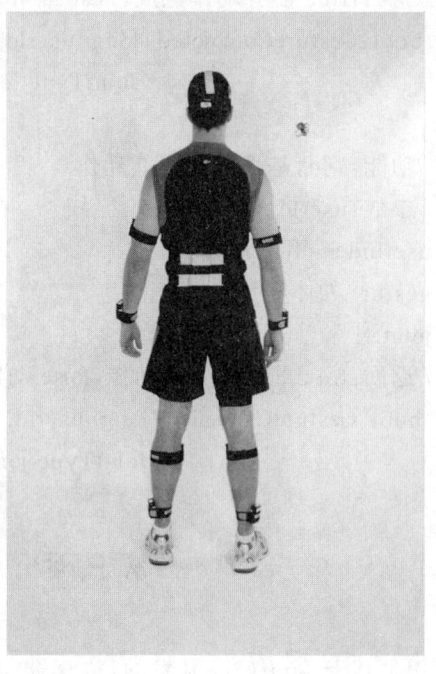

图 5-3 传感器的装配

(4)上臂传感器(Upper arm)装配在肘部上方二头肌侧部。
(5)前臂传感器(Forearm)装配在手腕上方,尺骨茎突背侧部。
(6)大腿传感器(Thigh)装配在膝盖上方大概 3 英寸(约 7.6cm)的位置。
(7)小腿传感器(Calf)装配在胫骨的中间位置。

此次的采集系统配置了 3 种传感器选项。①标准:头部、躯干、骨盆、手臂、腿部及足底压力传感器(图 5-4)。②脚踝:将前臂的传感器移到足部。③手腕:将小腿的传感器移到手掌。

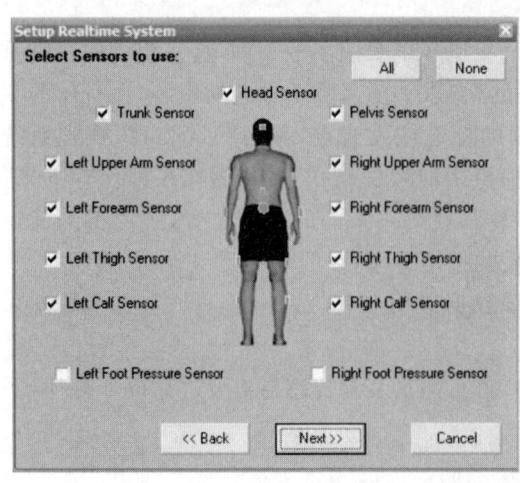
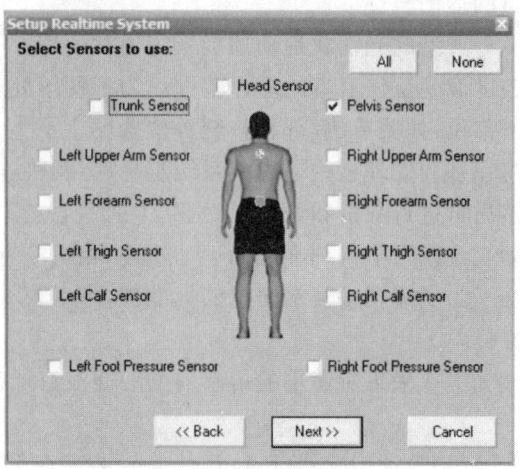

图 5-4　标准传感器选项　　　　　图 5-5　骨盆传感器选项

在选择使用传感器时,骨盆传感器是必须选择的(图 5-5),选择了骨盆传感器后,才可以选择躯干传感器(图 5-6)。选择头部传感器,从而必须选择躯干传感器和骨盆传感器(图 5-7)。选择前臂传感器,从而必须选择躯干传感器和盆骨传感器。选择大腿传感器,从而必须选择盆骨传感器。

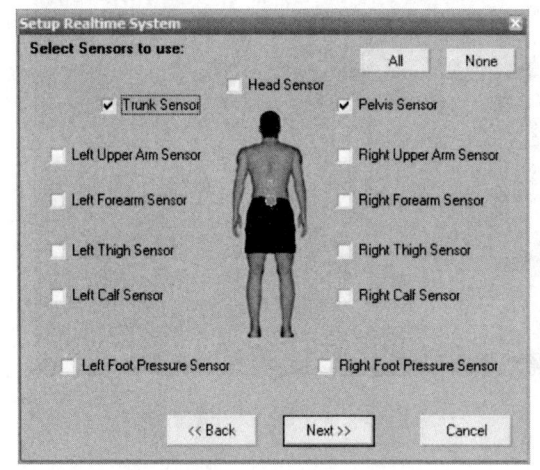

图 5-6　骨盆、躯干传感器选项

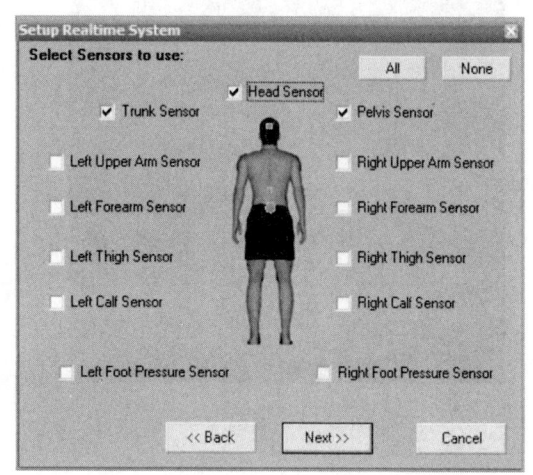

图 5-7　头部、躯干、骨盆传感器选项

二、人体模型的建立

就网格游戏建模部分来说,主要是分为以下几个部分,首先制作出角色的头部,然后以头部为标准设定出身体的比例和模型,再建立四肢(手臂和腿部)。下面我们主要介绍在 3ds Max 中的建模流程。

1. 角色头部模型的制作

(1)启动 3ds Max,在视图中创建一个 Box(长方体),调节其分段数,将 Length Segs(长度分段)、Width Segs(宽度分段)、Height Segs(高度分段)分别设置为 2、2、3,然后使用鼠标右键单击物体,在弹出的快捷菜单中选择"转换为可编辑多边形",将长方体转换为可编辑多边形。

(2)在顶点级别下调整脸部的形状,然后删除脸的一侧,如果竖向段数不够,可以通过边级别下的链接命令增加段数。

(3)制作头部基本模型,调整模型顶点。先调整出头部轮廓,再为模型添加更多的段数,调整头部的布线,完毕后删除头部后面的面(因为头部后面被头发遮挡,不需要表现出来),删除后可以节省系统部分资源。

(4)从各个角度观察模型,使用修剪命令制作出眼睛到嘴部轮廓的形状。挤出耳朵,并简单调整耳朵的外形,然后选择镜像命令将另一侧脸对称复制出来(图 5-8)。

(5)制作头发。根据后脑的形状,创建出立方体模型,将其转换为可编辑多边形后,调整头发的形状,最后通过镜像命令制作出另一侧的头发(图 5-9)。

(6)增加平滑组。选择元素层级,将头发模型选中。选择自动平滑命令为头发添加一个平滑组。

(7)将头发附加到头部模型,焊接头部和头发的点,选择头发模型和面部模型上的点,选择焊接命令将头发与脸部链接成一个整体。调整头发的形状,使两侧发型不对称(图 5-10)。

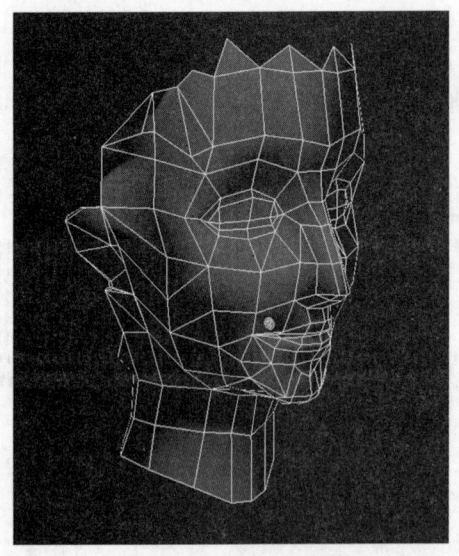
图 5-8 面部的模型

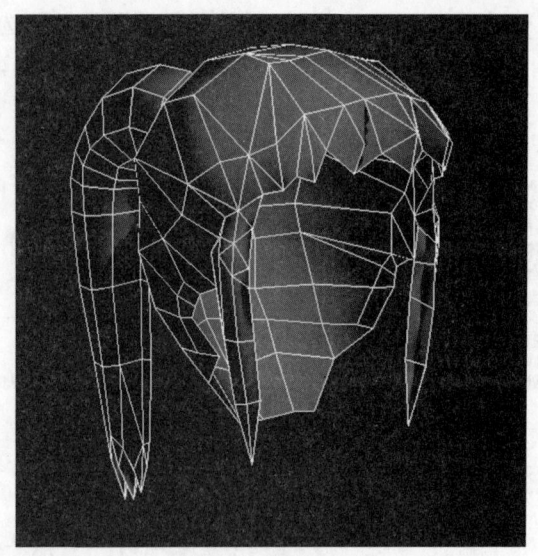
图 5-9 制作头发模型

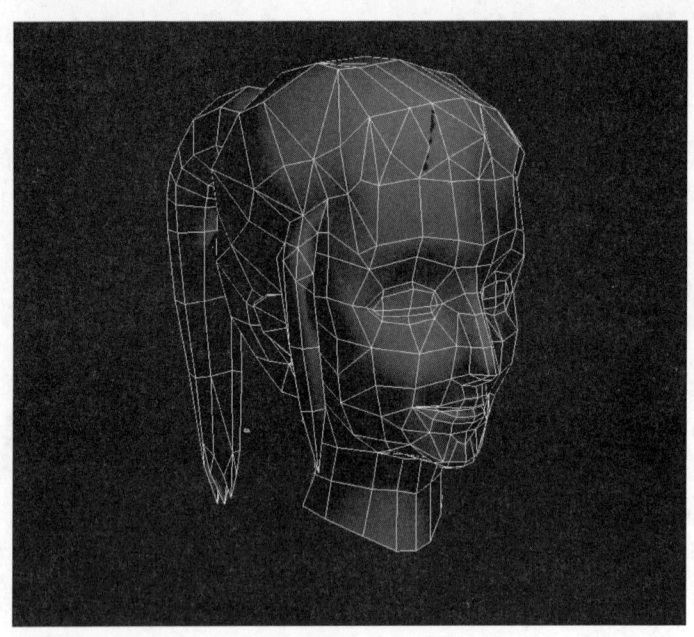
图 5-10 头发模型和面部模型的链接

2. 角色身体模型的制作

角色身体模型的制作分为以下几个步骤。

(1)创建一个基本长方体,并将其转化为可编辑多边形,然后根据女性角色的外形特征将胸部、腰部和臀部的大体结构调整处理,然后细化模型,并将手臂和腿部的衔接面删除。

(2)再次细化模型。根据人物原画的模型添加衣物、靴子等的纹理结构,制作时可以使用倒角等命令增加纹理的厚度,同时要尽量控制线段的数量,保持四边面。

(3)制作手臂。使用圆柱体模型,并且将圆柱体移动到手臂位置,将手臂摆成人形有利于之后的骨骼绑定,然后选择手臂上的边进行缩放,调整出手臂大体的轮廓;选择手臂上部的面,挤出衣袖的厚度,最后将手臂模型附加到身体上,并将连接处的顶点焊接到一起,完成手臂的制作(图 5-11)。

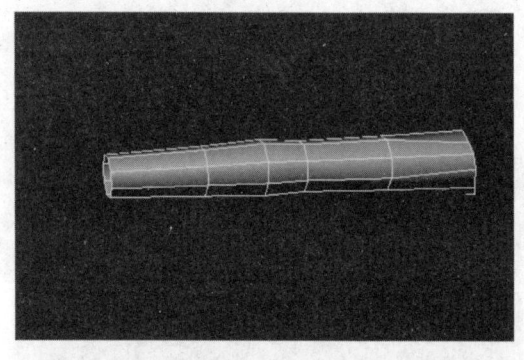

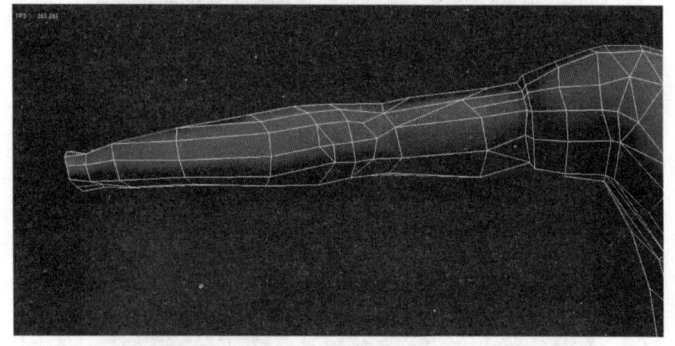

图 5-11　手臂的制作

(4)手部的制作可以用两种方法:一种是先从手掌开始,接着挤压出手指;另一种是先制作手指,再制作手掌,最后将两个对象焊接在一起(图 5-12)。细化手部纹路之后,将手部与手臂拼接到一起。

(5)腿部和靴子的制作方法与手臂和手部相同,创建圆柱体并调整模型,然后将制作好的腿部模型与身体焊接在一起,并调整布线结构,使线段更简洁流畅(图 5-13)。

(6)完成身体模型的制作,即可与头部模型拼接(图 5-14)。

3. 角色的 UV 制作

角色的 UV 制作是指使用 Unfold3D 插件分模型的 UV。Unfold3D 是一个独立的软件,这样使用起来可以不受 3D 软件的限制,通过导入主流 3D 软件都能够支持的 OBJ 文件格式来进行数据交换。角色的 UV 制作主要分为以下几个步骤。

(1)打开 3ds Max,调整头部模型(图 5-15)(面数很少)。

UV 的分布尽量重复利用,我们可以删掉对称的一半模型,在 Unfold3D 中展开完毕后,再复制另一半。由于我们的模型是不对称的,就全部展开。

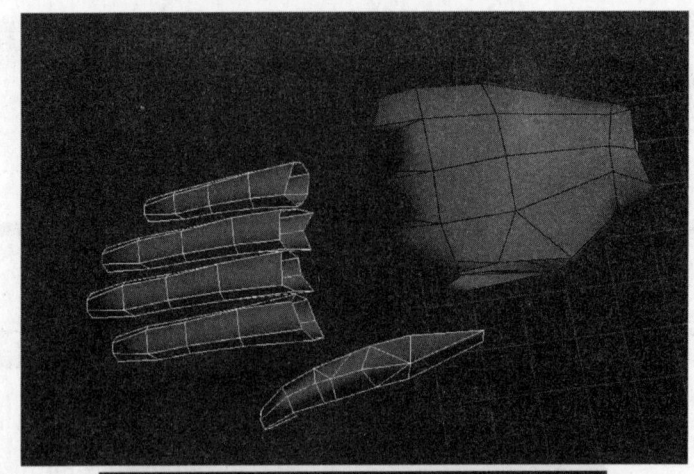

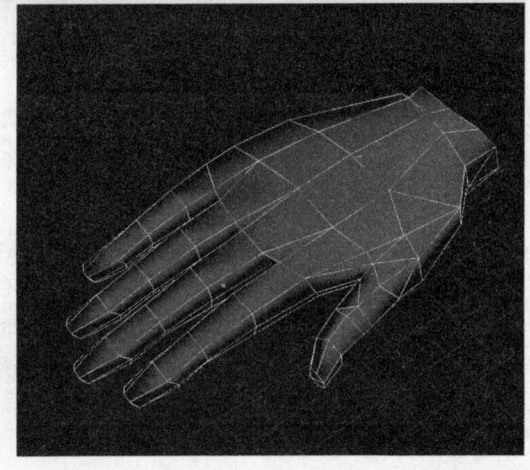

图 5-12 手部的制作

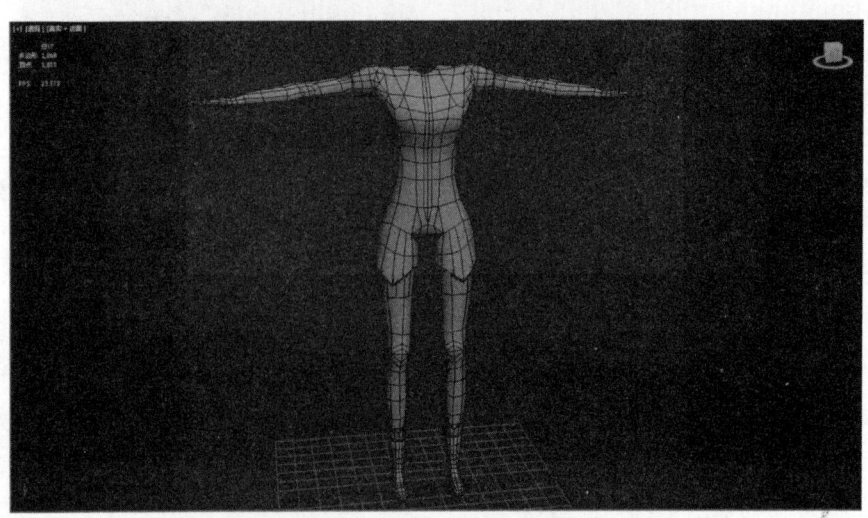

图 5-13 腿部和靴子的制作

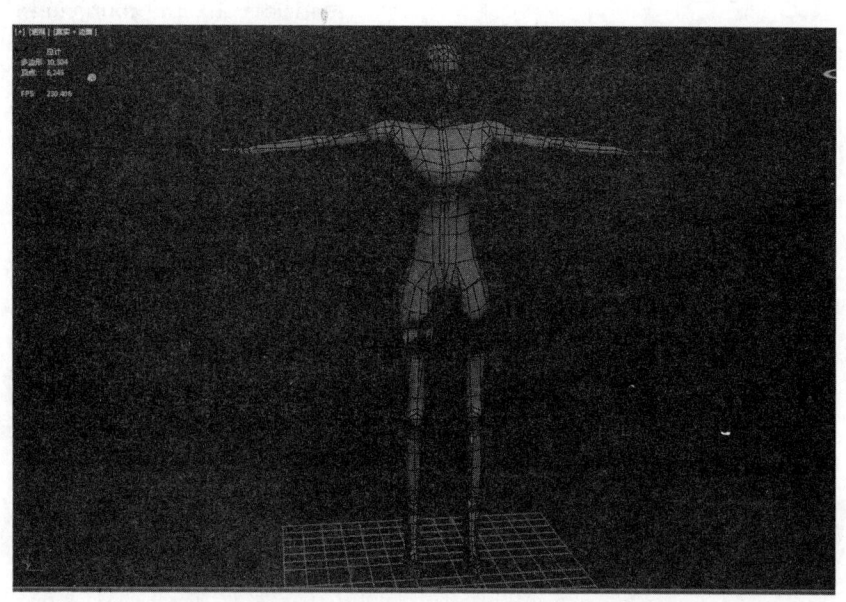

图 5-14 身体模型的制作

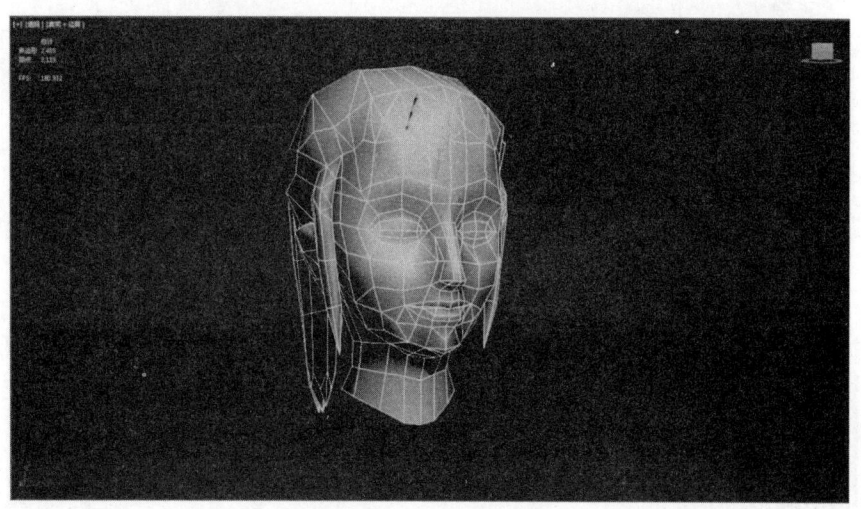

图 5-15 调整头部模型

(2)在导出 OBJ 格式之前,需要对模型进行一些必要的检查和修整。不能存在多余的游离点和重复边、重复面。使用 STL Check 工具查看模型是否存在这些缺陷和漏洞并加以修复(图 5-16)。

(3)选择我们需要导出的模型(图 5-17),导出被选择的物体,这里我们选择 OBJ 格式(图 5-18)。

需要注意的是,在 OBJ 格式选项里面要取消后两项的选择,否则 Unfold3D 会出现错误(图 5-19)。至此模型的导出工作基本结束。

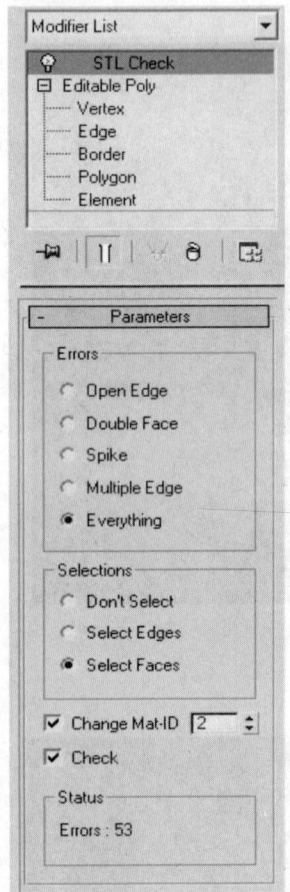
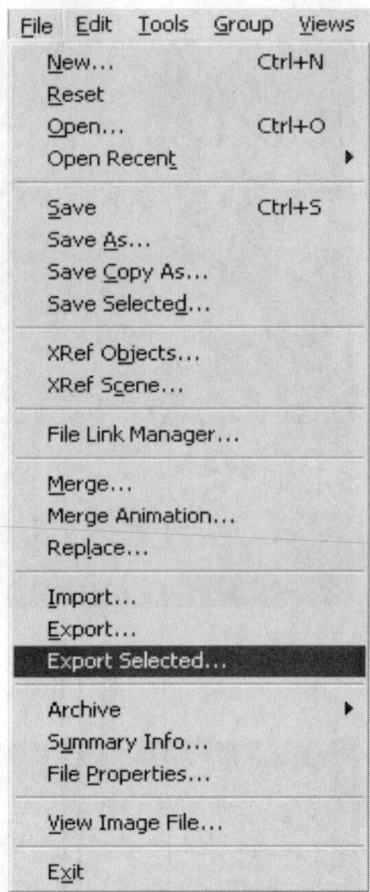

图 5-16　使用 STL Check 工具　　　　　图 5-17　选择导出的模型

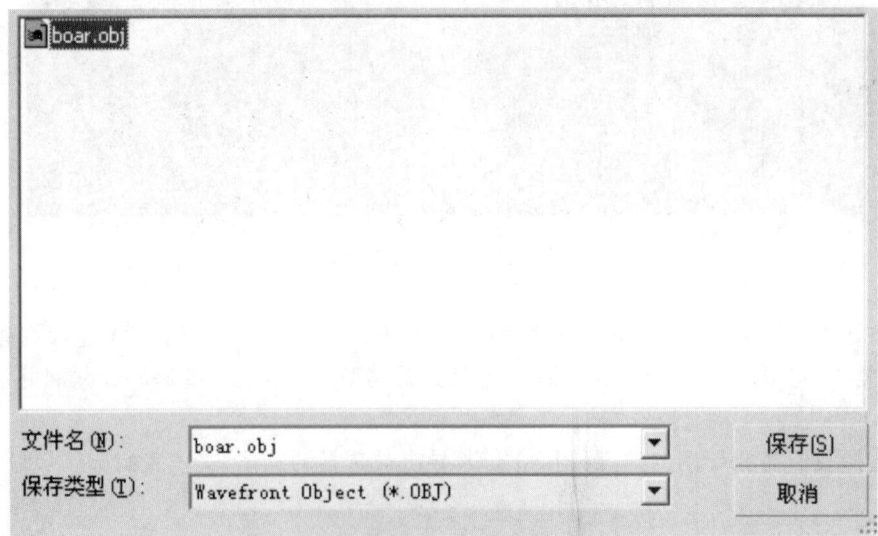

图 5-18　选择 OBJ 格式

第五章 平台设计与实现

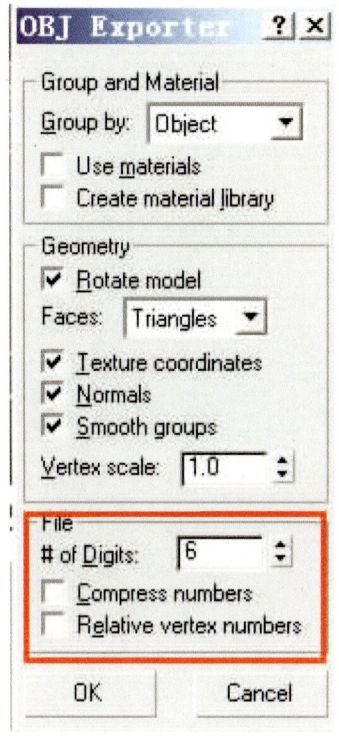

图 5-19 OBJ 格式的选项

（4）打开 Unfold3DLoad 出现我们导出的模型。我们看到，左边的视图显示的是 3D 模型，右面的视图显示的是 3D 模型的 UV 分布（图 5-20）。前面提到过，第一步我们需要设定鼠标和键盘键位的操作意义（即需要先设定 Mouse Bindings）。

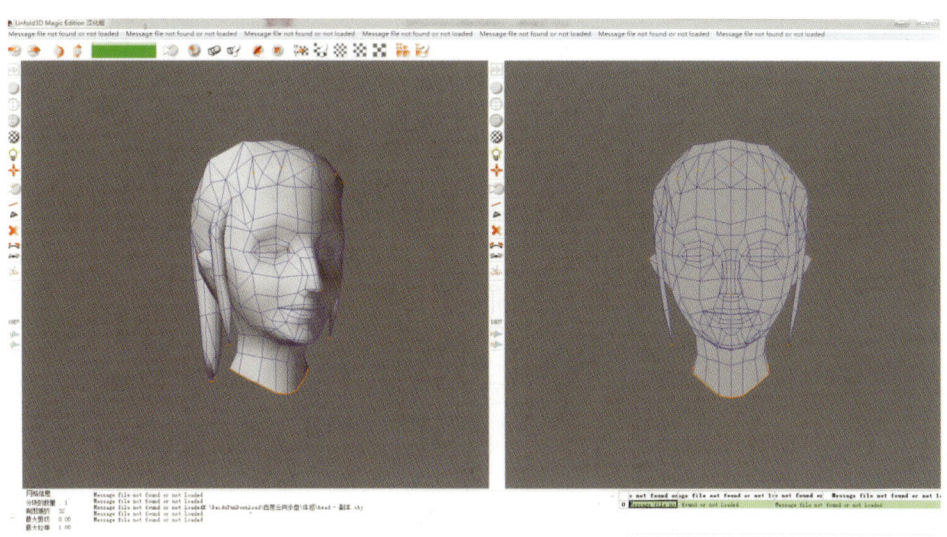

图 5-20 3D 模型和 3D 模型的 UV 分布

· 47 ·

这里选择默认的 Unfold3D 的按键和鼠标顺序(图 5-21)。预先展开一下,以便决定下一步的解决方案。Unfold3D 的原理是用户定义开放边,这个开放边会成为 UV 的开放边,然后 Unfold3D 会尽量均匀地平铺各个结构点来达到展开 UV 的目的。点击 按钮,预先展开一下,观察 UV 分布,得到如图 5-22 所示效果。

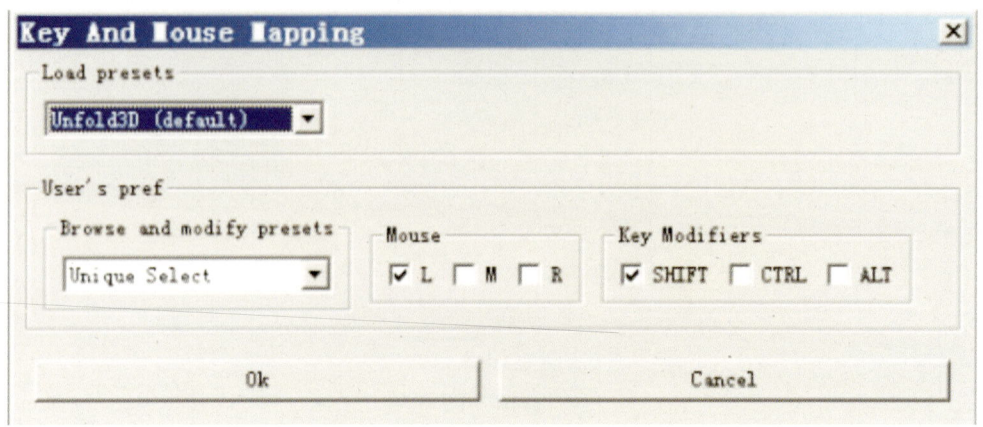

图 5-21 选择按键和鼠标顺序

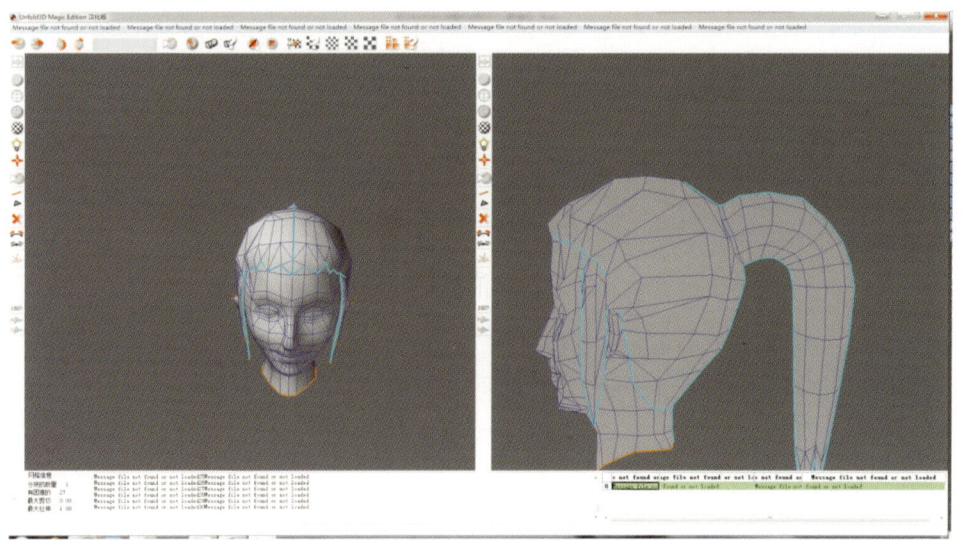

图 5-22 UV 分布效果图

(5)可以看到很多橙色的区域(图 5-23),其表示的是无法完整合理地展开 UV 的区域。这些区域同样显示在 3D 模型的视图里面。因为我们只有开始的模型轮廓的开放边,为了能够更加完整地划分 UV,我们需要拆分模型,选择的方式是按照刚刚设定的 MouseBindings 的设置来进行的。选择需要分割部分的边线,左键是选择,按住 shift 是增加选择。选好之后点击 按钮,分割模型。再次点击 按钮,自动展开 UV 得到如图 5-24 所示的 UV 分布。

图 5-23 橙色的区域

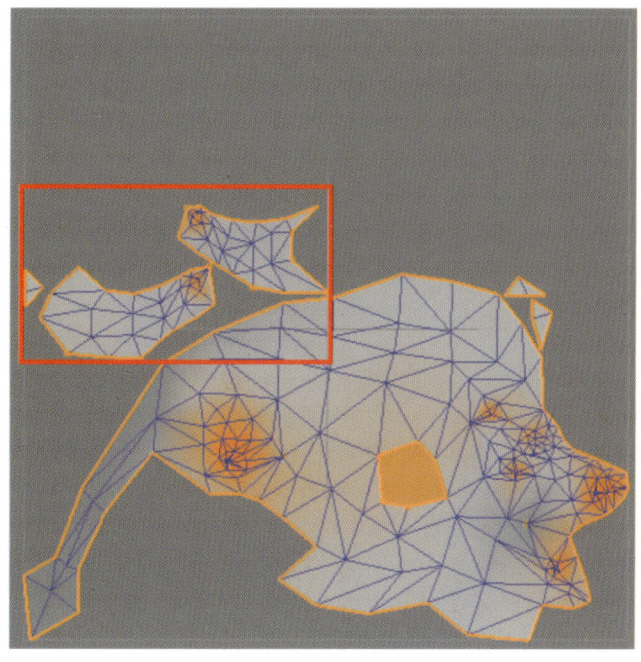

图 5-24 UV 的分布

此时可以看到刚刚无法分布均匀的耳朵部分的 UV 已经很好地展开,放在了红色框的区域里面。其他部分的操作也是同样的。

随着模型的橙色区域在减少(图5-25),最终消除 UV 分布不合理的区域,整个工作就可以完成了。当然,大家也可以根据自己的想法和规划去设计更加合理的 UV 分布方式。图5-25是分布好的 UV 范例,供大家参考。

图5-25 橙色区域在减少

这样,在 Unfold3D 里面的工作基本上就完成了。导出我们的模型成 OBJ 格式,然后在 3D 软件里面导入进来就可以了。

4. 贴图的绘制

贴图的绘制需要绘画师有很强的美术功底,能够对纹理进行深入分析,归纳出各种材质的绘制方法。绘画流程注意分为两种:一种是绘画贴图;另一种是拼贴贴图,绘画贴图主要是根据原画在模型的 UV 拓扑网格上绘制图案,而拼贴贴图主要是根据真实人物的照片进行图像处理,拼贴出角色的贴图。设计师需要根据角色特点来选择贴图方式,这里我们在 Photoshop 中进行贴图的绘制。

(1)面部的绘制。面部绘制主要是根据 UV 网格线,以及皮肤颜色和肤色过渡变化来绘制五官。绘制时要将眼睛、鼻子、嘴巴位置与网格线严丝合缝地对齐(图5-26)。这样在绘制完成后就不会产生贴图不对位的问题。

绘制主要分为3个部分:绘制皮肤大体颜色、绘制五官的明暗变化、绘制五官细节。绘制过程中要逐层深入,把握好画笔颜色的透明度,达到较好的渐变效果,同时善于使用减淡、加深及涂抹工具对过渡色进行柔化。

(2)毛发绘制。填充头发颜色,用中间色按照头发走向镜像绘画,再使用加深工具绘制头

图 5-26 面部的绘制

发的暗部,用减淡工具绘制头发的骨骼高光和亮部,绘画时可使用一些特效笔刷形状,使得绘画程度更细腻逼真。

(3)服饰布料绘制。绘制布料时要注意衣物褶皱的关系,绘制褶皱时要从暗部、中间色、亮部、反光、高光等几个色彩关系入手,同时还要注意褶皱的疏密程度。绘制服饰上的装饰物,如皮带、金属扣等,这些装饰物能够很好地体现模型的细节(图 5-27)。

图 5-27 服饰布料的绘制

绘制完成后将所有图层合并成一个图层,并保存为 TAG 文件,在图像通道中绘制 Alpha 透明通道,其中白色为显示部分,黑色为透明部分。

5. 添加贴图到模型

分别在 3ds Max 的材质编辑器中的漫反射颜色和不透明度贴图通道中添加贴图(图 5-28、图 5-29)。

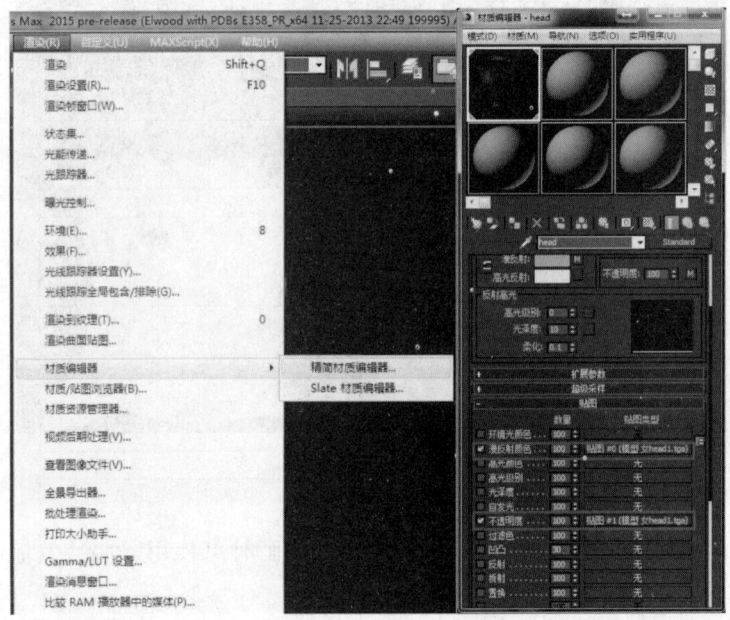

图 5-28 在材质编辑器中添加贴图

图 5-29 贴图模型的效果

6. 在 Maya 中的蒙皮绑定流程

这里我们采用无线传感器式动作捕捉录制的骨骼文件与模型绑定,利用 Maya 自带的脚本编辑器导入可以打开 BVH 动作捕捉文件的脚本,就可以成功导入带有录制好动作的骨骼到 Maya 场景中,然后就可以实现模型与骨骼的绑定(图 5-30、图 5-31)。

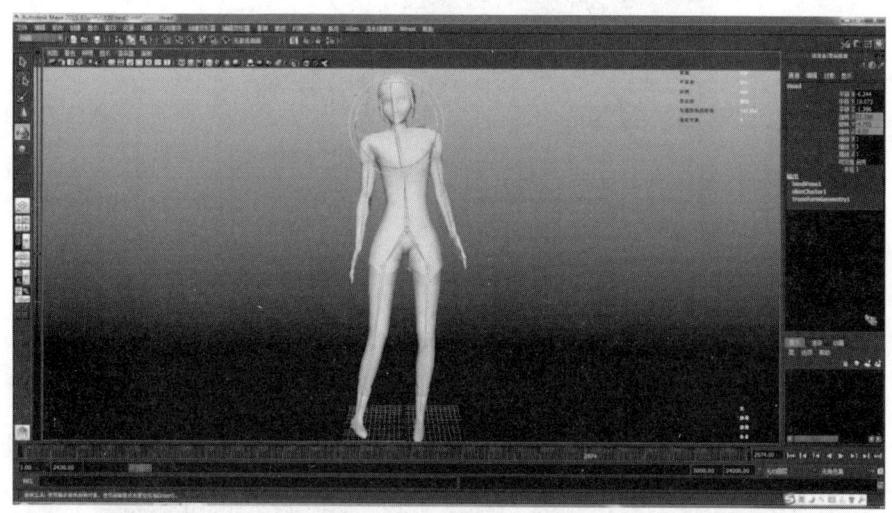

图 5-30 蒙皮部分

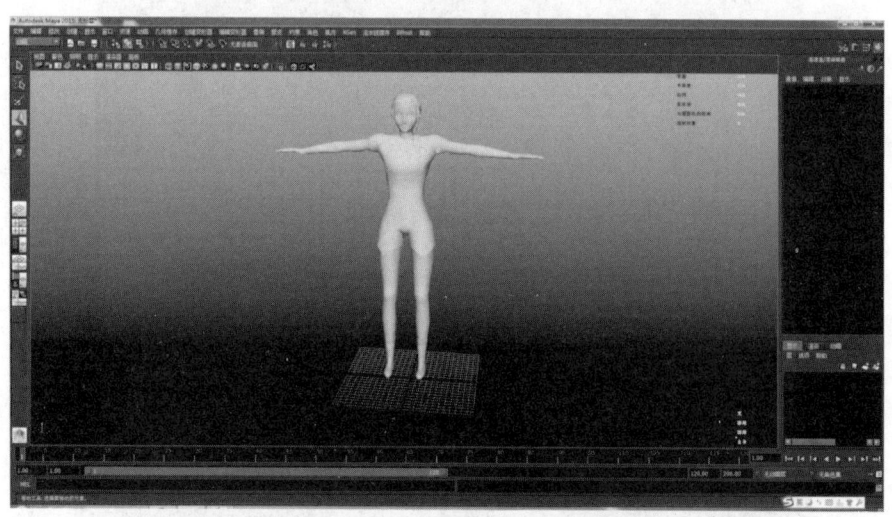

图 5-31 导入模型

运行脚本编辑器命令,打开 BVH 文件的脚本(图 5-32、图 5-33)。
利用脚本运行打开 BVH 文件(图 5-34、图 5-35)。
骨骼导入完成(图 5-36、图 5-37)。
调整骨骼尺寸,使其与模型吻合(图 5-38)。
将骨骼放入模型中匹配,选中要绑定的骨骼和模型对象(图 5-39)。

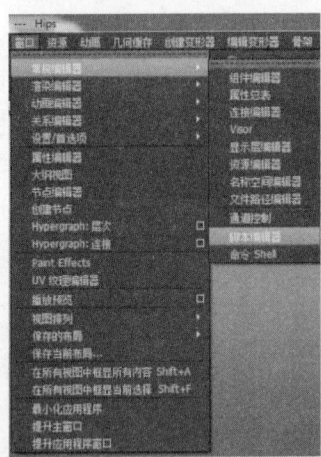

图 5-32 打开 BVH 文件的脚本

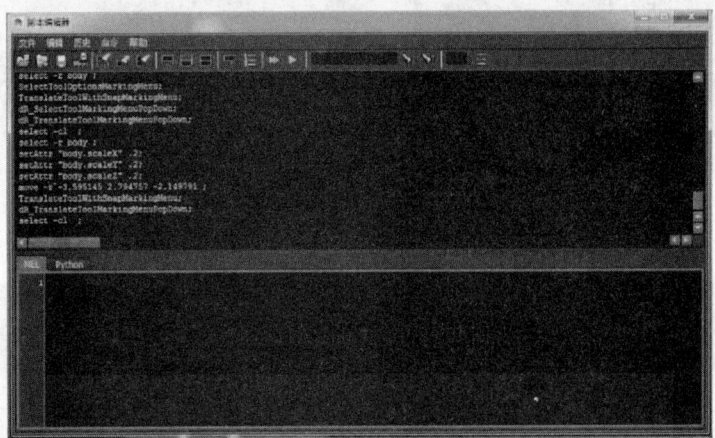

图 5-33 脚本编辑器

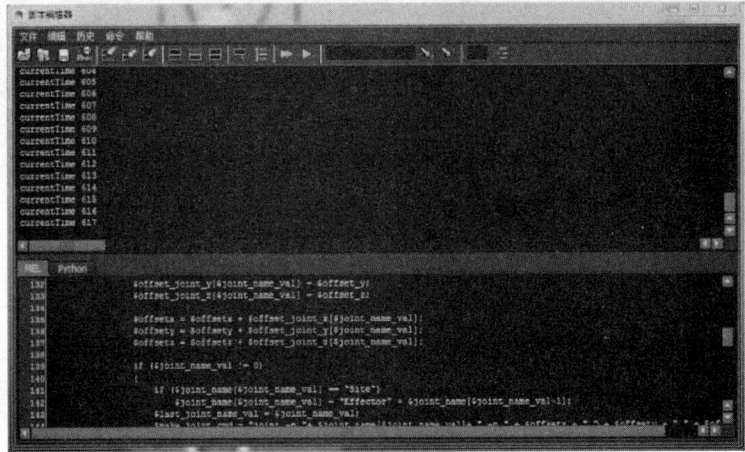

图 5-34 脚本运行

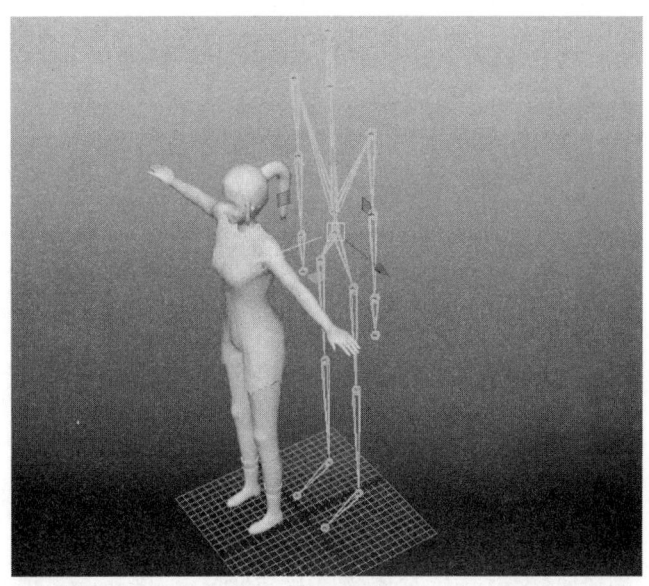

图 5-35 打开 BVH 文件

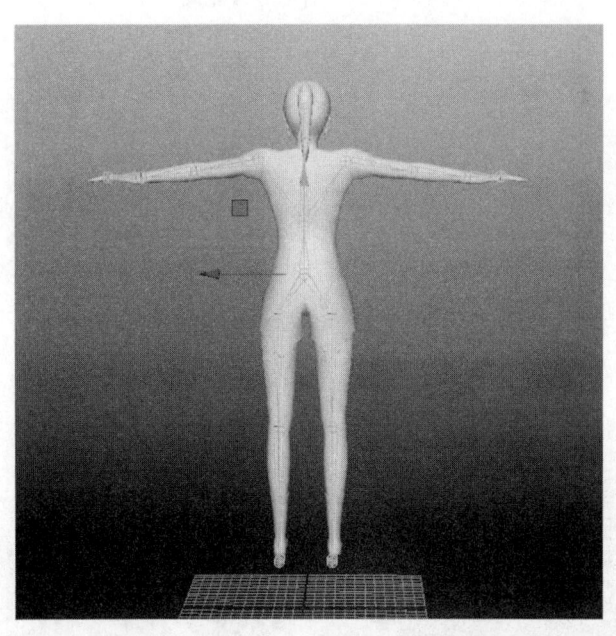

图 5-36 骨骼导入

使用平滑绑定命令,使模型蒙皮在骨骼上(图 5-40)。

执行绘制蒙皮权重画笔命令来使模型的细节处在跟随骨骼运动时产生的形变比较正常(图 5-41、图 5-42)。

观察动画的形变正常后即可选中要导出的对象,导出模型。注意要勾选导出动画选框,才会将模型骨骼的动作一并导出(图 5-43、图 5-44)。

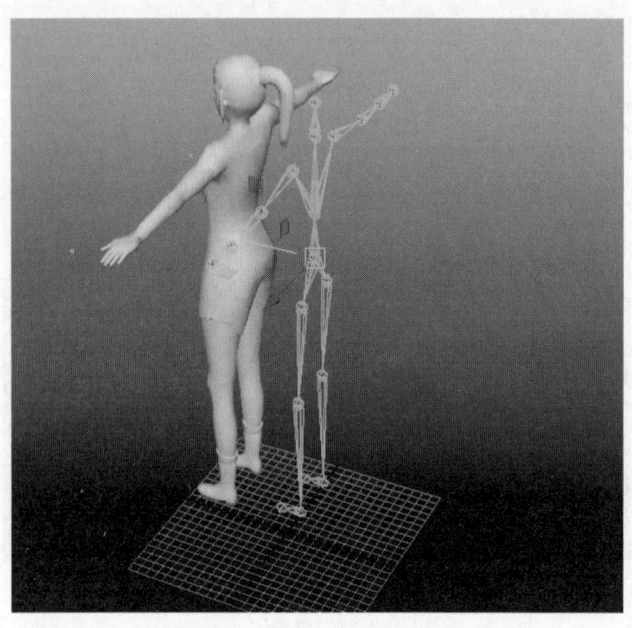

图 5-37 骨骼导入完成

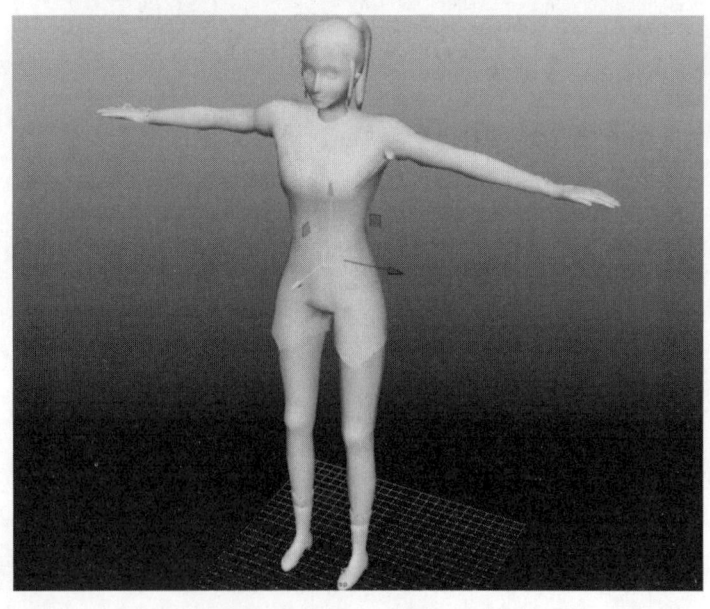

图 5-38 调整骨骼尺寸

虽然在 Max 中也有插件可以借助 Kinect 摄像头来录制骨骼动作,但相对 3ds Max 的 biped 动画制作技术,作者认为在 Maya 中绑定动作捕捉文件骨骼到模型,再进行调整,动作更精确,更方便快捷,也不会产生较大的误差点。

第五章　平台设计与实现

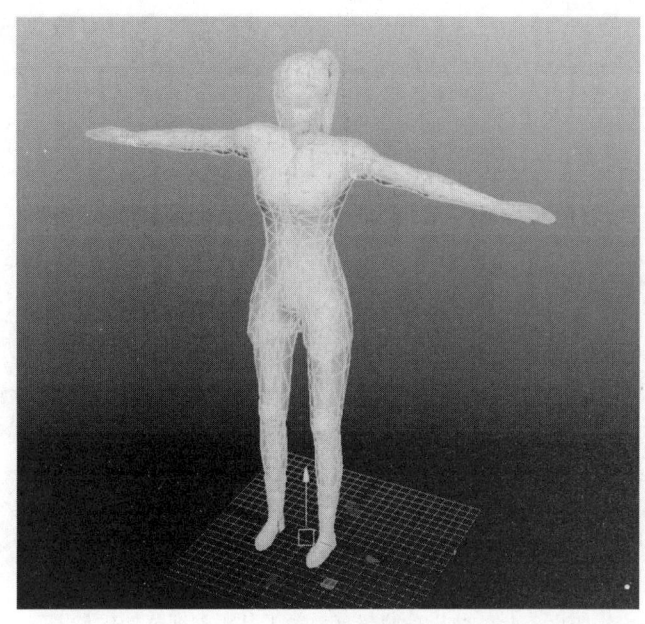

图 5-39　绑定的骨骼和模型对象

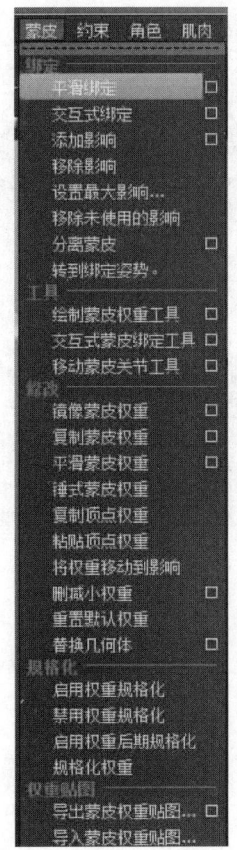

图 5-40　平滑绑定命令

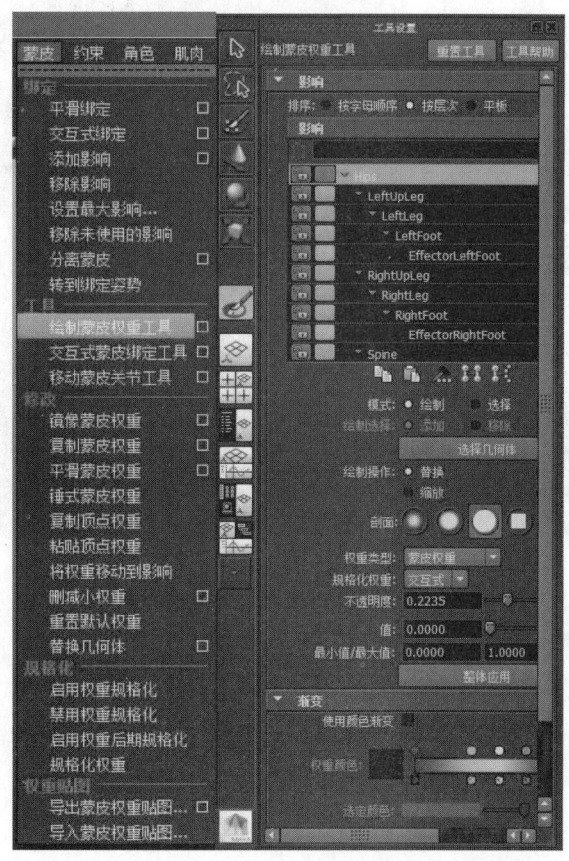

图 5-41　绘制蒙皮权重工具的使用

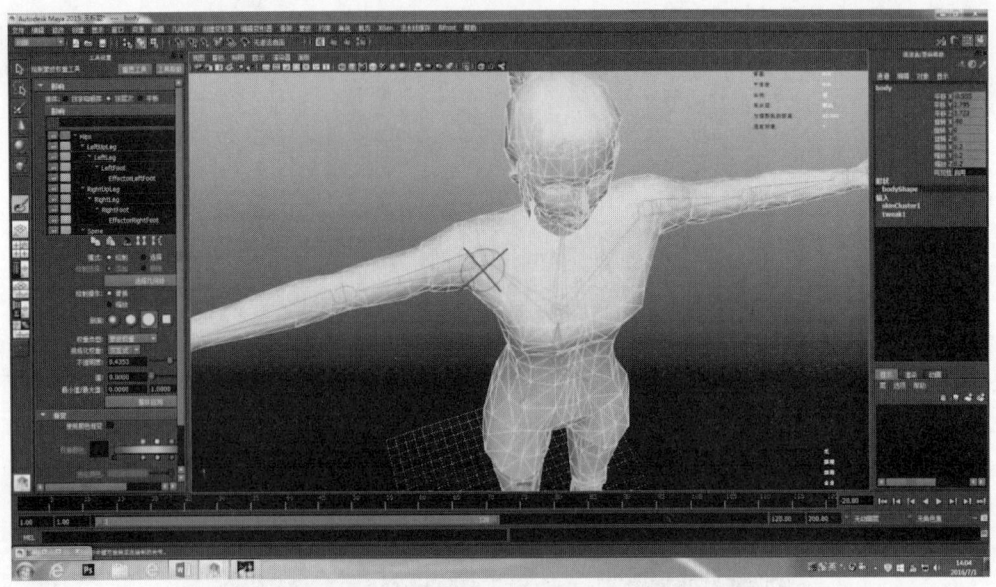

图 5-42 利用绘制权重画笔工具调整细节处权重

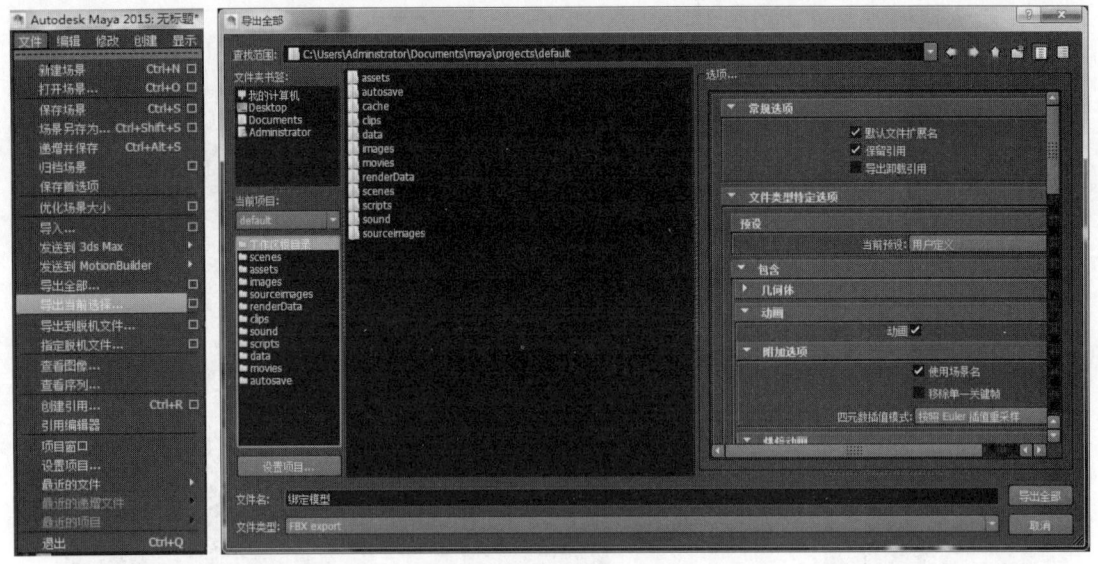

图 5-43 选择导出对象　　　　　图 5-44 导出模型

三、脚本编写

(一) 动画播放控制脚本

按钮控制动画的播放,具体如下:
public class PlayGame:MonoBehaviour {
　　//添加播放对象及动画

```
public GameObject target1;
public GameObject target2;
private GameObject man＝null ;
public const string all＝"Take 001";
private bool isPlayAnimation＝false;
//找到需要的对象
void Start () {
man＝GameObject.Find ("123");
man.GetComponent＜Animation＞() .GetComponent＜Animation＞() [all].speed＝0;
}
//暂停按钮控制
public void OnClick1(){
    if(isPlayAnimation)
    {
        Debug.Log("Stop");
        isPlayAnimation＝false;
        target1.SetActive(false);
        man.GetComponent＜Animation＞() .GetComponent＜Animation＞() [all].speed＝0;
            target2.SetActive(true);}
    }
//播放按钮控制
public void OnClick2(){
    if(! isPlayAnimation)
    {
        Debug.Log("play");//向控制台输出当前状态
        isPlayAnimation＝true;
        target1.SetActive(true);
//控制音乐播放
        man.GetComponent＜Animation＞() .GetComponent＜Animation＞() [all].speed＝1
        target2.SetActive(false);
    }
}
//返回主页面
    public void OnMouseDown1(){
        Application.LoadLevel("main");
    }
}
```

(二)音乐播放控制脚本

添加按钮点击事件来控制,具体实现如下:

```
Public class OpenScene:MonoBehaviour{
    //音乐选择
    public AudioSource music1;
    public AudioSource music2;
    //音乐按钮的外观图
    public Texture2D pause;
    public Texture2D play;
    private Texture2D playTest;
    //
    public const string all="all";

    private bool isPlayAnimation=true;
    void Start () {
    //初始化音量与音乐
        music1.volume=1;
        man=GameObject.Find ("part1");
    }
}
```

(三)多角度、多方向观看控制脚本

旋转主摄像机的方向使其始终指向观察对象,来实现多角度观看,具体实现如下:

```
public class Rotation:MonoBehaviour {
    //摄像机观察对象
    public Transform target;
    //初始化旋转信息
    private float xSpeed=500.0f;
    private float ySpeed=200.0f;
    private float x=-2.0f;
    private float y=-3.0f;
    private int yMinLimit=10;
    private int yMaxLimit=25;
    //摄像机与人物之间的距离
    private float normalDistance=2;

    private Vector3 CameraTarget;
    private Quaternion rotation=Quaternion.Euler(new Vector3(30f,0f,0f));
```

```
void Start () {
    CameraTarget=target.position;
    transform.LookAt(target);

    var angles=transform.eulerAngles;
    x=angles.y;
    y=angles.x-200;

}

void Update () {
//鼠标左键拖动控制旋转
if(Input.GetMouseButton(0))
        {//通过鼠标所在的坐标位置来确定拖动距离
        x+=Input.GetAxis("Mouse X")*xSpeed*0.02f;
        y-=Input.GetAxis("Mouse Y")*ySpeed*0.02f;

        y=ClampAngle(y, yMinLimit, yMaxLimit);
        //计算选择角度和坐标位置
        var rotation=Quaternion.Euler(y, x, 0);
        var position=rotation*new Vector3(0.0f, 0.0f,- normalDistance)+CameraTarget;

        transform.rotation=rotation;
        transform.position=position;

        }
    }
//限制旋转角度在-360°~360°之间
    static float ClampAngle (float angle, float min,float max)
    {
        if (angle<-360)
            angle+=360;
        if (angle>360)
            angle-=360;
        return Mathf.Clamp (angle, min, max);
    }
}
```

(四)太极拳人机交互娱乐功能模块实现

1. 人物模型控制脚本

人物模型控制也就是将人物模型中的骨骼与 Kinect 设备识别到的人体骨骼绑定在一起。为了使人物模型和用户的运动保持一致,将人物模型与人体骨骼进行匹配,骨骼控制模型运动。骨骼控制模型,也就是人物模型获取人体骨骼的空间坐标。具体实现如下:

```
[RequireComponent(typeof(Animator))]
public class AvatarController: MonoBehaviour
{
    //设置用户的索引编号
    public int playerIndex=0;

    //默认情况下,用户图像实际上是一个镜像数据
    public bool mirroredMovement=false;

    //判断人物模型是否垂直方向移动
    public bool verticalMovement=false;

    //模型在场景中的移动速度
    private int moveRate=1;

    //平滑度
    public float smoothFactor=5f;

    //人体骨骼的根节点
    private Transform bodyRoot;

    //判断模型是否进行旋转
    private GameObject offsetNode;

    //人体所有骨骼点集合
    private Transform[] bones;

    //人体骨骼旋转坐标
    private Quaternion[] initialRotations;
    private Quaternion[] initialLocalRotations;

    //人物模型的空间坐标
    private Vector3 initialPosition;
```

```
private Quaternion initialRotation;

private bool OffsetCalibrated=false;
private float XOffset, YOffset, ZOffset;

//创建一个 KinectManager 实例
private KinectManager kinectManager;

//用于存储每次获取 Transform 组件的值
private Transform _transformCache;
public new Transform transform
{
    get
    {
        if (!_transformCache) _transformCache=base.transform;
        return _transformCache;
    }
}

//功能:执行模型控制
public void Awake()
{
    //判断控制的人物模型是否存在
    if(bones!=null)
        return;

    //创建人体骨骼点的集合
    bones=new Transform[27];

    //初始化骨骼点的坐标
    initialRotations=new Quaternion[bones.Length];
    initialLocalRotations=new Quaternion[bones.Length];
    //initialDirections=new Vector3[bones.Length];

//设置父节点模型
offsetNode=new GameObject(name+"Ctrl") {layer=transform.gameObject.layer,
                                        tag=transform.gameObject.tag };
offsetNode.transform.position=transform.position;
offsetNode.transform.rotation=transform.rotation;
```

```csharp
        transform.parent=offsetNode.transform;
        transform.localPosition=Vector3.zero;
        transform.localRotation=Quaternion.identity;

        bodyRoot=transform;

        //人体骨骼无人物模型的匹配
        MapBones();

        //初始化模型旋转坐标
        GetInitialRotations();
}

//功能:实时更新模型数据库
public void UpdateAvatar(Int64 UserId)
{
        if(!transform.gameObject.activeInHierarchy)
            return;

        //获取 kinectManager 实例
        if(KinectManager==null)
        {
            kinectManager=KinectManager.Instance;
        }

        //移动人物模型到 Kinect 获取的空间位置上
        MoveAvatar(UserId);

        for (var boneIndex=0; boneIndex<bones.Length;boneIndex++)
        {
            if (!bones[boneIndex])
                continue;

            if(boneIndex2JointMap.ContainsKey(boneIndex))
            {
                KinectInterop.JointType joint=!mirroredMovement?boneIndex2JointMap
                                [boneIndex]: boneIndex2MirrorJointMap[boneIndex];
                TransformBone(UserId, joint, boneIndex,!mirroredMovement);
```

```
        }
        else if(specIndex2JointMap.ContainsKey(boneIndex))
        {
            //特殊骨骼点
            List<KinectInterop.JointType>alJoints = !mirroredMovement?
                specIndex2JointMap[boneIndex]: specIndex2MirrorJointMap[boneIndex];

            if(alJoints.Count>=2)
            {
                Vector3 baseDir=alJoints[0].ToString().EndsWith("Left")?
                    Vector3.left: Vector3.right;
                TransformSpecialBone(UserId, alJoints[0], alJoints[1], boneIndex,
                    baseDir,!mirroredMovement);
            }
        }
    }
}

//功能:设置骨骼点的空间位置坐标
public void ResetToInitialPosition()
{
    if(bones==null)
        return;

    if(offsetNode!=null)
    {
        offsetNode.transform.rotation=Quaternion.identity;
    }
    else
    {
        transform.rotation=Quaternion.identity;
    }

    //依次遍历每个骨骼点,设置骨骼点坐标
    for(int pass=0; pass<2; pass++){
        for(int i=0; i<bones.Length; i++)
        {
            if(bones[i]!=null)
```

```
                    {
                        bones[i].rotation=initialRotations[i];
                    }
            }

            if(bodyRoot!=null)
            {
                bodyRoot.localPosition=Vector3.zero;
                bodyRoot.localRotation=Quaternion.identity;
            }

            //存储空间坐标值
            if(offsetNode!=null)
            {
                offsetNode.transform.position=initialPosition;
                offsetNode.transform.rotation=initialRotation;
            }
            else
            {
                transform.position=initialPosition;
                transform.rotation=initialRotation;
            }
    }

//功能:对用户进行识别
public void SuccessfulCalibration(Int64 userId)
{
    //reset the models position
    if(offsetNode!=null)
    {
        offsetNode.transform.rotation=initialRotation;
    }
    else
    {
        transform.rotation=initialRotation;
    }
    OffsetCalibrated=false;
}
```

```csharp
//功能：使用 Kinect 获取的骨骼点坐标
void TransformBone(Int64 userId, KinectInterop.JointType joint, int boneIndex, bool flip)
{
    Transform boneTransform= bones[boneIndex];
    if(boneTransform==null||kinectManager==null)
        return;

    int iJoint=(int)joint;
    if(iJoint<0||!kinectManager.IsJointTracked(userId, iJoint))
        return;

    //获取骨骼关节点的定向信息
    Quaternion jointRotation=KinectManager.GetJointOrientation(userId, iJoint, flip);
    if(jointRotation==Quaternion.identity)
        return;

    //平滑过渡旋转坐标
    Quaternion newRotation=Kinect2AvatarRot(jointRotation, boneIndex);

    if(smoothFactor!=0f)
        boneTransform.rotation=Quaternion.Slerp(boneTransform.rotation, newRotation,
                                    smoothFactor*Time.deltaTime);
    else
        boneTransform.rotation=newRotation;
}

//功能：使用 Kinect 获取的特殊骨骼点旋转坐标
void TransformSpecialBone(Int64 userId, KinectInterop.JointType joint, KinectInterop.JointType jointParent, int boneIndex, Vector3 baseDir, bool flip)
{
    Transform boneTransform= bones[boneIndex];
    if(boneTransform==null||kinectManager==null)
        return;

    if(!kinectManager.IsJointTracked(userId, (int)joint)||
        !kinectManager.IsJointTracked(userId, (int)jointParent))
    {
        return;
    }
```

```
        Vector3 jointDir=kinectManager.GetJointDirection(userId, (int)joint, false, true);
        Quaternion jointRotation=Quaternion.FromToRotation(baseDir, jointDir);

        if(!flip)
        {
            Vector3 mirroredAngles=jointRotation.eulerAngles;
            mirroredAngles.y=-mirroredAngles.y;
            mirroredAngles.z=-mirroredAngles.z;

            jointRotation=Quaternion.Euler(mirroredAngles);
        }

        if(jointRotation!=Quaternion.identity)
        {
            //Smoothly transition to the new rotation
            Quaternion newRotation=Kinect2AvatarRot(jointRotation, boneIndex);

            if(smoothFactor!=0f)
               boneTransform.rotation = Quaternion.Slerp (boneTransform.rotation, newRotation,
                                                          smoothFactor*Time.deltaTime);
            else
               boneTransform.rotation=newRotation;
        }
    }

//功能:控制人物模型在场景中移动
void MoveAvatar(Int64 UserId)
{
        if(!kinectManager||!kinectManager.IsJointTracked (UserId, (int)KinectInterop.JointType.
                                                           SpineBase))
             return;

        //获取人体坐标并存储
        Vector3 trans=kinectManager.GetUserPosition(UserId);
        //移动人物模型
        if (!OffsetCalibrated)
        {
             OffsetCalibrated=true;
```

```
            XOffset=!mirroredMovement?trans.x*moveRate:-trans.x*moveRate;
            YOffset=trans.y*moveRate;
            ZOffset=-trans.z*moveRate;
    }

    //平滑过渡空间位置坐标
    Vector3 targetPos=Kinect2AvatarPos(trans, verticalMovement);

    if(bodyRoot!=null)
    {
        bodyRoot.localPosition=smoothFactor!=0f?
        Vector3.Lerp(bodyRoot.localPosition, targetPos, smoothFactor*Time.deltaTime):
            targetPos;
    }
    else
    {
        transform.localPosition=smoothFactor!=0f?
        Vector3.Lerp(transform.localPosition, targetPos, smoothFactor*Time.deltaTime):
            targetPos;
    }
}


//功能:将人体骨骼与人物模型进行匹配
void MapBones()
{//获取 Animator 动画组件,来控制人物模型的移动
    var animatorComponent=GetComponent<Animator>();

    for (int boneIndex=0; boneIndex<bones.Length; boneIndex++)
    {
        if (!boneIndex2MecanimMap.ContainsKey(boneIndex))
            continue;

        bones [boneIndex] = animatorComponent.GetBoneTransform(boneIndex2MecanimMap
                                                                [boneIndex]);
    }
}
```

```
//功能：捕捉骨骼的旋转坐标
void GetInitialRotations()
{
    //保存旋转坐标
    if(offsetNode!=null)
    {
        initialPosition=offsetNode.transform.position;
        initialRotation=offsetNode.transform.rotation;

        offsetNode.transform.rotation=Quaternion.identity;
    }
    else
    {
        initialPosition=transform.position;
        initialRotation=transform.rotation;

        transform.rotation=Quaternion.identity;
    }

    for (int i=0; i<bones.Length; i++)
    {
        if (bones[i]!=null)
        {
            initialRotations[i]=bones[i].rotation; //*Quaternion.Inverse(initialRotation);
            initialLocalRotations[i]=bones[i].localRotation;
        }
    }

    //恢复旋转坐标
    if(offsetNode!=null)
    {
        offsetNode.transform.rotation=initialRotation;
    }
    else
    {
        transform.rotation=initialRotation;
    }
}
```

```
//功能:将人体骨骼点旋转坐标传给人物模型,关键在于骨骼点的初始化时的旋转坐标与坐标
  差值
Quaternion Kinect2AvatarRot(Quaternion jointRotation, int boneIndex)
{
    Quaternion newRotation=jointRotation*initialRotations[boneIndex];

    if (offsetNode!=null)
    {
        Vector3 totalRotation=newRotation.eulerAngles+offsetNode.transform.rotation.
                              eulerAngles;
        newRotation=Quaternion.Euler(totalRotation);
    }

    return newRotation;
}

//功能:将人体骨骼点空间位置坐标传给人物模型,关键在于骨骼点的初始化时的空间位置坐
  标、移动速度、是否镜像
Vector3 Kinect2AvatarPos(Vector3 jointPosition, bool bMoveVertically)
{
    float xPos;

    if(!mirroredMovement)
        xPos=jointPosition.x*moveRate - XOffset;
    else
        xPos=-jointPosition.x*moveRate - XOffset;

    float yPos=jointPosition.y*moveRate - YOffset;
    float zPos=-jointPosition.z*moveRate - ZOffset;

    Vector3 newPosition=new Vector3(xPos, bMoveVertically?yPos：0f, zPos);

    return newPosition;
}

//功能:通过索引值获取人物模型骨骼点,用于人物模型与人体骨骼的匹配
private readonly Dictionary<int, HumanBodyBones>boneIndex2MecanimMap=new Dictionary
<int, HumanBodyBones>
{
```

```
            {0, HumanBodyBones.Hips},
            {1, HumanBodyBones.Spine},
            {2, HumanBodyBones.Chest},
            {3, HumanBodyBones.Neck},
            {4, HumanBodyBones.Head},

            {5, HumanBodyBones.LeftUpperArm},
            {6, HumanBodyBones.LeftLowerArm},
            {7, HumanBodyBones.LeftHand},
            {8, HumanBodyBones.LeftIndexProximal},

            {9, HumanBodyBones.LeftIndexIntermediate},
            {10, HumanBodyBones.LeftThumbProximal},

            {11, HumanBodyBones.RightUpperArm},
            {12, HumanBodyBones.RightLowerArm},
            {13, HumanBodyBones.RightHand},
            {14, HumanBodyBones.RightIndexProximal},

            {15, HumanBodyBones.RightIndexIntermediate},
            {16, HumanBodyBones.RightThumbProximal},

            {17, HumanBodyBones.LeftUpperLeg},
            {18, HumanBodyBones.LeftLowerLeg},
            {19, HumanBodyBones.LeftFoot},
            {20, HumanBodyBones.LeftToes},

            {21, HumanBodyBones.RightUpperLeg},
            {22, HumanBodyBones.RightLowerLeg},
            {23, HumanBodyBones.RightFoot},
            {24, HumanBodyBones.RightToes},

            {25, HumanBodyBones.LeftShoulder},
            {26, HumanBodyBones.RightShoulder},
        };
//功能：通过索引值获取人体骨骼点，用于人物模型与人体骨骼的匹配
private readonly Dictionary<int, KinectInterop.JointType>boneIndex2JointMap＝new
    Dictionary<int, KinectInterop.JointType>
{
```

```
{0, KinectInterop.JointType.SpineBase},
{1, KinectInterop.JointType.SpineMid},
{2, KinectInterop.JointType.SpineShoulder},
{3, KinectInterop.JointType.Neck},
{4, KinectInterop.JointType.Head},

{5, KinectInterop.JointType.ShoulderLeft},
{6, KinectInterop.JointType.ElbowLeft},
{7, KinectInterop.JointType.WristLeft},
{8, KinectInterop.JointType.HandLeft},

{9, KinectInterop.JointType.HandTipLeft},
{10,KinectInterop.JointType.ThumbLeft},

{11, KinectInterop.JointType.ShoulderRight},
{12, KinectInterop.JointType.ElbowRight},
{13, KinectInterop.JointType.WristRight},
{14, KinectInterop.JointType.HandRight},

{15, KinectInterop.JointType.HandTipRight},
{16, KinectInterop.JointType.ThumbRight},

{17, KinectInterop.JointType.HipLeft},
{18, KinectInterop.JointType.KneeLeft},
{19, KinectInterop.JointType.AnkleLeft},
{20, KinectInterop.JointType.FootLeft},

{21, KinectInterop.JointType.HipRight},
{22, KinectInterop.JointType.KneeRight},
{23, KinectInterop.JointType.AnkleRight},
{24, KinectInterop.JointType.FootRight},
};
//功能：通过索引值获取特殊人体骨骼点，用于人物模型与人体骨骼的匹配
private readonly Dictionary<int, List<KinectInterop.JointType>>specIndex2JointMap＝new
    Dictionary<int, List<KinectInterop.JointType>>
{
    {25, new List<KinectInterop.JointType>{KinectInterop.JointType.ShoulderLeft,
                                           KinectInterop.JointType.SpineShoulder} },
    {26, new List<KinectInterop.JointType>{KinectInterop.JointType.ShoulderRight,
```

                                    KinectInterop.JointType.SpineShoulder} },
};
//功能：通过索引值获取人体骨骼点的镜像点，用于人物模型与人体骨骼的匹配
private readonly Dictionary<int, KinectInterop.JointType>boneIndex2MirrorJointMap＝new
    Dictionary<int, KinectInterop.JointType>
{
    {0, KinectInterop.JointType.SpineBase},
    {1, KinectInterop.JointType.SpineMid},
    {2, KinectInterop.JointType.SpineShoulder},
    {3, KinectInterop.JointType.Neck},
    {4, KinectInterop.JointType.Head},

    {5, KinectInterop.JointType.ShoulderRight},
    {6, KinectInterop.JointType.ElbowRight},
    {7, KinectInterop.JointType.WristRight},
    {8, KinectInterop.JointType.HandRight},

    {9, KinectInterop.JointType.HandTipRight},
    {10, KinectInterop.JointType.ThumbRight},

    {11, KinectInterop.JointType.ShoulderLeft},
    {12, KinectInterop.JointType.ElbowLeft},
    {13, KinectInterop.JointType.WristLeft},
    {14, KinectInterop.JointType.HandLeft},

    {15, KinectInterop.JointType.HandTipLeft},
    {16, KinectInterop.JointType.ThumbLeft},

    {17, KinectInterop.JointType.HipRight},
    {18, KinectInterop.JointType.KneeRight},
    {19, KinectInterop.JointType.AnkleRight},
    {20, KinectInterop.JointType.FootRight},

    {21, KinectInterop.JointType.HipLeft},
    {22, KinectInterop.JointType.KneeLeft},
    {23, KinectInterop.JointType.AnkleLeft},
    {24, KinectInterop.JointType.FootLeft},
};
//功能：通过索引值获取人体特殊骨骼点的镜像点，用于人物模型与人体骨骼的匹配

```
private readonly Dictionary<int, List<KinectInterop.JointType>>specIndex2MirrorJointMap=
    new Dictionary<int, List<KinectInterop.JointType>>
{
    {25, new List<KinectInterop.JointType> {KinectInterop.JointType.ShoulderRight,
                                KinectInterop.JointType.SpineShoulder} },
    {26, new List<KinectInterop.JointType> {KinectInterop.JointType.ShoulderLeft,
                                KinectInterop.JointType.SpineShoulder} },
};
}
```

2. 从 Microsoft Kinect SDK 中获取数据脚本

NUI API 是 Kinect 的核心 API。它具有设备枚举的方法，支持"流处理"和"设备管理"的功能，具体包括：Kinect 传感器与计算机的连接、访问、关闭。访问从 Kinect 传感器上传输的图像和深度数据流。通过对图像和深度数据的处理来进行骨骼跟踪、数据坐标的变换。具体脚本实现如下：

```
public class KinectInterop
{
    public static class Constants
    {
        //Kinect 可被动跟踪最多6位玩家的形态和位置，可主动跟踪最多2位玩家的全身骨架
        public const int BodyCount=6;
        //Kinect 可识别的骨骼关节点的数量
        public const int JointCount=25;
        public const float MinTimeBetweenSameGestures=0.0f;
        public const float PoseCompleteDuration=1.0f;
        public const float ClickMaxDistance=0.05f;
        public const float ClickStayDuration=1.5f;
    }

    //数据帧的像素点
    public enum FrameSource：uint
    {
        TypeNone=0×0,
        TypeColor=0×1,
        TypeInfrared=0×2,
        TypeDepth=0×8,
        TypeBodyIndex=0×10,
        TypeBody=0×20,
        TypeAudio=0×40
```

```csharp
}
//骨骼点类型
//列出25个骨骼点的特定名称
public enum JointType : int
{
    SpineBase = 0,
    SpineMid = 1,
    Neck = 2,
    Head = 3,//头部
    ShoulderLeft = 4,//左肩
    ElbowLeft = 5,//左肘关节
    WristLeft = 6,//左腕关节
    HandLeft = 7,//左手
    ShoulderRight = 8,//右肩
    ElbowRight = 9,//右肘关节
    WristRight = 10,//右腕关节
    HandRight = 11,//右手
    HipLeft = 12,//左臀部
    KneeLeft = 13,//左膝盖
    AnkleLeft = 14,//左踝关节
    FootLeft = 15,//左脚
    HipRight = 16,//右臀部
    KneeRight = 17,//右膝盖
    AnkleRight = 18,//右踝关节
    FootRight = 19,//右脚
    SpineShoulder = 20,
    HandTipLeft = 21,
    ThumbLeft = 22,
    HandTipRight = 23,
    ThumbRight = 24
    //Count = 25
}
//骨骼关节点的前方向
public static readonly Vector3[] JointBaseDir =
{
    Vector3.zero,
    Vector3.up,
    Vector3.up,
    Vector3.up,
```

```
        Vector3.left,
        Vector3.left,
        Vector3.left,
        Vector3.left,
        Vector3.right,
        Vector3.right,
        Vector3.right,
        Vector3.right,
        Vector3.down,
        Vector3.down,
        Vector3.down,
        Vector3.forward,
        Vector3.down,
        Vector3.down,
        Vector3.down,
        Vector3.forward,
        Vector3.up,
        Vector3.left,
        Vector3.forward,
        Vector3.right,
        Vector3.forward
};
//骨骼点的跟踪状态
public enum TrackingState
{
        NotTracked=0,
        Inferred=1,
        Tracked=2
}
//手的状态
public enum HandState
{
        Unknown=0,
        NotTracked=1,
        Open=2,
        Closed=3,
        Lasso=4
}
//跟踪层度判断
```

```csharp
public enum TrackingConfidence
{
    Low=0,
    High=1
}
//传感器数据
public class SensorData
{
    public DepthSensorInterface sensorInterface;

    public int bodyCount;
    public int jointCount;

    public int colorImageWidth;
    public int colorImageHeight;

    public byte[] colorImage;
    public long lastColorFrameTime=0;

    public int depthImageWidth;
    public int depthImageHeight;

    public ushort[] depthImage;
    public long lastDepthFrameTime=0;

    public ushort[] infraredImage;
    public long lastInfraredFrameTime=0;

    public byte[] bodyIndexImage;
    public long lastBodyIndexFrameTime=0;
}
//Kinect 骨骼跟踪平滑处理的参数设置
public struct SmoothParameters
{
    public float smoothing;//平滑度属性:设置骨骼数据帧的平滑尺度
    public float correction;//修正属性
    public float prediction;//预测帧尺度属性,平滑化所需预测骨骼帧的数目
    public float jitterRadius;//抖动半径属性
    public float maxDeviationRadius;//最大偏离半径属性
```

}
//人体骨骼关节点数据
public struct JointData
{
    //传感器接口中的参数
    public JointType jointType;
    public TrackingState trackingState;
    public Vector3 kinectPos;
    public Vector3 position;
    public Quaternion orientation;//deprecated

    //用于计算的参数
    public Vector3 direction;
    public Quaternion normalRotation;
    public Quaternion mirroredRotation;
}
//人体数据
public struct BodyData
{
    //传感器接口中的参数
    public Int64 liTrackingId;
    public Vector3 position;
    public Quaternion orientation;
    public JointData[] joint;

    //用于计算的参数
    public Quaternion normalRotation;
    public Quaternion mirroredRotation;

    public Vector3 hipsDirection;
    public Vector3 shouldersDirection;
    public float bodyTurnAngle;

    public Vector3 leftThumbDirection;
    public Vector3 leftHandDirection;
    public Vector3 leftThumbForward;
    public float leftThumbAngle;

    public Vector3 rightThumbDirection;

```csharp
        public Vector3 rightHandDirection;
        public Vector3 rightThumbForward;
        public float rightThumbAngle;

        public HandState leftHandState;
        public TrackingConfidence leftHandConfidence;
        public HandState rightHandState;
        public TrackingConfidence rightHandConfidence;

        public uint dwClippedEdges;
        public short bIsTracked;
        public short bIsRestricted;
    }
    //人体帧数据
    public struct BodyFrameData
    {
        public Int64 liRelativeTime;
        [MarshalAsAttribute(UnmanagedType.ByValArray, SizeConst=6,
                    ArraySubType=UnmanagedType.Struct)]
        public BodyData[] bodyData;
        public UnityEngine.Vector4 floorClipPlane;

        public BodyFrameData(int bodyCount, int jointCount)
        {
            liRelativeTime=0;
            floorClipPlane=UnityEngine.Vector4.zero;

            bodyData=new BodyData[bodyCount];

            for(int i=0; i<bodyCount; i++)
            {
                bodyData[i].joint=new JointData[jointCount];
            }
        }
    }

//初始化可用传感器的接口
public static List<DepthSensorInterface>InitSensorInterfaces(ref bool bNeedRestart)
{
```

```csharp
List<DepthSensorInterface> listInterfaces = new List<DepthSensorInterface>();

var typeInterface = typeof(DepthSensorInterface);
Type[] typesAvailable = typeInterface.Assembly.GetTypes();

foreach(Type type in typesAvailable)
{
    if(typeInterface.IsAssignableFrom(type) && type!=typeInterface)
    {
        DepthSensorInterface sensorInt = null;

        try
        {
            sensorInt = (DepthSensorInterface)Activator.CreateInstance(type);

            bool bIntNeedRestart = false;
            if(sensorInt.InitSensorInterface(ref bIntNeedRestart))
            {
                bNeedRestart| = bIntNeedRestart;
            }
            else
            {
                sensorInt.FreeSensorInterface();
                sensorInt = null;
                continue;
            }

            if(sensorInt.GetSensorsCount()<=0)
            {
                sensorInt.FreeSensorInterface();
                sensorInt = null;
            }
        }
        catch (Exception)
        {
            if(sensorInt!=null)
            {
                try
                {
```

```
                    sensorInt.FreeSensorInterface();
                }
                catch (Exception)
                {
                    //do nothing
                }
                finally
                {
                    sensorInt=null;
                }
            }
        }

        if(sensorInt!=null)
        {
            listInterfaces.Add(sensorInt);
        }
    }
    return listInterfaces;
}

//功能:打开默认传感器,默认为第一个
public static SensorData OpenDefaultSensor(List<DepthSensorInterface>listInterfaces,
    FrameSource dwFlags, float sensorAngle, bool bUseMultiSource)
{
    SensorData sensorData=null;

    if(listInterfaces==null)
        return sensorData;

    foreach(DepthSensorInterface sensorInt in listInterfaces)
    {
        try
        {
            if(sensorData==null)
            {//打开传感器
                sensorData=sensorInt.OpenDefaultSensor(dwFlags, sensorAngle,
                                                        bUseMultiSource);
```

```
                if(sensorData!=null)
                {
                    sensorData.sensorInterface=sensorInt;
                    Debug.Log("Interface used: "+sensorInt.GetType().Name);
                }
            }
            else
            {
                sensorInt.FreeSensorInterface();
            }
        }
        catch (Exception ex)
        {
            Debug.LogError("Initialization of sensor failed");
            Debug.LogError(ex.ToString());

            try
            {
                sensorInt.FreeSensorInterface();
            }
            catch (Exception)
            {
            }
        }
    }
    return sensorData;
}

//功能:关闭传感器
public static void CloseSensor(SensorData sensorData)
{
    if(sensorData!=null && sensorData.sensorInterface!=null)
    {
        //使用关闭的方法 sensorData.sensorInterface.CloseSensor(sensorData);
    }
}

//功能:获取最新的传感器数据
```

```csharp
public static bool UpdateSensorData(SensorData sensorData)
{
    bool bResult=false;

    if(sensorData.sensorInterface!=null)
    {//调用获取数据方法
        bResult=sensorData.sensorInterface.UpdateSensorData(sensorData);
    }
    return bResult;
}

//功能:获取镜像骨骼点
public static JointType GetMirrorJoint(JointType joint)
{
    switch(joint)
    {//取该骨骼点的对称点
      case JointType.ShoulderLeft:
          return JointType.ShoulderRight;
      case JointType.ElbowLeft:
          return JointType.ElbowRight;
      case JointType.WristLeft:
          return JointType.WristRight;
      case JointType.HandLeft:
          return JointType.HandRight;

      case JointType.ShoulderRight:
          return JointType.ShoulderLeft;
      case JointType.ElbowRight:
          return JointType.ElbowLeft;
      case JointType.WristRight:
          return JointType.WristLeft;
      case JointType.HandRight:
          return JointType.HandLeft;

      case JointType.HipLeft:
          return JointType.HipRight;
      case JointType.KneeLeft:
          return JointType.KneeRight;
      case JointType.AnkleLeft:
```

```
                return JointType.AnkleRight;
            case JointType.FootLeft:
                return JointType.FootRight;

            case JointType.HipRight:
                return JointType.HipLeft;
            case JointType.KneeRight:
                return JointType.KneeLeft;
            case JointType.AnkleRight:
                return JointType.AnkleLeft;
            case JointType.FootRight:
                return JointType.FootLeft;

            case JointType.HandTipLeft:
                return JointType.HandTipRight;
            case JointType.ThumbLeft:
                return JointType.ThumbRight;

            case JointType.HandTipRight:
                return JointType.HandTipLeft;
            case JointType.ThumbRight:
                return JointType.ThumbLeft;
        }
//输入骨骼点的镜像骨骼点
        return joint;
}


//功能:获取最新多种资源帧,包括彩色图像帧、深度图像帧、骨骼跟踪数据流
public static bool GetMultiSourceFrame(SensorData sensorData)
{
        bool bResult=false;

        if(sensorData.sensorInterface!=null)
        {//调取多种资源帧的方法
            bResult=sensorData.sensorInterface.GetMultiSourceFrame(sensorData);
        }
        return bResult;
}
```

```
//功能:释放多源帧
public static void FreeMultiSourceFrame(SensorData sensorData)
{
    if(sensorData.sensorInterface!=null)
    {
    //调用释放多源帧的方法
      sensorData.sensorInterface.FreeMultiSourceFrame(sensorData);
    }
}

//功能:请求骨骼数据帧
public static bool PollBodyFrame(SensorData sensorData, ref BodyFrameData bodyFrame, ref
    Matrix4×4 kinectToWorld)
{
    bool bNewFrame=false;

    if(sensorData.sensorInterface!=null)
    {//调用请求骨骼帧的方法
      bNewFrame=sensorData.sensorInterface.PollBodyFrame(sensorData, ref bodyFrame,
                                                 ref kinectToWorld);

    if(bNewFrame)
      {
        for(int i=0; i<sensorData.bodyCount; i++)
        {
            if(bodyFrame.bodyData[i].bIsTracked!=0)
            {
                //计算骨骼点方向
                for(int j=0; j<sensorData.jointCount; j++)
                {
                    if(j==0)
                    {
                        bodyFrame.bodyData[i].joint[j].direction=Vector3.zero;
                    }
                    else
                    {
                     int jParent = (int)sensorData.sensorInterface.GetParentJoint(bodyFrame.
                                bodyData[i].joint[j].jointType);

                        if(bodyFrame.bodyData[i].joint[j].trackingState!=
```

```
                        TrackingState.NotTracked && bodyFrame.bodyData [i]. joint [jParent].
                        trackingState!=TrackingState.NotTracked)
                        {
                          bodyFrame.bodyData[i].joint[j].direction=bodyFrame.bodyData[i].joint[j].
                              position - bodyFrame.bodyData[i].joint[jParent].position;
                        }
                      }
                    }
                  }
                }
              }
            }
          }
        }
        return bNewFrame;
}

//功能:请求彩色图像帧
public static bool PollColorFrame(SensorData sensorData)
{
    bool bNewFrame=false;

    if(sensorData.sensorInterface!=null)
    {//调用请求彩色图像帧的方法
      bNewFrame=sensorData.sensorInterface.PollColorFrame(sensorData);
    }

    return bNewFrame;
}

//功能:请求深度图像帧
public static bool PollDepthFrame(SensorData sensorData)
{
    bool bNewFrame=false;

    if(sensorData.sensorInterface!=null)
    {//调用请求深度图像帧方法
      bNewFrame=sensorData.sensorInterface.PollDepthFrame(sensorData);
    }
    return bNewFrame;
}
```

```csharp
//功能:请求红外数据帧
public static bool PollInfraredFrame(SensorData sensorData)
{
    bool bNewFrame=false;

    if(sensorData.sensorInterface!=null)
    {//调用请求红外数据帧
     bNewFrame=sensorData.sensorInterface.PollInfraredFrame(sensorData);
    }
    return bNewFrame;
}

//功能:将骨骼空间三维坐标转为彩色图像二维坐标
public static Vector2 MapSpacePointToDepthCoords(SensorData sensorData, Vector3 kinectPos)
{
    Vector2 vPoint=Vector2.zero;

    if(sensorData.sensorInterface!=null)
    {//调用骨骼空间坐标转为彩色图像的方法
     vPoint=sensorData.sensorInterface.MapSpacePointToDepthCoords(sensorData,
                                                                   kinectPos);
    }
    return vPoint;
}

//功能:将深度图像二维坐标点转为骨骼空间三维坐标点
public static Vector3 MapDepthPointToSpaceCoords(SensorData sensorData, Vector2 depthPos,
    ushort depthVal)
{
    Vector3 vPoint=Vector3.zero;

    if(sensorData.sensorInterface!=null)
    {//调用深度图像坐标转为二维坐标的方法
     vPoint=sensorData.sensorInterface.MapDepthPointToSpaceCoords(sensorData, depthPos,
                                                                   depthVal);
    }
    return vPoint;
}
```

```csharp
//功能:将深度图像坐标点转为彩色图像坐标点
public static Vector2 MapDepthPointToColorCoords(SensorData sensorData, Vector2 depthPos,
                                                 ushort depthVal)
{
    Vector2 vPoint = Vector2.zero;

    if(sensorData.sensorInterface!=null)
    {//调用深度图像坐标转为二维坐标的方法
        vPoint = sensorData.sensorInterface.MapDepthPointToColorCoords(sensorData, depthPos,
                                                                       depthVal);
    }
    return vPoint;
}


//功能:将深度图像帧转为彩色图像坐标点
public static bool MapDepthFrameToColorCoords(SensorData sensorData,
                                              ref Vector2[] vColorCoords)
{
    bool bResult = false;

    if(sensorData.sensorInterface!=null)
    {//调用深度图像帧转为二维坐标的方法
        bResult = sensorData.sensorInterface.MapDepthFrameToColorCoords(sensorData, ref
                                                                        vColorCoords);
    }
    return bResult;
}


//功能:将传感器获取的数据传给模型
public static bool CopyResourceFile(string targetFilePath, string resFileName,
                                    ref bool bOneCopied, ref bool bAllCopied)
{
    TextAsset textRes = Resources.Load(resFileName, typeof(TextAsset)) as TextAsset;
    if(textRes == null)
    {
        bOneCopied = false;
        bAllCopied = false;
```

```
            return false;
    }
    FileInfo targetFile=new FileInfo(targetFilePath);
    if(!targetFile.Directory.Exists)
    {//创建目标目录
        targetFile.Directory.Create();
    }

    if(!targetFile.Exists||targetFile.Length!=textRes.bytes.Length)
    {
        if(textRes!=null)
        {//新建文件
            using (FileStream fileStream = new FileStream (targetFilePath, FileMode.Create,
                                            FileAccess.Write, FileShare.Read))
            {
                fileStream.Write(textRes.bytes, 0, textRes.bytes.Length);
            }

            bool bFileCopied=File.Exists(targetFilePath);

            bOneCopied=bOneCopied||bFileCopied;
            bAllCopied=bAllCopied && bFileCopied;

            return bFileCopied;
        }
    }
    return false;
  }
}
```

3. 从Kinect设备中获取数据脚本

```
public class KinectManager: MonoBehaviour
{
    //传感器距离地面的高度
    public float sensorHeight=1.0f;
    //传感器提高的角度
    public float sensorAngle=0f;
    //是否去接收和计算用户映射
    public bool computeUserMap=false;
```

//是否去接收颜色映射
public bool computeColorMap=false;
//是否接收和计算红外线映射
public bool computeInfraredMap=false;
//是否显示用户映射在图形界面上
public bool displayUserMap=false;
//是否显示颜色映射在图形界面上
public bool displayColorMap=false;
//是否显示骨骼线在用户映射上
public bool displaySkeletonLines=false;

//显示映射宽度的百分比,通过使用深度和颜色的映射来指定图形的宽度,作为相机的宽度百分比。高度通过宽度来计算
//如果百分比为零,那就通过内部的计算去匹配深度图的骨骼的宽和高
public float DisplayMapsWidthPercent=20f;
//是否使用多源阅读
public bool useMultiSourceReader=false;
//用户与Kinect之间的最短距离,为了提高骨骼数据的质量
public float minUserDistance=0.5f;
//用户距离Kinect的最远距离。如果值为0意味着没有最远距离限制
public float maxUserDistance=0f;
//是否检测最近用户
public bool detectClosestUser=true;
//是否忽视推测骨骼点。也就是,是否只使用跟踪到的骨骼点
public bool ignoreInferredJoints=true;
//平滑参数的选择
public enum Smoothing: int {None, Default, Medium 中间, Aggressive 可提升的}
public Smoothing smoothing=Smoothing.Default;
//是否使用骨骼定位限制,也就是,是否使用额外的滤器
public bool useBoneOrientationConstraints=true;
//实例一个 AvatarController 对象列表,也就是实例一个列表,里面的元素都是Avatar Controller类型的。AvatarController 的对象列表将被用户控制
public List<AvatarController>avatarControllers;
//校准每个用户的静态姿势
public KinectGestures.Gestures playerCalibrationPose;
//用户姿势集
public List<KinectGestures.Gestures>playerCommonGestures;

```csharp
//两个被检测的姿势间相隔的最短时间。
public float minTimeBetweenGestures = 0.7f;

//姿势监听者,这个监听者必须执行姿势监听者接口
public List<MonoBehaviour> gestureListeners;

//校准文本框,用来显示信息
public GUIText calibrationText;

//判断 Kinect 是否被初始化,这个变量就是拿来跟踪用。
private bool kinectInitialized = false;

//一个 KinectManager 类的实例
//private 只有在声明他的类和结构体中才能用。
private static KinectManager instance = null;

//可用的传感器接口集
private List<DepthSensorInterface> sensorInterfaces = null;

//传感器数据,主要的传感器数据结构
private KinectInterop.SensorData sensorData = null;

//深度图像映射
private Color32[] usersHistogramImage;
private ushort[] usersPrevState;
private float[] usersHistogramMap;

private Texture2D usersLblTex;
private Rect usersMapRect;
private int usersMapSize;

//彩色图像映射
//private KinectInterop.ColorBuffer colorImage;
private Texture2D usersClrTex;
private Rect usersClrRect;
private int usersClrSize;

//用来存放身体帧数据
private KinectInterop.BodyFrameData bodyFrame;
```

```csharp
//所有的用户 Id
//Dictionary<[key],[value]>通过 key 去找对应的值
private List<Int64>alUserIds;
//通过用户的 Id 值去找对应的用户索引值
private Dictionary<Int64, int>dictUserIdToIndex;

//第一个用户 Id,或是最靠近的那个用户的 Id
private Int64 liPrimaryUserId=0;

//将 Kinect 中的坐标转为世界坐标
private Matrix4×4 KinectToWorld=Matrix4x4.zero;
//private Matrix4×4 mOrient=Matrix4x4.zero;

//用户 Id 和用户姿势的数据
private Dictionary<Int64, KinectGestures.GestureData>playerCalibrationData=new
    Dictionary<Int64, KinectGestures.GestureData>();

//用户 Id 与用户姿势集数据
private Dictionary<Int64, List<KinectGestures.GestureData>>playerGesturesData=new
    Dictionary<Int64, List<KinectGestures.GestureData>>();
//用户跟踪姿势跟踪时间
private Dictionary<Int64, float>gesturesTrackingAtTime=new Dictionary<Int64, float>();

//姿势监听器集。监听器必须使用姿势监听器接口
public List<KinectGestures.GestureListenerInterface>gestureListenerInts;

//身体过滤器实例
private JointPositionsFilter jointPositionFilter=null;
private BoneOrientationsConstraint boneConstraintsFilter=null;

//获取 KinectManager 类的实例
public static KinectManager Instance
{
    get
    {
        return instance;
    }
}
```

```csharp
//判断Kinect是否初始化,通过判断KinectManager的实例是否为空
public static bool IsKinectInitialized()
{
    return instance!=null?instance.kinectInitialized:false;
}

//判断Kinect是否初始化
public bool IsInitialized()
{
    return kinectInitialized;
}

//检测到的人体的数量,通过判断KinecInterop中的sensorData是否为空
public int GetSensorBodyCount()
{
    return sensorData!=null?sensorData.bodyCount:0;
}

//获取传感器中的骨骼点数量,通过判断KinecInterop中的sensorData是否为空
public int GetSensorJointCount()
{
    return sensorData!=null?sensorData.jointCount:0;
}

//Joint:代表Kinect跟踪到的骨骼中的某一关节点
//功能:获取关节点的索引值,也就是传入一个骨骼点名称,转化为JointType中骨骼点的
//    索引值,例如Neck=2,
//sensorData是KinectInterop中的一个类
//sensorInterface是sensorData类中一个DepthSensorInterface实例
//GetJointIndex();为DepthSensorInterface接口中的一个方法
public int GetJointIndex(KinectInterop.JointType joint)
{
    if(sensorData!=null && sensorData.sensorInterface!=null)
    {
        return sensorData.sensorInterface.GetJointIndex(joint);
    }
```

```
        //fallback - index matches the joint
        return (int)joint;
}

//功能:通过骨骼点的索引值获取骨骼点的名称
public KinectInterop.JointType GetJointAtIndex(int index)
{
        if(sensorData!=null && sensorData.sensorInterface!=null)
        {
                return sensorData.sensorInterface.GetJointAtIndex(index);
        }

        //fallback - index matches the joint
        return (KinectInterop.JointType)index;
}

//功能:返回当前骨骼点的上一个节点
public KinectInterop.JointType GetParentJoint(KinectInterop.JointType joint)
{
        if(sensorData!=null && sensorData.sensorInterface!=null)
        {
                return sensorData.sensorInterface.GetParentJoint(joint);
        }

        //fall back - return the same joint (i.e. end - joint)
        return joint;
}

//获取 Kinect 中彩色图的宽度
public int GetColorImageWidth()
{
        return sensorData!=null?sensorData.colorImageWidth:0;
}

//功能:获取 Kinect 中彩色图的高度
public int GetColorImageHeight()
{
        return sensorData!=null?sensorData.colorImageHeight:0;
}
```

```csharp
//功能:获取 Kinect 中深度图的宽度
public int GetDepthImageWidth()
{
    return sensorData!=null?sensorData.depthImageWidth:0;
}

//功能:获取 Kinect 中深度图的高度
public int GetDepthImageHeight()
{
    return sensorData!=null?sensorData.depthImageHeight:0;
}

//获取未加工的深度图数据,前提是在 ComputeUserMap =true 时,才调用这个方法
public ushort[] GetRawDepthMap()
{
    return sensorData!=null?sensorData.depthImage:null;
}

//获取未加工的红外图数据,前提是在 ComputeUserMap =true 时,才调用这个方法
public ushort[] GetRawInfraredMap()
{
    return sensorData!=null?sensorData.infraredImage:null;
}

//功能:返回用户的深度图的柱状图结构,前提是在 ComputeUserMap =true 时,才调用这个方法
//Texture :结构、质地
public Texture2D GetUsersLblTex()
{
    return usersLblTex;
}

//功能:获取用户的彩色图结构,前提是在 ComputeUserMap =true 时,才调用这个方法
public Texture2D GetUsersClrTex()
{
    return usersClrTex;
}
```

```csharp
//功能:判断是否有用户被检测到
public bool IsUserDetected()
{
    return kinectInitialized && (alUserIds.Count>0);
}

//功能:校准用户,也就是判断该用户的 Id 是否存在过
public bool IsUserCalibrated(Int64 userId)
{
    return dictUserIdToIndex.ContainsKey(userId);
}

//功能:获取当前检测到的用户数量
public int GetUsersCount()
{
    return alUserIds.Count;
}

//功能:通过索引值获取用户 Id
public Int64 GetUserIdByIndex(int i)
{
    if(i>=0 && i<alUserIds.Count)
    {
        return alUserIds[i];
    }
    return 0;
}

//功能:获取最近用户的 Id
public Int64 GetPrimaryUserId()
{
    return liPrimaryUserId;
}

//功能:设置新的主用户 Id
public bool SetPrimaryUserId(Int64 userId)
{
    bool bResult=false;
```

```
    if(alUserIds.Contains(userId) || (userId==0))
    {//修改主 Id
      liPrimaryUserId=userId;
      bResult=true;
    }

    return bResult;
}

//功能:获取用户人体数据
public KinectInterop.BodyData GetUserBodyData(Int64 userId)
{
//判断该用户 Id 是否存在 if(dictUserIdToIndex.ContainsKey(userId))
    {
        int index=dictUserIdToIndex[userId];

        if(index>=0 && index<sensorData.bodyCount)
        {//通过索引值获取该用户的人体数据
            return bodyFrame.bodyData[index];
        }
    }
    return new KinectInterop.BodyData();
}


//功能:获取用户空间坐标值
public Vector3 GetUserPosition(Int64 userId)
{
    //判断该用户 Id 是否存在 if(dictUserIdToIndex.ContainsKey(userId))
        {
            int index=dictUserIdToIndex[userId];

            if(index>=0 && index<sensorData.bodyCount &&
                bodyFrame.bodyData[index].bIsTracked!=0)
            {//通过索引值获取该用户空间坐标
                return bodyFrame.bodyData[index].position;
            }
        }
        return Vector3.zero;
}
```

```
//功能:获取用户旋转坐标值
public Quaternion GetUserOrientation(Int64 userId, bool flip)
{
    //判断该用户 Id 是否存在 if(dictUserIdToIndex.ContainsKey(userId))
        {
            int index= dictUserIdToIndex[userId];

            if(index>=0 && index<sensorData.bodyCount &&
                bodyFrame.bodyData[index].bIsTracked!=0)
            {
                if(flip)//通过索引值获取人体正常旋转坐标
                    return bodyFrame.bodyData[index].normalRotation;
                else//通过索引值获取镜像旋转坐标
                    return bodyFrame.bodyData[index].mirroredRotation;
            }
        }
        return Quaternion.identity;
}


//功能:获取骨骼跟踪状态
public KinectInterop.TrackingState GetJointTrackingState(Int64 userId, int joint)
{
    //判断该用户 Id 是否存在 if(dictUserIdToIndex.ContainsKey(userId))
    {//获取用户索引值
        int index= dictUserIdToIndex[userId];

        if(index>=0 && index<sensorData.bodyCount &&
            bodyFrame.bodyData[index].bIsTracked!=0)
        {
            if(joint>=0 && joint<sensorData.jointCount)
            {//返回该骨骼点的跟踪状态
                return bodyFrame.bodyData[index].joint[joint].trackingState;
            }
        }
    }
    return KinectInterop.TrackingState.NotTracked;
}
```

```csharp
//功能:判断关节点是否被跟踪
public bool IsJointTracked(Int64 userId, int joint)
{
    //判断该用户 Id 是否存在 if(dictUserIdToIndex.ContainsKey(userId))
    {//获取用户索引值
        int index=dictUserIdToIndex[userId];

        if(index>=0 && index<sensorData.bodyCount &&
            bodyFrame.bodyData[index].bIsTracked!=0)
        {//判断骨骼点是否存在
            if(joint>=0 && joint<sensorData.jointCount)
            {
                KinectInterop.JointData jointData=bodyFrame.bodyData[index].joint[joint];
                return ignoreInferredJoints?(jointData.trackingState==KinectInterop.
                                    TrackingState.Tracked): (jointData.trackingState!
                                    =KinectInterop.TrackingState.NotTracked);
            }
        }
    }
    return false;
}

//获取骨骼空间坐标
public Vector3 GetJointKinectPosition(Int64 userId, int joint)
{
    if(dictUserIdToIndex.ContainsKey(userId))
    {
        int index=dictUserIdToIndex[userId];

        if(index>=0 && index<sensorData.bodyCount &&
            bodyFrame.bodyData[index].bIsTracked!=0)
        {
            if(joint>=0 && joint<sensorData.jointCount)
            {
                //创建骨骼点
                KinectInterop.JointData jointData=bodyFrame.bodyData[index].joint[joint];
                //返回骨骼点坐标 return jointData.kinectPos;
            }
        }
```

```
            }
            return Vector3.zero;

//功能:获取骨骼点坐标
    public Vector3 GetJointPosition(Int64 userId, int joint)
    {
        if(dictUserIdToIndex.ContainsKey(userId))
        {
            int index=dictUserIdToIndex[userId];

            if(index>=0 && index<sensorData.bodyCount &&
                bodyFrame.bodyData[index].bIsTracked!=0)
            {
            if(joint>=0 && joint<sensorData.jointCount)
                {
        //创建骨骼点
            KinectInterop.JointData jointData=bodyFrame.bodyData[index].joint[joint];
        //返回骨骼点坐标 return jointData.position;
                }
            }
        }
        return Vector3.zero;
}

//功能:获取骨骼方向
public Vector3 GetJointDirection(Int64 userId, int joint, bool flipX, bool flipZ)
{
//判断该用户 Id 是否存在 if(dictUserIdToIndex.ContainsKey(userId))
    {
        int index=dictUserIdToIndex[userId];
        //判断是否存在该索引值及该用户是否被跟踪
        if(index>=0 && index<sensorData.bodyCount &&
            bodyFrame.bodyData[index].bIsTracked!=0)
        {//判断是否存在该关节点
            if(joint>=0 && joint<sensorData.jointCount)
            {
//创建关节点
    KinectInterop.JointData jointData=bodyFrame.bodyData[index].joint[joint];
//获取关节点方向
```

```
            Vector3 jointDir=jointData.direction;
                if(flipX)
                    jointDir.x=-jointDir.x;
                if(flipZ)
                    jointDir.z=-jointDir.z;
                return jointDir;
            }
        }
    }
    return Vector3.zero;
}

//功能:获取两个骨骼点之间的方向
public Vector3 GetDirectionBetweenJoints(Int64 userId, int firstJoint, int secondJoint, bool flipX,
     bool flipZ)
{
//判断该用户 Id 是否存在
if(dictUserIdToIndex.ContainsKey(userId))
    {
            int index=dictUserIdToIndex[userId];
            //判断该索引值是否存在及该用户是否被跟踪
            if(index>=0 && index<sensorData.bodyCount &&
                bodyFrame.bodyData[index].bIsTracked!=0)
            {
                KinectInterop.BodyData bodyData=bodyFrame.bodyData[index];

                if(firstJoint>=0 && firstJoint<sensorData.jointCount &&
                    secondJoint>=0 && secondJoint<sensorData.jointCount)
                {//获取第一个关节点的空间坐标
                    Vector3 firstJointPos=bodyData.joint[firstJoint].position;
                    //获取第二个关节点的空间坐标
                    Vector3 secondJointPos=bodyData.joint[secondJoint].position;
                    //计算两关节点的方向
                    Vector3 jointDir=secondJointPos-firstJointPos;

                    if(flipX)
                        jointDir.x=-jointDir.x;
                    if(flipZ)
                        jointDir.z=-jointDir.z;
```

```
            return jointDir;
        }
    }
}
    return Vector3.zero;
}

//功能: 获取骨骼点的旋转坐标
public Quaternion GetJointOrientation(Int64 userId, int joint, bool flip)
{
    //判断该用户 Id 是否存在 if(dictUserIdToIndex.ContainsKey(userId))
    {
        int index= dictUserIdToIndex[userId];
        //判断该索引值是否存在及该用户是否被跟踪
        if(index>=0 && index<sensorData.bodyCount &&
            bodyFrame.bodyData[index].bIsTracked!=0)
        {
            if(flip)
    //获取人体骨骼正常旋转坐标
            return bodyFrame.bodyData[index].joint[joint].normalRotation;
                else
    //获取人体骨骼镜像坐标
            return bodyFrame.bodyData[index].joint[joint].mirroredRotation;
        }
    }
        return Quaternion.identity;
}
        public bool IsLeftHandConfidenceHigh(Int64 userId)
{
        if(dictUserIdToIndex.ContainsKey(userId))
        {
            int index= dictUserIdToIndex[userId];

            if(index>=0 && index<sensorData.bodyCount &&
                bodyFrame.bodyData[index].bIsTracked!=0)
            {
                return (bodyFrame.bodyData[index].leftHandConfidence==KinectInterop.
                    TrackingConfidence.High);
            }
```

```
            }
            return false;
        }
        public bool IsRightHandConfidenceHigh(Int64 userId)
        {
            if(dictUserIdToIndex.ContainsKey(userId))
            {
                int index= dictUserIdToIndex[userId];

                if(index>=0 && index<sensorData.bodyCount &&
                    bodyFrame.bodyData[index].bIsTracked!=0)
                {
                    return (bodyFrame.bodyData[index].rightHandConfidence==
                        KinectInterop.TrackingConfidence.High);
                }
            }
            return false;
        }

//功能:获取左手的跟踪状态
public KinectInterop.HandState GetLeftHandState(Int64 userId)
{
    //判断该用户 Id 是否存在
    if(dictUserIdToIndex.ContainsKey(userId))
    {
        int index= dictUserIdToIndex[userId];
    //判断该索引值是否存在,并且该人体骨骼是否被跟踪
        if(index>=0 && index<sensorData.bodyCount &&
            bodyFrame.bodyData[index].bIsTracked!=0)
        {
    //获取左手的跟踪状态
         return bodyFrame.bodyData[index].leftHandState;
        }
    }
    return KinectInterop.HandState.NotTracked;
}

//功能:获取右手的跟踪状态
public KinectInterop.HandState GetRightHandState(Int64 userId)
```

```
{
//判断该用户 Id 是否存在
    if(dictUserIdToIndex.ContainsKey(userId))
    {
        int index=dictUserIdToIndex[userId];
        //判断该索引值是否存在,并且该人体骨骼是否被跟踪
        if(index>=0 && index<sensorData.bodyCount &&
            bodyFrame.bodyData[index].bIsTracked!=0)
        {//获取右手的跟踪状态
            return bodyFrame.bodyData[index].rightHandState;
        }
    }
    return KinectInterop.HandState.NotTracked;
}


//功能:获取左手交互区域
public bool GetLeftHandInteractionBox(Int64 userId, ref Vector3 leftBotBack,
    ref Vector3 rightTopFront, bool bValidBox)
{
    //判断该用户 Id 是否存在 if(dictUserIdToIndex.ContainsKey(userId))
    {
        int index=dictUserIdToIndex[userId];
        //判断该索引值是否存在,并且该人体骨骼是否被跟踪
            if(index>=0 && index<sensorData.bodyCount &&
                bodyFrame.bodyData[index].bIsTracked!=0)
        {//创建人体骨骼
            KinectInterop.BodyData bodyData=bodyFrame.bodyData[index];
            bool bResult=true;

        //判断人体右肩与左臀部跟踪状态
        if(bodyData.joint[(int)KinectInterop.JointType.ShoulderRight].trackingState==
            KinectInterop.TrackingState.Tracked &&
            bodyData.joint[(int)KinectInterop.JointType.HipLeft].trackingState==
                KinectInterop.TrackingState.Tracked)
            {//右上角的 x 轴坐标为右肩的坐标
                rightTopFront.x=bodyData.joint[(int)KinectInterop.JointType.ShoulderRight].
                            position.x;
            //左下角的 x 坐标为左臀部的坐标
                leftBotBack.x=rightTopFront.x-2*(rightTopFront.x-bodyData.joint[(int)
```

```
                    KinectInterop.JointType.HipLeft].position.x);
        }
        else
        {
            bResult=bValidBox;
        }
//判断人体右肩与右臀部跟踪状态
if(bodyData.joint[(int)KinectInterop.JointType.HipRight].trackingState==
    KinectInterop.TrackingState.Tracked &&
      bodyData.joint[(int)KinectInterop.JointType.ShoulderRight].trackingState==
        KinectInterop.TrackingState.Tracked)
        {//左下角的 y 坐标为右臀部的坐标
         leftBotBack.y=bodyData.joint[(int)KinectInterop.JointType.HipRight].position.y;
        //右上角的 y 轴坐标为右肩的坐标
         rightTopFront.y=bodyData.joint[(int)KinectInterop.JointType.ShoulderRight].position.y;
            float fDelta=(rightTopFront.y - leftBotBack.y)*0.35f; //* 2 / 3;
            leftBotBack.y+=fDelta;
            rightTopFront.y+=fDelta;
        }
        else
        {
            bResult=bValidBox;
        }

//判断脊柱底部是否被跟踪
if(bodyData.joint[(int)KinectInterop.JointType.SpineBase].trackingState==
    KinectInterop.TrackingState.Tracked)
        {//左下角的 z 坐标为脊柱底部的坐标
         leftBotBack.z=bodyData.joint[(int)KinectInterop.JointType.SpineBase].position.z;
        //计算右上角的 z 坐标
         rightTopFront.z=leftBotBack.z -0.5f;
            }
            else
            {
                bResult=bValidBox;
            }
            return bResult;
        }
```

        }

        return false;
}

//功能:获取右手的交互区域
public bool GetRightHandInteractionBox(Int64 userId, ref Vector3 leftBotBack,
ref Vector3 rightTopFront, bool bValidBox)
{
    //判断该用户 Id 是否存在
      if(dictUserIdToIndex.ContainsKey(userId))
    {
        int index=dictUserIdToIndex[userId];
        //判断该索引值是否存在,并且该人体骨骼是否被跟踪
        if(index>=0 && index<sensorData.bodyCount &&
            bodyFrame.bodyData[index].bIsTracked!=0)
        {//创建人体骨骼
            KinectInterop.BodyData bodyData=bodyFrame.bodyData[index];
            bool bResult=true;

            //判断人体右肩与右臀部跟踪状态
                if(bodyData.joint[(int)KinectInterop.JointType.ShoulderLeft].trackingState==
                    KinectInterop.TrackingState.Tracked &&
                bodyData.joint[(int)KinectInterop.JointType.HipRight].trackingState==
                    KinectInterop.TrackingState.Tracked);
            {
                //左下角的 x 轴坐标为左肩的坐标
                leftBotBack.x=bodyData.joint[(int)KinectInterop.JointType.ShoulderLeft].
                            position.x;
                //计算右上角的坐标
                rightTopFront.x=leftBotBack.x+2*(bodyData.joint[(int)KinectInterop.JointType.
                            HipRight].position.x-leftBotBack.x);
            }
            else
            {
                bResult=bValidBox;
            }

//判断人体左肩与左臀部跟踪状态

```
if(bodyData.joint[(int)KinectInterop.JointType.HipLeft].trackingState==
    KinectInterop.TrackingState.Tracked &&
        bodyData.joint[(int)KinectInterop.JointType.ShoulderLeft].trackingState==
            KinectInterop.TrackingState.Tracked)
        {
    //左下角的y轴坐标为左臀部的坐标
      leftBotBack.y=bodyData.joint[(int)KinectInterop.JointType.HipLeft].position.y;
    //右上角的y坐标为左肩的坐标
      rightTopFront.y=bodyData.joint[(int)KinectInterop.JointType.ShoulderLeft].position.y;

            float fDelta=(rightTopFront.y - leftBotBack.y)*0.35f; //*2/3;
            leftBotBack.y+=fDelta;
            rightTopFront.y+=fDelta;
        }
        else
        {
            bResult=bValidBox;
        }


    //判断脊柱底部是否被跟踪
    if(bodyData.joint[(int)KinectInterop.JointType.SpineBase].trackingState==
        KinectInterop.TrackingState.Tracked)
        {//左下角的z轴坐标为脊柱底部的坐标
            leftBotBack.z=bodyData.joint[(int)KinectInterop.JointType.SpineBase].position.z;
            rightTopFront.z=leftBotBack.z -0.5f;
        }
        else
        {
            bResult=bValidBox;
        }
        return bResult;
    }
}

return false;
}

//功能: 获取深度图像
public ushort GetDepthForPixel(int x, int y)
```

```
{//判断传感器数据与深度图像数据是否存在
    if(sensorData!=null && sensorData.depthImage!=null)
    {
        int index=y*sensorData.depthImageWidth+x;

        if(index>=0 && index<sensorData.depthImage.Length)
        {
        //返回深度图像 return sensorData.depthImage[index];
        }
    }
    return 0;
}

//功能:将深度图像帧的点坐标转为骨骼数据帧中的点坐标
public Vector3 MapDepthPointToSpaceCoords(Vector2 posPoint, ushort depthValue,
    bool bWorldCoords)
{//初始化 Kinect 坐标
    Vector3 posKinect=Vector3.zero;

    if(kinectInitialized)
    {//深度图像帧的某一点坐标转为骨骼数据帧中某一点坐标
    posKinect=KinectInterop.MapDepthPointToSpaceCoords(sensorData, posPoint, depthValue);

        if(bWorldCoords)
        {//设置多点坐标
            posKinect=kinectToWorld.MultiplyPoint3x4(posKinect);
        }
    }
    //返回骨骼空间三维坐标
    return posKinect;
}

//功能:将骨骼空间坐标转为深度图像坐标
public Vector2 MapSpacePointToDepthCoords(Vector3 posPoint)
    {//初始化深度图像坐标
    Vector2 posDepth=Vector2.zero;

    if(kinectInitialized)
    {//将骨骼空间坐标转为深度图像坐标
```

```csharp
        posDepth=KinectInterop.MapSpacePointToDepthCoords(sensorData, posPoint);
    }
    return posDepth;
}

//功能:深度图像坐标转为彩色图像坐标
public Vector2 MapDepthPointToColorCoords(Vector2 posPoint, ushort depthValue)
{//初始化彩色图像坐标
    Vector2 posColor=Vector3.zero;

    if(kinectInitialized)
    {//调用深度图像坐标转为彩色图像坐标的方法
        posColor=KinectInterop.MapDepthPointToColorCoords(sensorData, posPoint,
                                                           depthValue);
    }

    return posColor;
}

//功能:清除当前用户
public void ClearKinectUsers()
{
    if(!kinectInitialized)
        return;

    //移除当前用户
    for(int i=alUserIds.Count -1; i>=0; i--)
    {
        Int64 userId=alUserIds[i];
        RemoveUser(userId);
    }
    ResetFilters();
}

//功能:重新设置过滤器
public void ResetFilters()
{
    if(jointPositionFilter!=null)
    {
```

```
        jointPositionFilter.Reset();
    }
}

//功能:添加一个姿势到姿势列表中
public void DetectGesture(Int64 UserId, KinectGestures.Gestures gesture)
    {//添加新动作
    List<KinectGestures.GestureData>gesturesData=playerGesturesData.ContainsKey
(UserId)?playerGesturesData[UserId]: new List<KinectGestures.GestureData>();
    //获取姿势索引值
    int index=GetGestureIndex(gesture, ref gesturesData);

    if(index>=0)
    {//该姿势已经存在不添加
     DeleteGesture(UserId, gesture);
    }
    //创建姿势
    KinectGestures.GestureData gestureData=new KinectGestures.GestureData();
    //姿势属性赋值
    gestureData.userId=UserId;
    gestureData.gesture=gesture;
    gestureData.state=0;
    gestureData.joint=0;
    gestureData.progress=0f;
    gestureData.complete=false;
    gestureData.cancelled=false;

    gestureData.checkForGestures=new List<KinectGestures.Gestures>();
    //判断姿势类型
    switch(gesture)
    {
    case KinectGestures.Gestures.ZoomIn:
        gestureData.checkForGestures.Add(KinectGestures.Gestures.ZoomOut);
        gestureData.checkForGestures.Add(KinectGestures.Gestures.Wheel);
        break;

    case KinectGestures.Gestures.ZoomOut:
        gestureData.checkForGestures.Add(KinectGestures.Gestures.ZoomIn);
        gestureData.checkForGestures.Add(KinectGestures.Gestures.Wheel);
```

```csharp
            break;

        case KinectGestures.Gestures.Wheel:
            gestureData.checkForGestures.Add(KinectGestures.Gestures.ZoomIn);
            gestureData.checkForGestures.Add(KinectGestures.Gestures.ZoomOut);
            break;
        }
    //添加动作
        gesturesData.Add(gestureData);
        playerGesturesData[UserId] = gesturesData;

        if(!gesturesTrackingAtTime.ContainsKey(UserId))
        {
            gesturesTrackingAtTime[UserId] = 0f;
        }
    }

//功能:重设姿势数据
public bool ResetGesture(Int64 UserId, KinectGestures.Gestures gesture)
{
    List<KinectGestures.GestureData> gesturesData =
        playerGesturesData.ContainsKey(UserId)?playerGesturesData[UserId]: null;
    int index = gesturesData!=null?GetGestureIndex(gesture, ref gesturesData):-1;
    if(index<0)
        return false;

    KinectGestures.GestureData gestureData = gesturesData[index];

    gestureData.state = 0;
    gestureData.joint = 0;
    gestureData.progress = 0f;
    gestureData.complete = false;
    gestureData.cancelled = false;
    gestureData.startTrackingAtTime = Time.realtimeSinceStartup +
        KinectInterop.Constants.MinTimeBetweenSameGestures;

    gesturesData[index] = gestureData;
    playerGesturesData[UserId] = gesturesData;
```

```
        return true;
    }

//功能:重设用户所有的姿势
public void ResetPlayerGestures(Int64 UserId)
{
    List<KinectGestures.GestureData> gesturesData=
        playerGesturesData.ContainsKey(UserId)?playerGesturesData[UserId]: null;

    if(gesturesData!=null)
    {
        int listSize=gesturesData.Count;

        for(int i=0; i<listSize; i++)
        {
            ResetGesture(UserId, gesturesData[i].gesture);
        }
    }
}

//功能:删除给定的姿势
public bool DeleteGesture(Int64 UserId, KinectGestures.Gestures gesture)
{
    List<KinectGestures.GestureData> gesturesData=
        playerGesturesData.ContainsKey(UserId)?playerGesturesData[UserId]: null;
    int index=gesturesData!=null?GetGestureIndex(gesture, ref gesturesData):-1;
    if(index<0)
        return false;

    gesturesData.RemoveAt(index);
    playerGesturesData[UserId]=gesturesData;

    return true;
}

//功能:清除检测到的姿势列表
public void ClearGestures(Int64 UserId)
{
    List<KinectGestures.GestureData> gesturesData=
```

```
        playerGesturesData.ContainsKey(UserId)?playerGesturesData[UserId]:null;

    if(gesturesData!=null)
    {
        gesturesData.Clear();
        playerGesturesData[UserId]=gesturesData;
    }
}

//功能:获取检测到的动态手势数量,这种手势是在手势集范围中
public int GetGesturesCount(Int64 UserId)
{
    List<KinectGestures.GestureData>gesturesData=
        playerGesturesData.ContainsKey(UserId)?playerGesturesData[UserId]:null;

    if(gesturesData!=null)
    {
        return gesturesData.Count;
    }
    return 0;
}

//功能:获取检测到的手势集
public List<KinectGestures.Gestures>GetGesturesList(Int64 UserId)
{
    List<KinectGestures.Gestures>list=new List<KinectGestures.Gestures>();
    List<KinectGestures.GestureData>gesturesData=
        playerGesturesData.ContainsKey(UserId)?playerGesturesData[UserId]:null;

    if(gesturesData!=null)
    {
        foreach(KinectGestures.GestureData data in gesturesData) list.Add(data.gesture);
    }
    return list;
}

//功能:判断手势是否被检测到,如果使用的手势是在手势集中,则返回 True
public bool IsGestureDetected(Int64 UserId, KinectGestures.Gestures gesture)
{
```

```
    List<KinectGestures.GestureData>gesturesData=
        playerGesturesData.ContainsKey(UserId)?playerGesturesData[UserId]:null;
    int index=gesturesData!=null?GetGestureIndex(gesture, ref gesturesData):-1;

    return index>=0;
}

//功能:判断手势是否完全
public bool IsGestureComplete(Int64 UserId, KinectGestures.Gestures gesture,
                              bool bResetOnComplete)
{
    List<KinectGestures.GestureData>gesturesData=
        playerGesturesData.ContainsKey(UserId)?playerGesturesData[UserId]:null;
    int index=gesturesData!=null?GetGestureIndex(gesture, ref gesturesData):-1;

    if(index>=0)
    {
        KinectGestures.GestureData gestureData=gesturesData[index];

        if(bResetOnComplete && gestureData.complete)
        {
            ResetPlayerGestures(UserId);
            return true;
        }

        return gestureData.complete;
    }
    return false;
}

//功能:判断是否取消手势,
public bool IsGestureCancelled(Int64 UserId, KinectGestures.Gestures gesture)
{
    List<KinectGestures.GestureData>gesturesData=
        playerGesturesData.ContainsKey(UserId)?playerGesturesData[UserId]:null;
    int index=gesturesData!=null?GetGestureIndex(gesture, ref gesturesData):-1;

    if(index>=0)
    {
```

```csharp
            KinectGestures.GestureData gestureData=gesturesData[index];
            return gestureData.cancelled;
        }
        return false;
}

//功能:获取用户手势进度
public float GetGestureProgress(Int64 UserId, KinectGestures.Gestures gesture)
{
    List<KinectGestures.GestureData> gesturesData=
        playerGesturesData.ContainsKey(UserId)?playerGesturesData[UserId]:null;
    int index=gesturesData!=null?GetGestureIndex(gesture, ref gesturesData):-1;

    if(index>=0)
    {
        KinectGestures.GestureData gestureData=gesturesData[index];
        return gestureData.progress;
    }
    return 0f;
}

//功能:获取用户手势在屏幕上的位置,通过判断用户手势数据中是否包含用户 Id
//ContainsKey(UserId) 判断是否包含指定键名
//ref 添加在参数前,参数进入方法后参数值被更改了,则保存更改后的值;而不加 ref,参数进
    入方法后参数值被修改了,回来后参数值还是最开始的值,即在方法中的修改没有用
public Vector3 GetGestureScreenPos(Int64 UserId, KinectGestures.Gestures gesture)
{
    List<KinectGestures.GestureData> gesturesData=
        playerGesturesData.ContainsKey(UserId)?playerGesturesData[UserId]:null;
    int index=gesturesData!=null?GetGestureIndex(gesture, ref gesturesData):-1;

    if(index>=0)
    {
        KinectGestures.GestureData gestureData=gesturesData[index];
        return gestureData.screenPos;
    }
    return Vector3.zero;
}
//这个脚本的内部方法
```

```csharp
void Awake()
{
    try
    {//初始化传感器接口
        bool bNeedRestart=false;
        sensorInterfaces=KinectInterop.InitSensorInterfaces(ref bNeedRestart);

        if(bNeedRestart)
        {
            //载入界面
            Application.LoadLevel(Application.loadedLevel);
        }
    }
    catch (Exception ex)
    {
        Debug.LogError(ex.ToString());

        if(calibrationText!=null)
        {
            calibrationText.GetComponent<GUIText>().text=ex.Message;
        }
    }
}

void Start()
{
    try
    {
        //初始化默认传感器
        KinectInterop.FrameSource dwFlags=KinectInterop.FrameSource.TypeBody;
        if(computeUserMap)
            dwFlags|=KinectInterop.FrameSource.TypeDepth | KinectInterop.FrameSource.
                TypeBodyIndex;
        if(computeColorMap)
            dwFlags|=KinectInterop.FrameSource.TypeColor;
        if(computeInfraredMap)
            dwFlags|=KinectInterop.FrameSource.TypeInfrared;
```

```csharp
        //打开默认传感器
        sensorData=KinectInterop.OpenDefaultSensor(sensorInterfaces, dwFlags, sensorAngle,
                                useMultiSourceReader);
        if (sensorData==null)
        {
            throw new Exception("OpenDefaultSensor failed");
        }

        //创建 Kinect 坐标转为世界坐标的矩阵
            Quaternion quatTiltAngle=new Quaternion();
            quatTiltAngle.eulerAngles=new Vector3(- sensorAngle, 0.0f, 0.0f);

                kinectToWorld.SetTRS(new Vector3(0.0f, sensorHeight, 0.0f), quatTiltAngle,
                                Vector3.one);
    }
    catch(DllNotFoundException ex)
    {
        string message=ex.Message+" cannot be loaded. Please check the Kinect SDK
                            installation.";

        Debug.LogError(message);
        Debug.LogException(ex);

        if(calibrationText!=null)
        {
            calibrationText.GetComponent<GUIText>().text=message;
        }
        return;
    }
    catch(Exception ex)
    {
        string message=ex.Message;

        Debug.LogError(message);
        Debug.LogException(ex);

        if(calibrationText!=null)
        {
            calibrationText.GetComponent<GUIText>().text=message;
```

```
        }
        return;
}

//设置实例
instance=this;

//初始化骨骼结构
bodyFrame=new KinectInterop.BodyFrameData(sensorData.bodyCount, KinectInterop.Constants.
                                JointCount); //设置关节数量

//新建骨骼跟踪平滑处理的参数
  KinectInterop.SmoothParameters smoothParameters=new KinectInterop.SmoothParameters();

switch(smoothing)
{
    case Smoothing.Default:
        //默认情况各参数值
        smoothParameters.smoothing=0.5f;
        smoothParameters.correction=0.5f;
        smoothParameters.prediction=0.5f;
        smoothParameters.jitterRadius=0.05f;
        smoothParameters.maxDeviationRadius=0.04f;
        break;
    case Smoothing.Medium:
        //中等平滑度
        smoothParameters.smoothing=0.5f;
        smoothParameters.correction=0.1f;
        smoothParameters.prediction=0.5f;
        smoothParameters.jitterRadius=0.1f;
        smoothParameters.maxDeviationRadius=0.1f;
        break;
    case Smoothing.Aggressive:
        smoothParameters.smoothing=0.7f;
        smoothParameters.correction=0.3f;
        smoothParameters.prediction=1.0f;
        smoothParameters.jitterRadius=1.0f;
        smoothParameters.maxDeviationRadius=1.0f;
        break;
```

}

//初始化数据过滤器
jointPositionFilter=new JointPositionsFilter();
jointPositionFilter.Init(smoothParameters);

//初始化骨骼旋转限制
if(useBoneOrientationConstraints)
{
    boneConstraintsFilter= new BoneOrientationsConstraint();
    boneConstraintsFilter.AddDefaultConstraints();
}

//获取主摄像机的视角矩形宽的大小
Rect cameraRect=Camera.main.pixelRect;

//计算映射宽和高的百分比
if(DisplayMapsWidthPercent==0f)
{
    DisplayMapsWidthPercent=(sensorData.depthImageWidth / 2)*100 / cameraRect.width;
}
//将用户显示在主摄像机中
if(computeUserMap)
{//计算映射宽的百分比
    float displayMapsWidthPercent=DisplayMapsWidthPercent / 100f;
    //计算映射高的百分比
    float displayMapsHeightPercent=displayMapsWidthPercent*sensorData.depthImageHeight/
                                    sensorData.depthImageWidth;
    //计算显示在主摄像机中的宽高大小
    float displayWidth=cameraRect.width*displayMapsWidthPercent;
    float displayHeight=cameraRect.width*displayMapsHeightPercent;

//初始化用户的标签图
    usersLblTex=new Texture2D(sensorData.depthImageWidth, sensorData.depthImageHeight);
    usersMapRect=new Rect(cameraRect.width − displayWidth, cameraRect.height, displayWidth,
                          − displayHeight);
//计算深度图像的分辨率
    usersMapSize=sensorData.depthImageWidth*sensorData.depthImageHeight;
    usersHistogramImage=new Color32[usersMapSize];

```csharp
        usersPrevState＝new ushort[usersMapSize];
        usersHistogramMap＝new float[5001];
}
//将彩色图像映射到主摄像机中显示
if(computeColorMap)
{//计算映射宽的百分比
    float displayMapsWidthPercent＝DisplayMapsWidthPercent / 100f;
//计算映射高的百分比
    float displayMapsHeightPercent ＝ displayMapsWidthPercent * sensorData.colorImageHeight/
                            sensorData.colorImageWidth;
//计算显示在主摄像机中的宽高大小
    float displayWidth＝cameraRect.width*displayMapsWidthPercent;
    float displayHeight＝cameraRect.width*displayMapsHeightPercent;

//初始化彩色图像映射的相关值
    usersClrTex＝new Texture2D(sensorData.colorImageWidth, sensorData.colorImageHeight,
                        TextureFormat.RGBA32, false);
    usersClrRect＝new Rect(cameraRect.width - displayWidth, cameraRect.height, displayWidth,
                        - displayHeight);
    usersClrSize＝sensorData.colorImageWidth*sensorData.colorImageHeight;
}

//自动查找场景中能够控制的人物模型
if(avatarControllers.Count＝＝0)
{
    AvatarController[] avatars＝FindObjectsOfType(typeof(AvatarController)) as
                        AvatarController[];

    foreach(AvatarController avatar in avatars)
    {
        avatarControllers.Add(avatar);
    }
}

    //初始化包含所有用户的用户列表
    alUserIds＝new List<Int64>();
    dictUserIdToIndex＝new Dictionary<Int64, int>();

    kinectInitialized＝true;
```

```
        DontDestroyOnLoad(gameObject);

        //GUI Text.
        if(calibrationText!=null)
        {
            calibrationText.GetComponent<GUIText>().text="WAITING FOR USERS";
        }
        Debug.Log("Waiting for users.");
    }

    void OnApplicationQuit()
    {
        //在应用退出时关闭传感器
        if(kinectInitialized)
        {
            KinectInterop.CloseSensor(sensorData);
            instance=null;
        }
    }

    void OnGUI()
    {//显示映射后的图像
        if(kinectInitialized)
        {
            if(computeUserMap && displayUserMap)
            {
                GUI.DrawTexture(usersMapRect, usersLblTex);
            }
            else if(computeColorMap && displayColorMap)
            {
                GUI.DrawTexture(usersClrRect, usersClrTex);
            }
        }
    }

    void Update()
    {
        if(kinectInitialized)
        {//更新传感器数据
```

```
KinectInterop.UpdateSensorData(sensorData);

if(useMultiSourceReader)
{//获取多源帧
KinectInterop.GetMultiSourceFrame(sensorData);
}

if(computeColorMap)
{
    if(KinectInterop.PollColorFrame(sensorData))
    {//更新彩色图像映射
        UpdateColorMap();
    }
}

if(computeUserMap)
{
    if(KinectInterop.PollDepthFrame(sensorData))
    {//更新用户映射
        UpdateUserMap();
    }
}

if(computeInfraredMap)
{
    if(KinectInterop.PollInfraredFrame(sensorData))
    {//更新红外图像映射
    UpdateInfraredMap();
    }
}

if(KinectInterop.PollBodyFrame(sensorData, ref bodyFrame, ref kinectToWorld))
{

    if(smoothing!=Smoothing.None)
    {//更新过滤器
    jointPositionFilter.UpdateFilter(ref bodyFrame);
    }
```

```
            ProcessBodyFrameData();
    }

    if(useMultiSourceReader)
    {//释放多源帧
        KinectInterop.FreeMultiSourceFrame(sensorData);
    }
    //遍历模型,更新人物模型
    foreach (AvatarController controller in avatarControllers)
    {
        int userIndex= controller.playerIndex;

        if((userIndex>=0) && (userIndex<alUserIds.Count))
        {
            Int64 userId=alUserIds[userIndex];
            controller.UpdateAvatar(userId);
        }
    }

    foreach(Int64 userId in alUserIds)
    {
        if(!playerGesturesData.ContainsKey(userId))
            continue;

        //检测用户第一个姿势
        CheckForGestures(userId);

        //检测用户的完整姿势
        List<KinectGestures.GestureData> gesturesData = playerGesturesData[userId];
        foreach(KinectGestures.GestureData gestureData in gesturesData)
        {
        //完整动作
        if(gestureData.complete)
        {//遍历姿势监听器,重设用户动作
            foreach(KinectGestures.GestureListenerInterface listener in gestureListeners)
            {
                if(listener.GestureCompleted(userId, 0, gestureData.gesture, (KinectInterop.
                        JointType) gestureData. joint, gestureData.
                        screenPos))
```

```
                {
                    ResetPlayerGestures(userId);
                }
            }
        }
        //取消动作
            else if(gestureData.cancelled)
            {
            foreach(KinectGestures.GestureListenerInterface listener in gestureListeners)
                {
                    if(listener.GestureCancelled(userId, 0, gestureData.gesture, (KinectInterop.
                                JointType)gestureData.joint))
                    {
                        ResetGesture(userId, gestureData.gesture);
                    }
                }
            }
            else if(gestureData.progress>=0.1f)
            {
                foreach(KinectGestures.GestureListenerInterface listener in gestureListeners)
                {
                    listener.GestureInProgress(userId, 0, gestureData.gesture, gestureData.
                                progress, (KinectInterop. JointType ) gestureData.
                                joint, gestureData.screenPos);
                }
            }
        }
    }
}

//功能: 更新彩色图像
void UpdateColorMap()
{
    usersClrTex.LoadRawTextureData(sensorData.colorImage);
    usersClrTex.Apply();
}
```

```
//功能:更新用户直方图
void UpdateUserMap()
{
    if(KinectInterop.PollUserHistogramFrame(ref userHistogramImage, computeColorMap))
    {//调用更新用户直方图方法
        UpdateUserHistogramImage();
        usersLblTex.SetPixels32(usersHistogramImage);

        //画出骨骼线
        if(displaySkeletonLines)
        {
            for(int i=0; i<alUserIds.Count; i++)
            {//初始化骨骼线 Id
                Int64 liUserId=alUserIds[i];
                //将 Id 转为索引值
                int index=dictUserIdToIndex[liUserId];

                if(index>=0 && index<sensorData.bodyCount)
                {//画出骨骼
                    DrawSkeleton(usersLblTex, ref bodyFrame.bodyData[index]);
                }
            }
        }
        usersLblTex.Apply();
    }
}

//更新直方图
void UpdateUserHistogramImage()
{
    int numOfPoints=0;
    Array.Clear(usersHistogramMap, 0, usersHistogramMap.Length);

    //计算累积直方图的深度
    for (int i=0; i<usersMapSize; i++)
    {
        //仅计算深度图像
        if (sensorData.bodyIndexImage[i]!=255)
        {
```

```
            ushort depth=sensorData.depthImage[i];
            if(depth>5000)
                depth=5000;

            usersHistogramMap[depth]++;
            numOfPoints++;
        }
    }
    //关节点数大于零
    if (numOfPoints>0)
    {
        for (int i=1; i<usersHistogramMap.Length; i++)
        {
            usersHistogramMap[i]+=usersHistogramMap[i-1];
        }

        for (int i=0; i<usersHistogramMap.Length; i++)
        {
            usersHistogramMap[i]=1.0f -(usersHistogramMap[i]/numOfPoints);
        }
    }


    Vector2[] colorCoords=null;

    if(sensorData.colorImage!=null)
    {
        colorCoords=new Vector2[sensorData.depthImageWidth*sensorData.
                        depthImageHeight];

        if(!KinectInterop.MapDepthFrameToColorCoords(sensorData, ref colorCoords))
        {
            colorCoords=null;
        }
    }

    //Create the actual users texture based on label map and depth histogram Color32 clrClear=
        Color.clear;
    for (int i=0; i<usersMapSize; i++)
    {
```

```
ushort userMap=sensorData.bodyIndexImage[i];
ushort userDepth=sensorData.depthImage[i];

if(userDepth>5000)
    userDepth=5000;

ushort nowUserPixel=userMap!=255?(ushort)((userMap<<13)|userDepth):
                                userDepth;
ushort wasUserPixel=usersPrevState[i];

//画出变化的像素
if(nowUserPixel!=wasUserPixel)
{
    usersPrevState[i]=nowUserPixel;

    if (userMap==255)
    {
        usersHistogramImage[i]=clrClear;
    }
    else
    {
        if(sensorData.colorImage!=null)
        {
            Vector2 vColorPos=Vector2.zero;

            if(colorCoords!=null)
            {
                vColorPos.x=colorCoords[i].x;
                vColorPos.y=colorCoords[i].y;
            }
            else
            {
                Vector2 vDepthPos=Vector2.zero;
                vDepthPos.x=i% sensorData.depthImageWidth;
                vDepthPos.y=i/sensorData.depthImageWidth;
                vColorPos=KinectInterop.MapDepthPointToColorCoords
                        (sensorData, vDepthPos, userDepth);
            }
```

```csharp
if(!float.IsInfinity(vColorPos.x) &&!float.IsInfinity(vColorPos.y))
{
    int cx=(int)vColorPos.x;
    int cy=(int)vColorPos.y;
    int colorIndex=cx+cy*sensorData.colorImageWidth;

    if(colorIndex>=0 && colorIndex<usersClrSize)
    {
        int ci=colorIndex<<2;
        Color32 colorPixel= new Color32(sensorData.colorImage[ci],
                            sensorData.colorImage[ci+1],
                            sensorData.colorImage[ci+2], 230);

        usersHistogramImage[i]=colorPixel;
    }
}
else
{
    //通过深度直方图创建混合彩色图像
    float histDepth=usersHistogramMap[userDepth];
    Color c=new Color(histDepth, histDepth, histDepth, 0.9f);

    switch(userMap % 4)
    {
    case 0:
        usersHistogramImage[i]=Color.red*c;
        break;
    case 1:
        usersHistogramImage[i]=Color.green*c;
        break;
    case 2:
        usersHistogramImage[i]=Color.blue*c;
        break;
    case 3:
        usersHistogramImage[i]=Color.magenta*c;
        break;
    }
}
```

            }
        }
    }
}

//功能:处理人体帧数据
private void ProcessBodyFrameData()
{
    List<Int64> addedUsers = new List<Int64>();
    List<int> addedIndexes = new List<int>();

    List<Int64> lostUsers = new List<Int64>();
    lostUsers.AddRange(alUserIds);

    for(int i=0; i<sensorData.bodyCount; i++)
    {
        KinectInterop.BodyData bodyData = bodyFrame.bodyData[i];
        Int64 userId = bodyData.liTrackingId;

        if(bodyData.bIsTracked!=0 && Mathf.Abs(bodyData.position.z)>=minUserDistance
            && (maxUserDistance<=0f || Mathf.Abs(bodyData.position.z)<=maxUserDistance))
        {//获取人体坐标
            Vector3 bodyPos = bodyData.position;

            if(liPrimaryUserId==0)
            {//判断是否为最近用户
                bool bClosestUser = true;
                int iClosestUserIndex = i;

                if(detectClosestUser)
                {
                    for(int j=0; j<sensorData.bodyCount; j++)
                    {
                        if(j!=i)
                        {
                            KinectInterop.BodyData bodyDataOther =
                                bodyFrame.bodyData[j];
                            if((bodyDataOther.bIsTracked!=0)&&
                                (Mathf.Abs(bodyDataOther.position.z)<

```
                            Mathf.Abs(bodyPos.z)))
                        {
                            bClosestUser=false;
                            iClosestUserIndex=j;
                            break;
                        }
                    }
                }
            }
            if(bClosestUser)
            {//添加第一个或最近用户 Id 到新用户列表里
                if(!addedUsers.Contains(userId))
                {
                    addedUsers.Add(userId);
                    addedIndexes.Add(iClosestUserIndex);
                }
            }
        }

//添加用户 Id 到新用户列表
if(!addedUsers.Contains(userId))
{
    addedUsers.Add(userId);
    addedIndexes.Add(i);
}

//将 Kinect 坐标转为世界坐标
bodyFrame.bodyData[i].position=bodyPos;

//判断左臀部、脊柱底部、右臀部是否被跟踪
if(bodyData.joint[(int)KinectInterop.JointType.HipLeft].trackingState==
        KinectInterop.TrackingState.NotTracked &&
    bodyData.joint[(int)KinectInterop.JointType.SpineBase].trackingState!=
        KinectInterop.TrackingState.NotTracked &&
    bodyData.joint[(int)KinectInterop.JointType.HipRight].trackingState!=
        KinectInterop.TrackingState.NotTracked)
{
//将左臀部的跟踪状态设置为通过相邻点来推测
    bodyData.joint[(int)KinectInterop.JointType.HipLeft].trackingState=
```

```
        KinectInterop.TrackingState.Inferred;

//计算左臀部关节点的坐标
    bodyData.joint[(int)KinectInterop.JointType.HipLeft].kinectPos=
        bodyData.joint[(int)KinectInterop.JointType.SpineBase].kinectPos+
   (bodyData.joint[(int)KinectInterop.JointType.SpineBase].kinectPos-
        bodyData.joint[(int)KinectInterop.JointType.HipRight].kinectPos);
    bodyData.joint[(int)KinectInterop.JointType.HipLeft].position=
        bodyData.joint[(int)KinectInterop.JointType.SpineBase].position+
   (bodyData.joint[(int)KinectInterop.JointType.SpineBase].position-
        bodyData.joint[(int)KinectInterop.JointType.HipRight].position);
    bodyData.joint[(int)KinectInterop.JointType.HipLeft].direction=
        bodyData.joint[(int)KinectInterop.JointType.HipLeft].position-
    bodyData.joint[(int)KinectInterop.JointType.SpineBase].position;
}

//判断右臀部、脊柱底部、左臀部关节点是否被跟踪
    if(bodyData.joint[(int)KinectInterop.JointType.HipRight].trackingState==
        KinectInterop.TrackingState.NotTracked &&
    bodyData.joint[(int)KinectInterop.JointType.SpineBase].trackingState!=
        KinectInterop.TrackingState.NotTracked &&
    bodyData.joint[(int)KinectInterop.JointType.HipLeft].trackingState!=
        KinectInterop.TrackingState.NotTracked)
{
//将右臀部的跟踪状态设置为通过相邻点来推测
    bodyData.joint[(int)KinectInterop.JointType.HipRight].trackingState=
        KinectInterop.TrackingState.Inferred;

//计算右臀部关节点的坐标
    bodyData.joint[(int)KinectInterop.JointType.HipRight].kinectPos=
        bodyData.joint[(int)KinectInterop.JointType.SpineBase].kinectPos+
   (bodyData.joint[(int)KinectInterop.JointType.SpineBase].kinectPos-
        bodyData.joint[(int)KinectInterop.JointType.HipLeft].kinectPos);
    bodyData.joint[(int)KinectInterop.JointType.HipRight].position=
        bodyData.joint[(int)KinectInterop.JointType.SpineBase].position+
   (bodyData.joint[(int)KinectInterop.JointType.SpineBase].position-
        bodyData.joint[(int)KinectInterop.JointType.HipLeft].position);
    bodyData.joint[(int)KinectInterop.JointType.HipRight].direction=
        bodyData.joint[(int)KinectInterop.JointType.HipRight].position-
```

```
            bodyData.joint[(int)KinectInterop.JointType.SpineBase].position;
    }

    //判断左肩、双肩中央、右肩关节点是否被跟踪
    if((bodyData.joint[(int)KinectInterop.JointType.ShoulderLeft].trackingState==
            KinectInterop.TrackingState.NotTracked &&
        bodyData.joint[(int)KinectInterop.JointType.SpineShoulder].trackingState!=
            KinectInterop.TrackingState.NotTracked &&
        bodyData.joint[(int)KinectInterop.JointType.ShoulderRight].trackingState!=
            KinectInterop.TrackingState.NotTracked))
    {
        //将脊柱中央的跟踪状态设置为通过相邻点来推测
        bodyData.joint[(int)KinectInterop.JointType.ShoulderLeft].trackingState=
            KinectInterop.TrackingState.Inferred;

        //计算左肩关节点的坐标
        bodyData.joint[(int)KinectInterop.JointType.ShoulderLeft].kinectPos=
            bodyData.joint[(int)KinectInterop.JointType.SpineShoulder].kinectPos+
            (bodyData.joint[(int)KinectInterop.JointType.SpineShoulder].kinectPos−
            bodyData.joint[(int)KinectInterop.JointType.ShoulderRight].kinectPos);
        bodyData.joint[(int)KinectInterop.JointType.ShoulderLeft].position=
            bodyData.joint[(int)KinectInterop.JointType.SpineShoulder].position+
            (bodyData.joint[(int)KinectInterop.JointType.SpineShoulder].position−
            bodyData.joint[(int)KinectInterop.JointType.ShoulderRight].position);
        bodyData.joint[(int)KinectInterop.JointType.ShoulderLeft].direction=
            bodyData.joint[(int)KinectInterop.JointType.ShoulderLeft].position−
            bodyData.joint[(int)KinectInterop.JointType.SpineShoulder].position;
    }

    //判断左肩、双肩中央、右肩关节点是否被跟踪
    if((bodyData.joint[(int)KinectInterop.JointType.ShoulderRight].trackingState==
            KinectInterop.TrackingState.NotTracked &&
        bodyData.joint[(int)KinectInterop.JointType.SpineShoulder].trackingState!=
            KinectInterop.TrackingState.NotTracked &&
        bodyData.joint[(int)KinectInterop.JointType.ShoulderLeft].trackingState!=
            KinectInterop.TrackingState.NotTracked))
    {
        //将右肩的跟踪状态设置为通过相邻点来推测
        bodyData.joint[(int)KinectInterop.JointType.ShoulderRight].trackingState=
```

```
           KinectInterop.TrackingState.Inferred;

    //计算右肩关节点的坐标
    bodyData.joint[(int)KinectInterop.JointType.ShoulderRight].kinectPos＝
        bodyData.joint[(int)KinectInterop.JointType.SpineShoulder].kinectPos＋
        (bodyData.joint[(int)KinectInterop.JointType.SpineShoulder].kinectPos－
        bodyData.joint[(int)KinectInterop.JointType.ShoulderLeft].kinectPos);
    bodyData.joint[(int)KinectInterop.JointType.ShoulderRight].position＝
        bodyData.joint[(int)KinectInterop.JointType.SpineShoulder].position＋
        (bodyData.joint[(int)KinectInterop.JointType.SpineShoulder].position－
        bodyData.joint[(int)KinectInterop.JointType.ShoulderLeft].position);
    bodyData.joint[(int)KinectInterop.JointType.ShoulderRight].direction＝
        bodyData.joint[(int)KinectInterop.JointType.ShoulderRight].position－
        bodyData.joint[(int)KinectInterop.JointType.SpineShoulder].position;
}

//判断左臀部、右臀部关节点是否被跟踪
if(bodyData.joint[(int)KinectInterop.JointType.HipLeft].trackingState!＝
        KinectInterop.TrackingState.NotTracked &&
    bodyData.joint[(int)KinectInterop.JointType.HipRight].trackingState!＝
        KinectInterop.TrackingState.NotTracked)
{//计算右臀部的坐标
Vector3 posRHip＝bodyData.joint[(int)KinectInterop.JointType.HipRight].position;
Vector3 posLHip＝bodyData.joint[(int)KinectInterop.JointType.HipLeft].position;
bodyData.hipsDirection＝posRHip－posLHip;
bodyData.hipsDirection －＝Vector3.Project(bodyData.hipsDirection, Vector3.up);
}

//判断左肩部、右肩部关节点是否被跟踪
if(bodyData.joint[(int)KinectInterop.JointType.ShoulderLeft].trackingState!＝
    KinectInterop.TrackingState.NotTracked &&
bodyData.joint[(int)KinectInterop.JointType.ShoulderRight].trackingState!＝
        KinectInterop.TrackingState.NotTracked);
{//计算右肩部的坐标
  Vector3 posRShoulder＝bodyData.joint[(int)KinectInterop.JointType.ShoulderRight].
                        position;
  Vector3 posLShoulder＝bodyData.joint[(int)KinectInterop.JointType.ShoulderLeft].
                        position;
//计算肩部的方向
```

```
bodyData.shouldersDirection=posRShoulder-posLShoulder;
bodyData.shouldersDirection -= Vector3.Project(bodyData.shouldersDirection,
                                               Vector3.up);

Vector3 shouldersDir=bodyData.shouldersDirection;
shouldersDir.z=-shouldersDir.z;

Quaternion turnRot=Quaternion.FromToRotation(Vector3.right, shouldersDir);
bodyData.bodyTurnAngle=turnRot.eulerAngles.y;
}

//判断左腕、左手关节点是否被跟踪
if(bodyData.joint[(int)KinectInterop.JointType.WristLeft].trackingState!=
        KinectInterop.TrackingState.NotTracked &&
    bodyData.joint[(int)KinectInterop.JointType.HandLeft].trackingState!=
        KinectInterop.TrackingState.NotTracked)
{//初始化左肩的坐标
Vector3 pos1=bodyData.joint[(int)KinectInterop.JointType.WristLeft].position;
//初始化左手的坐标
Vector3 pos2=bodyData.joint[(int)KinectInterop.JointType.HandLeft].position;

//判断左手方向 bodyData.leftHandDirection=pos2-pos1;
}

//判断左手方向是否为零,左腕和左手指关节是否被跟踪
if(bodyData.leftHandDirection!=Vector3.zero &&
    bodyData.joint[(int)KinectInterop.JointType.WristLeft].trackingState!=
        KinectInterop.TrackingState.NotTracked &&
    bodyData.joint[(int)KinectInterop.JointType.ThumbLeft].trackingState!=
        KinectInterop.TrackingState.NotTracked)
{//初始化左腕关节的坐标
Vector3 pos1=bodyData.joint[(int)KinectInterop.JointType.WristLeft].position;
//初始化左手指关节的坐标
Vector3 pos2=bodyData.joint[(int)KinectInterop.JointType.ThumbLeft].position;

//计算左手指方向
bodyData.leftThumbDirection=pos2-pos1;
bodyData.leftThumbDirection -= Vector3.Project(bodyData.leftThumbDirection,
                                               bodyData.leftHandDirection);
```

```
            bodyData.leftThumbAngle＝bodyData.bodyTurnAngle;
        }
//判断右腕和左手关节是否被跟踪
if(bodyData.joint[(int)KinectInterop.JointType.WristRight].trackingState!＝
        KinectInterop.TrackingState.NotTracked &&
    bodyData.joint[(int)KinectInterop.JointType.HandRight].trackingState!＝
        KinectInterop.TrackingState.NotTracked)
{//初始化右腕、右手关节的坐标
Vector3 pos1＝bodyData.joint[(int)KinectInterop.JointType.WristRight].position;
Vector3 pos2＝bodyData.joint[(int)KinectInterop.JointType.HandRight].position;
//计算右手方向
bodyData.rightHandDirection＝pos2－pos1;
}

//判断右手方向是否为零，右腕和右手指关节是否被跟踪
if(bodyData.rightHandDirection!＝Vector3.zero &&
    bodyData.joint[(int)KinectInterop.JointType.WristRight].trackingState!＝
        KinectInterop.TrackingState.NotTracked &&
    bodyData.joint[(int)KinectInterop.JointType.ThumbRight].trackingState!＝
        KinectInterop.TrackingState.NotTracked)
{//初始化右腕、右手指关节的坐标
Vector3 pos1＝bodyData.joint[(int)KinectInterop.JointType.WristRight].position;
Vector3 pos2＝bodyData.joint[(int)KinectInterop.JointType.ThumbRight].position;
//计算右手指方向
bodyData.rightThumbDirection＝pos2－pos1;
   bodyData.rightThumbDirection －＝ Vector3.Project (bodyData.rightThumbDirection,
                                        bodyData.rightHandDirection);
bodyData.rightThumbAngle＝bodyData.bodyTurnAngle;
}
//判断左膝、左踝和左脚关节是否被跟踪
if(bodyData.joint[(int)KinectInterop.JointType.KneeLeft].trackingState!＝
        KinectInterop.TrackingState.NotTracked &&
    bodyData.joint[(int)KinectInterop.JointType.AnkleLeft].trackingState!＝
        KinectInterop.TrackingState.NotTracked &&
    bodyData.joint[(int)KinectInterop.JointType.FootLeft].trackingState!＝
        KinectInterop.TrackingState.NotTracked)
    {
    Vector3 vFootProjected＝Vector3.Project(bodyData.joint[(int)KinectInterop.JointType.
                            FootLeft].direction, bodyData.joint[(int)
```

KinectInterop.JointType.AnkleLeft].direction);
//计算关节坐标与方向
bodyData.joint[(int)KinectInterop.JointType.AnkleLeft].kinectPos＋＝vFootProjected;
bodyData.joint[(int)KinectInterop.JointType.AnkleLeft].position＋＝vFootProjected;
bodyData.joint[(int)KinectInterop.JointType.FootLeft].direction－＝vFootProjected;
}

//判断右膝、右踝和右脚关节是否被跟踪
if(bodyData.joint[(int)KinectInterop.JointType.KneeRight].trackingState!＝
        KinectInterop.TrackingState.NotTracked &&
    bodyData.joint[(int)KinectInterop.JointType.AnkleRight].trackingState!＝
        KinectInterop.TrackingState.NotTracked &&
    bodyData.joint[(int)KinectInterop.JointType.FootRight].trackingState!＝
        KinectInterop.TrackingState.NotTracked)
{
    Vector3 vFootProjected ＝ Vector3.Project(bodyData.joint[(int)KinectInterop.JointType.
                        FootRight].direction, bodyData.joint[(int)
                        KinectInterop.JointType.AnkleRight].direction);
//计算关节坐标与方向
bodyData.joint[(int)KinectInterop.JointType.AnkleRight].kinectPos＋＝vFootProjected;
bodyData.joint[(int)KinectInterop.JointType.AnkleRight].position＋＝vFootProjected;
bodyData.joint[(int)KinectInterop.JointType.FootRight].direction－＝vFootProjected;
//计算人体关节点的世界坐标
CalculateJointOrients(ref bodyData);

if(sensorData!＝null && sensorData.sensorInterface!＝null)
{
//修改关节点旋转坐标
sensorData.sensorInterface.FixJointOrientations(sensorData, ref bodyData);
}

//过滤器旋转限制
if(useBoneOrientationConstraints && boneConstraintsFilter!＝null)
{
    boneConstraintsFilter.Constrain(ref bodyData);
}

lostUsers.Remove(userId);
bodyFrame.bodyData[i]＝bodyData;

```csharp
        }
    }

    //移除丢失的用户
    if(lostUsers.Count>0)
    {
        foreach(Int64 userId in lostUsers)
        {
            RemoveUser(userId);
        }
        lostUsers.Clear();
    }

    //验证新检测到的用户
    if(addedUsers.Count>0)
    {
        for(int i=0; i<addedUsers.Count; i++)
        {
            Int64 userId=addedUsers[i];
            int userIndex=addedIndexes[i];
            CalibrateUser(userId, userIndex);
        }
        addedUsers.Clear();
        addedIndexes.Clear();
    }
}

//功能:添加用户 Id 到用户列表
void CalibrateUser(Int64 userId, int bodyIndex)
{
    if(!alUserIds.Contains(userId))
    {
        if(CheckForCalibrationPose(userId, bodyIndex, playerCalibrationPose))
        {
            int uidIndex=alUserIds.Count;
            Debug.Log("Adding user "+uidIndex+",ID:"+userId+",Index: "+bodyIndex);

            alUserIds.Add(userId);
            dictUserIdToIndex[userId]=bodyIndex;
```

```
if(liPrimaryUserId==0)
{
    liPrimaryUserId=userId;

    if(liPrimaryUserId!=0)
    {
        if(calibrationText!=null && calibrationText.GetComponent<GUIText>().
            text!="")
        {
            calibrationText.GetComponent<GUIText>().text="";
        }
    }
}

for(int i=0; i<avatarControllers.Count; i++)
{
    AvatarController avatar=avatarControllers[i];

    if(avatar && avatar.playerIndex==uidIndex)
    {
        avatar.SuccessfulCalibration(userId);
    }
}

//检测姿势
foreach(KinectGestures.Gestures gesture in playerCommonGestures)
{
    DetectGesture(userId, gesture);
}

//把新用户通知给姿势监听器
foreach(KinectGestures.GestureListenerInterface listener in gestureListeners)
{
    listener.UserDetected(userId, 0);
}
ResetFilters();
        }
    }
}
```

```csharp
//功能:移除丢失的用户的 Id
void RemoveUser(Int64 userId)
{
    int uidIndex=alUserIds.IndexOf(userId);
    Debug.Log("Removing user "+uidIndex+", ID: "+userId);

    for(int i=0; i<avatarControllers.Count; i++)
    {
        AvatarController avatar=avatarControllers[i];

        if(avatar && avatar.playerIndex>=uidIndex && avatar.playerIndex<alUserIds.Count)
        {
            avatar.ResetToInitialPosition();
        }
    }

    //把丢失的用户通知给姿势监听器
    foreach(KinectGestures.GestureListenerInterface listener in gestureListeners)
    {
        listener.UserLost(userId, 0);
    }
    //清除该用户的姿势列表和校验数据
    if(playerCalibrationData.ContainsKey(userId))
    {
        playerCalibrationData.Remove(userId);
    }
    //清除过期的数据列表中的校验数据
    List<Int64>alCaldataKeys=new List<Int64>(playerCalibrationData.Keys);

    foreach(Int64 calUserId in alCalDataKeys)
    {
        KinectGestures.GestureData gestureData=playerCalibrationData[calUserId];

        if((gestureData.timestamp+60f)<Time.realtimeSinceStartup)
        {
            playerCalibrationData.Remove(calUserId);
        }
    }
```

```csharp
alCalDataKeys.Clear();
//移除总体用户列表
alUserIds.Remove(userId);
dictUserIdToIndex.Remove(userId);

if(liPrimaryUserId==userId)
{
    if(alUserIds.Count>0)
    {
        liPrimaryUserId=alUserIds[0];
    }
    else
    {
        liPrimaryUserId=0;
    }
}

for(int i=0; i<avatarControllers.Count; i++)
{
    AvatarController avatar=avatarControllers[i];

    if(avatar && avatar.playerIndex>=uidIndex && avatar.playerIndex<alUserIds.Count)
    {
        avatar.SuccessfulCalibration(alUserIds[avatar.playerIndex]);
    }
}

if(liPrimaryUserId==0)
{
    Debug.Log("Waiting for users.");

    if(calibrationText!=null)
    {
        calibrationText.GetComponent<GUIText>().text="WAITING FOR USERS";
    }
}
}
```

```
//功能:在给出的结构上画出骨骼
private void DrawSkeleton(Texture2D aTexture, ref KinectInterop.BodyData bodyData)
{
    int jointsCount=sensorData.jointCount;

    for(int i=0; i<jointsCount; i++)
    {
        int parent=(int)sensorData.sensorInterface.GetParentJoint((KinectInterop.JointType)i);

        if(bodyData.joint[i].trackingState!=KinectInterop.TrackingState.NotTracked &&
            bodyData.joint[parent].trackingState!=KinectInterop.TrackingState.NotTracked)
        {
            Vector2 posParent = KinectInterop.MapSpacePointToDepthCoords (sensorData,
                bodyData.joint[parent].kinectPos);
            Vector2 posJoint=KinectInterop.MapSpacePointToDepthCoords(sensorData,
                bodyData.joint[i].kinectPos);

            if(posParent!=Vector2.zero && posJoint!=Vector2.zero)
            {
                DrawLine(aTexture, (int)posParent.x, (int)posParent.y, (int)posJoint.x,
                    (int)pos Joint.y, Color.yellow);
            }
        }
    }
}

//功能:在结构中画出线
private void DrawLine(Texture2D a_Texture, int x1, int y1, int x2, int y2, Color a_Color)
{
    int width=sensorData!=null?sensorData.depthImageWidth:0;
    int height=sensorData!=null?sensorData.depthImageHeight:0;

    int dy=y2-y1;
    int dx=x2-x1;

    int stepy=1;
    if (dy<0)
    {
        dy=-dy;
```

```
            stepy=-1;
}

int stepx=1;
if (dx<0)
{
    dx=-dx;
    stepx=-1;
}

dy<<=1;
dx<<=1;

if(x1>=0 && x1<width && y1>=0 && y1<height)
    for(int x=-1; x<=1; x++)
        for(int y=-1; y<=1; y++)
            a_Texture.SetPixel(x1+x, y1+y, a_Color);

if (dx>dy)
{
    int fraction=dy -(dx>>1);

    while (x1!=x2)
    {
        if (fraction>=0)
        {
            y1+=stepy;
            fraction -=dx;
        }

        x1+=stepx;
        fraction+=dy;

        if(x1>=0 && x1<width && y1>=0 && y1<height)
            for(int x=-1; x<=1; x++)
                for(int y=-1; y<=1; y++)
                    a_Texture.SetPixel(x1+x, y1+y, a_Color);
    }
}
```

```
            else
            {
                int fraction=dx-(dy>>1);

                while (y1!=y2)
                {
                    if (fraction>=0)
                    {
                        x1+=stepx;
                        fraction-=dy;
                    }

                    y1+=stepy;
                    fraction+=dx;

                    if(x1>=0 && x1<width && y1>=0 && y1<height)
                        for(int x=-1; x<=1; x++)
                            for(int y=-1; y<=1; y++)
                                a_Texture.SetPixel(x1+x, y1+y, a_Color);
                }
            }
        }
}

//功能:计算人体关节点的旋转
private void CalculateJointOrients(ref KinectInterop.BodyData bodyData)
{
    int jointCount=bodyData.joint.Length;

    for(int j=0; j<jointCount; j++)
    {
        int joint=j;

        KinectInterop.JointData jointData=bodyData.joint[joint];
        bool bJointValid=ignoreInferredJoints?jointData.trackingState==
            KinectInterop.TrackingState.Tracked: jointData.trackingState!=
            KinectInterop.TrackingState.NotTracked;

        if(bJointValid)
        {
```

```
int nextJoint=(int)sensorData.sensorInterface.GetNextJoint((KinectInterop.JointType)
                                                          joint);
if(nextJoint!=joint && nextJoint>=0 && nextJoint<sensorData.jointCount)
{
    KinectInterop.JointData nextJointData=bodyData.joint[nextJoint];
    bool bNextJointValid=ignoreInferredJoints?nextJointData.trackingState==
        KinectInterop.TrackingState.Tracked:nextJointData.trackingState!=
        KinectInterop.TrackingState.NotTracked;

    if(bNextJointValid)
    {
        Vector3 baseDir=KinectInterop.JointBaseDir[nextJoint];
        Vector3 jointDir=nextJointData.direction;
        jointDir.z=-jointDir.z;

        if((joint==(int)KinectInterop.JointType.ShoulderLeft)||
          (joint==(int)KinectInterop.JointType.ElbowLeft)||
          (joint==(int)KinectInterop.JointType.WristLeft)||
          (joint==(int)KinectInterop.JointType.HandLeft))
        {
            float angle=-bodyData.leftThumbAngle;
            Vector3 axis=jointDir;
            Quaternion armTurnRotation=Quaternion.AngleAxis(angle, axis);

            jointData.normalRotation=armTurnRotation*Quaternion.FromToRotation
                            (baseDir, jointDir);
        }
        else if((joint==(int)KinectInterop.JointType.ShoulderRight)||
               (joint==(int)KinectInterop.JointType.ElbowRight)||
               (joint==(int)KinectInterop.JointType.WristRight)||
               (joint==(int)KinectInterop.JointType.HandRight))
        {
            float angle=-bodyData.rightThumbAngle;
            Vector3 axis=jointDir;
            Quaternion armTurnRotation=Quaternion.AngleAxis(angle, axis);

            jointData.normalRotation=armTurnRotation*Quaternion.FromToRotation
                            (baseDir, jointDir);
        }
```

```
        else
        {
            jointData.normalRotation=Quaternion.FromToRotation(baseDir, jointDir);
        }

        if((joint==(int)KinectInterop.JointType.SpineBase)||
            (joint==(int)KinectInterop.JointType.SpineMid)||
            (joint==(int)KinectInterop.JointType.SpineShoulder)||
            (joint==(int)KinectInterop.JointType.Neck)||
            (joint==(int)KinectInterop.JointType.HipLeft)||
            (joint==(int)KinectInterop.JointType.HipRight)||
            (joint==(int)KinectInterop.JointType.KneeLeft)||
            (joint==(int)KinectInterop.JointType.KneeRight)||
            (joint==(int)KinectInterop.JointType.AnkleLeft)||
            (joint==(int)KinectInterop.JointType.AnkleRight))
        {
            baseDir=Vector3.right;
            jointDir=bodyData.shouldersDirection;
            jointDir.z=-jointDir.z;

            jointData.normalRotation *=Quaternion.FromToRotation(baseDir,
                                                                  jointDir);
        }

    jointData.mirroredRotation=Quaternion.FromToRotation(baseDir, jointDir);

    Vector3 mirroredAngles=jointData.normalRotation.eulerAngles;
    mirroredAngles.y=-mirroredAngles.y;
    mirroredAngles.z=-mirroredAngles.z;
    jointData.mirroredRotation=Quaternion.Euler(mirroredAngles);
    }
}
else
{
    jointData.normalRotation=Quaternion.identity;
    jointData.mirroredRotation=Quaternion.identity;
}
}
```

```csharp
        bodyData.joint[joint]=jointData;

        if(joint==(int)KinectInterop.JointType.SpineBase)
        {
            bodyData.normalRotation=jointData.normalRotation;
            bodyData.mirroredRotation=jointData.mirroredRotation;
        }
    }
}

//功能:检测姿势的状态
private void CheckForGestures(Int64 UserId)
{
    if(!playerGesturesData.ContainsKey(UserId)||!gesturesTrackingAtTime.ContainsKey
        (UserId))
        return;

    //检测姿势
    if(Time.realtimeSinceStartup>=gesturesTrackingAtTime[UserId])
    {
        //获取关节点空间坐标
        int iAllJointsCount=sensorData.jointCount;
        bool[] playerJointsTracked=new bool[iAllJointsCount];
        Vector3[] playerJointsPos=new Vector3[iAllJointsCount];

        int[] aiNeededJointIndexes=KinectGestures.GetNeededJointIndexes();
        int iNeededJointsCount=aiNeededJointIndexes.Length;

        for(int i=0; i<iNeededJointsCount; i++)
        {
            int joint=aiNeededJointIndexes[i];

            if(joint>=0 && IsJointTracked(UserId, joint))
            {
                playerJointsTracked[joint]=true;
                playerJointsPos[joint]=GetJointPosition(UserId, joint);
            }
        }
```

```
//检测关节点
List<KinectGestures.GestureData> gesturesData = playerGesturesData[UserId];

int listGestureSize = gesturesData.Count;
float timestampNow = Time.realtimeSinceStartup;

for(int g = 0; g < listGestureSize; g++)
{
    KinectGestures.GestureData gestureData = gesturesData[g];

    if((timestampNow >= gestureData.startTrackingAtTime) &&
        !IsConflictingGestureInProgress(gestureData, ref gesturesData))
    {
        KinectGestures.CheckForGesture(UserId, ref gestureData, Time.realtime
                            SinceStartup,ref playerJointsPos,
                            ref playerJointsTracked);
        gesturesData[g] = gestureData;

        if(gestureData.complete)
        {
            gesturesTrackingAtTime[UserId] = timestampNow + minTimeBetweenGestures;
        }
    }
}

playerGesturesData[UserId] = gesturesData;
}
}

private bool IsConflictingGestureInProgress(KinectGestures.GestureData gestureData, ref List<
                            KinectGestures.GestureData> gesturesData)
{
    foreach(KinectGestures.Gestures gesture in gestureData.checkForGestures)
    {
        int index = GetGestureIndex(gesture, ref gesturesData);

        if(index >= 0)
        {
            if(gesturesData[index].progress > 0f)
```

```
                return true;
            }
        }
        return false;
    }

//功能:获取姿势索引
private int GetGestureIndex(KinectGestures.Gestures gesture,
                    ref List<KinectGestures.GestureData> gesturesData)
{
    int listSize = gesturesData.Count;

    for(int i=0; i<listSize; i++)
    {
        if(gesturesData[i].gesture==gesture)
            return i;
    }
    return -1;
}

//功能:检测校验姿势
private bool CheckForCalibrationPose(Int64 UserId, int bodyIndex,
                            KinectGestures.Gestures calibrationGesture)
{
    if(calibrationGesture==KinectGestures.Gestures.None)
        return true;

    KinectGestures.GestureData gestureData = playerCalibrationData.ContainsKey(UserId)?
        playerCalibrationData[UserId]: new KinectGestures.GestureData();

    //初始化姿势数据
    if(gestureData.userId!=UserId)
    {
        gestureData.userId = UserId;
        gestureData.gesture = calibrationGesture;
        gestureData.state = 0;
        gestureData.timestamp = Time.realtimeSinceStartup;
        gestureData.joint = 0;
        gestureData.progress = 0f;
```

```
        gestureData.complete=false;
        gestureData.cancelled=false;
    }

    //获取关节点的空间坐标并跟踪
    int iAllJointsCount=sensorData.jointCount;
    bool[] playerJointsTracked=new bool[iAllJointsCount];
    Vector3[] playerJointsPos=new Vector3[iAllJointsCount];
    int[] aiNeededJointIndexes=KinectGestures.GetNeededJointIndexes();
    int iNeededJointsCount=aiNeededJointIndexes.Length;
    for(int i=0; i<iNeededJointsCount; i++)
    {
        int joint=aiNeededJointIndexes[i];

        if(joint>=0)
        {
            KinectInterop.JointData jointData=bodyFrame.bodyData[bodyIndex].joint[joint];
            playerJointsTracked[joint]=jointData.trackingState!=
                KinectInterop.TrackingState.NotTracked;
            playerJointsPos[joint]=jointData.kinectPos;
        }
    }

    //检测姿势处理
    KinectGestures.CheckForGesture(UserId, ref gestureData, Time.realtimeSinceStartup,
                    ref playerJointsPos, ref playerJointsTracked);
    playerCalibrationData[UserId]=gestureData;

    //检测姿势是否完整
    if(gestureData.complete)
    {
        gestureData.userId=0;
        playerCalibrationData[UserId]=gestureData;
        return true;
    }
    return false;
    }
}
```

4. 动作识别脚本

动作识别的基础是骨骼跟踪，识别内容包含肢体运动、手势以及静态姿势。本平台使用的是手势识别。手势识别大致分为算法匹配、模板匹配、神经网路和支持向量机、统计分析和机器学习。本书主要采用"模板匹配"的思路，通过手势动作序列和预设的模板数据进行匹配，测量两者之间的相似度来完成识别任务。

```csharp
public class KinectGestures
{
//动作姿势类型
public enum Gestures
    {
        None=0,
        RaiseRightHand,
        RaiseLeftHand,
        Psi,
        Tpose,
        Stop,
        Wave,
        SwipeLeft,
        SwipeRight,
        SwipeUp,
        SwipeDown,
        ZoomOut,
        ZoomIn,
        Wheel,
        Jump,
        Squat,
        Push,
        Pull
    }

//动作姿势数据
public struct GestureData
{
    public long userId;
    public Gestures gesture;
    public int state;
    public float timestamp;
    public int joint;
    public Vector3 jointPos;
```

```csharp
    public Vector3 screenPos;
    public float tagFloat;
    public Vector3 tagVector;
    public Vector3 tagVector2;
    public float progress;
    public bool complete;
    public bool cancelled;
    public List<Gestures> checkForGestures;
    public float startTrackingAtTime;
}

//获取人体骨骼关节点的索引
private const int leftHandIndex=(int)KinectInterop.JointType.HandLeft;
private const int rightHandIndex=(int)KinectInterop.JointType.HandRight;

private const int leftElbowIndex=(int)KinectInterop.JointType.ElbowLeft;
private const int rightElbowIndex=(int)KinectInterop.JointType.ElbowRight;

private const int leftShoulderIndex=(int)KinectInterop.JointType.ShoulderLeft;
private const int rightShoulderIndex=(int)KinectInterop.JointType.ShoulderRight;

private const int hipCenterIndex=(int)KinectInterop.JointType.SpineBase;
private const int shoulderCenterIndex=(int)KinectInterop.JointType.SpineShoulder;

private const int leftHipIndex=(int)KinectInterop.JointType.HipLeft;
private const int rightHipIndex=(int)KinectInterop.JointType.HipRight;

//需要用到的关节点索引
private static int[] neededJointIndexes = {
    leftHandIndex, rightHandIndex, leftElbowIndex, rightElbowIndex, leftShoulderIndex,
    rightShoulderIndex, hipCenterIndex, shoulderCenterIndex, leftHipIndex, rightHipIndex
};

//获取所需关节点索引值数组
public static int[] GetNeededJointIndexes()
{
    return neededJointIndexes;
}
```

//设置运动关节点的信息
```
private static void SetGestureJoint(ref GestureData gestureData, float timestamp, int joint,
                    Vector3 jointPos)
{
    gestureData.joint=joint;
    gestureData.jointPos=jointPos;
    gestureData.timestamp=timestamp;
    gestureData.state++;
}
```
//功能:设置动作取消时的动作信息
```
private static void SetGestureCancelled(ref GestureData gestureData)
{
    gestureData.state=0;
    gestureData.progress=0f;
    gestureData.cancelled=true;
}
```
//功能:检查用户动作是否完成
```
private static void CheckPoseComplete (ref GestureData gestureData, float timestamp, Vector3
                    jointPos, bool isInPose, float durationToComplete)
{
    if(isInPose)
    {
        float timeLeft=timestamp - gestureData.timestamp;
        gestureData.progress=durationToComplete>0f?Mathf.Clamp01(timeLeft/duration
                                                ToComplete):1.0f;

        if(timeLeft>=durationToComplete)
        {
            gestureData.timestamp=timestamp;
            gestureData.jointPos=jointPos;
            gestureData.state++;
            gestureData.complete=true;
        }
    }
    else
    {
        SetGestureCancelled(ref gestureData);
    }
}
```

//功能:设置屏幕坐标
```
private static void SetScreenPos(long userId, ref GestureData gestureData, ref Vector3[] jointsPos,
                ref bool[] jointsTracked)
{
    Vector3 handPos = jointsPos[rightHandIndex];
    bool calculateCoords = false;
    if(gestureData.joint == rightHandIndex)
    {
        if(jointsTracked[rightHandIndex] /**&& jointsTracked[rightElbowIndex] &&
            jointsTracked[rightShoulderIndex]*/)
        {
            calculateCoords = true;
        }
    }
    else if(gestureData.joint == leftHandIndex)
    {
        if(jointsTracked[leftHandIndex] /**&& jointsTracked[leftElbowIndex] &&
            jointsTracked[leftShoulderIndex]*/)
        {
            handPos = jointsPos[leftHandIndex];
            calculateCoords = true;
        }
    }

    if(calculateCoords)
    {

        if(jointsTracked[hipCenterIndex] && jointsTracked[shoulderCenterIndex] &&
            jointsTracked[leftShoulderIndex] && jointsTracked[rightShoulderIndex])
        {
            Vector3 shoulderToHips = jointsPos[shoulderCenterIndex] —
                            jointsPos[hipCenterIndex];
            Vector3 rightToLeft = jointsPos[rightShoulderIndex] — jointsPos[leftShoulderIndex];

            gestureData.tagVector2.x = rightToLeft.x; //* 1.2f;
            gestureData.tagVector2.y = shoulderToHips.y; //* 1.2f;

            if(gestureData.joint == rightHandIndex)
            {
```

```
                gestureData.tagVector.x=jointsPos[rightShoulderIndex].x-
                            gestureData.tagVector2.x/2;
                gestureData.tagVector.y=jointsPos[hipCenterIndex].y;
            }
            else
            {
                gestureData.tagVector.x=jointsPos[leftShoulderIndex].x-
                            gestureData.tagVector2.x/2;
                gestureData.tagVector.y=jointsPos[hipCenterIndex].y;
            }
        }

        if(gestureData.tagVector2.x!=0 && gestureData.tagVector2.y!=0)
        {
            Vector3 relHandPos=handPos-gestureData.tagVector;
            gestureData.screenPos.x=Mathf.Clamp01(relHandPos.x/gestureData.tagVector2.x);
            gestureData.screenPos.y=Mathf.Clamp01(relHandPos.y/gestureData.tagVector2.y);
        }
    }
}
//功能:设置焦点
private static void SetZoomFactor(long userId, ref GestureData gestureData, float initialZoom,
                    ref Vector3[] jointsPos, ref bool[] jointsTracked)
{
    Vector3 vectorZooming=jointsPos[rightHandIndex]-jointsPos[leftHandIndex];

    if(gestureData.tagFloat==0f || gestureData.userId!=userId)
    {
        gestureData.tagFloat=0.5f; //this is 100%
    }

    float distZooming=vectorZooming.magnitude;
    gestureData.screenPos.z=initialZoom+(distZooming / gestureData.tagFloat);
}
//功能:设置翻转角度
private static void SetWheelRotation(long userId, ref GestureData gestureData, Vector3 initialPos,
                    Vector3 currentPos)
{
    float angle=Vector3.Angle(initialPos, currentPos)*Mathf.Sign(currentPos.y-initialPos.y);
```

```
        gestureData.screenPos.z=angle;
}

//功能:识别人体完整的动作
public static void CheckForGesture(long userId, ref GestureData gestureData, float timestamp,
                    ref Vector3[] jointsPos, ref bool[] jointsTracked)
{
    if(gestureData.complete)
        return;

    switch(gestureData.gesture)
    {
        //举起右手
        case Gestures.RaiseRightHand:
            switch(gestureData.state)
            {
                case 0:    //姿势检测
                    if (jointsTracked[rightHandIndex] && jointsTracked[rightShoulderIndex] &&
                        (jointsPos[rightHandIndex].y－jointsPos[rightShoulderIndex].y)>0.1f)
                    {
                        SetGestureJoint(ref gestureData, timestamp, rightHandIndex,
                                jointsPos[rightHandIndex]);
                    }
                    break;

                case 1:    //姿势完成
                    bool isInPose=jointsTracked[rightHandIndex] &&
                        jointsTracked[rightShoulderIndex]&&(jointsPos[rightHandIndex].y－
                        jointsPos[rightShoulderIndex].y)>0.1f;

                    Vector3 jointPos=jointsPos[gestureData.joint];
                    CheckPoseComplete(ref gestureData, timestamp, jointPos, isInPose,
                            KinectInterop.Constants.PoseCompleteDuration);
                    break;
            }
            break;

        //举起左手
        case Gestures.RaiseLeftHand:
```

```
switch(gestureData.state)
{
    case 0:    //姿势检测
        if (jointsTracked[leftHandIndex] && jointsTracked[leftShoulderIndex] &&
            (jointsPos[leftHandIndex].y－jointsPos[leftShoulderIndex].y)＞0.1f)
        {
            SetGestureJoint(ref gestureData, timestamp, leftHandIndex,
                    jointsPos[leftHandIndex]);
        }
        break;


    case 1:    //姿势完成
        bool isInPose＝jointsTracked[leftHandIndex] &&
            jointsTracked[leftShoulderIndex] && (jointsPos[leftHandIndex].y－
            jointsPos[leftShoulderIndex].y)＞0.1f;

        Vector3 jointPos＝jointsPos[gestureData.joint];
        CheckPoseComplete(ref gestureData, timestamp, jointPos, isInPose,
                KinectInterop.Constants.PoseCompleteDuration);
        break;
}
break;
//
case Gestures.Psi:
    switch(gestureData.state)
    {
        case 0:    //姿势检测
            if (jointsTracked[rightHandIndex] && jointsTracked[rightShoulderIndex] &&
                (jointsPos[rightHandIndex].y－jointsPos[rightShoulderIndex].y)＞0.1f &&
                jointsTracked[leftHandIndex] && jointsTracked[leftShoulderIndex] &&
                (jointsPos[leftHandIndex].y－jointsPos[leftShoulderIndex].y)＞0.1f)
            {
                SetGestureJoint(ref gestureData, timestamp, rightHandIndex,
                        jointsPos[rightHandIndex]);
            }
            break;

        case 1:    //姿势完成
            boolisInPose＝jointsTracked[rightHandIndex] &&
```

```csharp
                    jointsTracked[rightShoulderIndex]&&(jointsPos[rightHandIndex].y-
                    jointsPos[rightShoulderIndex].y)>0.1f &&
                    jointsTracked[leftHandIndex] &&
                    jointsTracked[leftShoulderIndex] &&(jointsPos[leftHandIndex].y-
                    jointsPos[leftShoulderIndex].y)>0.1f;

                    Vector3 jointPos=jointsPos[gestureData.joint];
                    CheckPoseComplete(ref gestureData, timestamp, jointPos, isInPose,
                            KinectInterop.Constants.PoseCompleteDuration);
                    break;
            }
        break;

//
        case Gestures.Tpose:
            switch(gestureData.state)
            {
                case 0:     //姿势检测
                    if(jointsTracked [rightHandIndex] && jointsTracked [rightElbowIndex] &&
                        jointsTracked[rightShoulderIndex] &&
                        Mathf.Abs(jointsPos[rightElbowIndex].y-
                            jointsPos[rightShoulderIndex].y)<0.1f &&    //0.07f
                        Mathf.Abs(jointsPos[rightHandIndex].y-
                            jointsPos[rightShoulderIndex].y)<0.1f &&    //0.7f
                        jointsTracked[leftHandIndex] && jointsTracked[leftElbowIndex] &&
                        jointsTracked[leftShoulderIndex] &&
                        Mathf.Abs(jointsPos[leftElbowIndex].y-
                            jointsPos[leftShoulderIndex].y)<0.1f &&
                        Mathf.Abs(jointsPos[leftHandIndex].y-
                            jointsPos[leftShoulderIndex].y)<0.1f)
                    {
                        SetGestureJoint(ref gestureData, timestamp, rightHandIndex,
                                jointsPos[rightHandIndex]);
                    }
                    break;

                case 1:     //姿势完成
                    bool isInPose=jointsTracked[rightHandIndex] &&
                            jointsTracked[rightElbowIndex] &&
```

```
                    jointsTracked[rightShoulderIndex] &&
                Mathf.Abs(jointsPos[rightElbowIndex].y-
                    jointsPos[rightShoulderIndex].y)<0.1f &&    //0.7f
                Mathf.Abs(jointsPos[rightHandIndex].y-
                    jointsPos[rightShoulderIndex].y)<0.1f &&    //0.7f
                jointsTracked[leftHandIndex] && jointsTracked[leftElbowIndex] &&
                    jointsTracked[leftShoulderIndex] &&
                Mathf.Abs(jointsPos[leftElbowIndex].y-
                    jointsPos[leftShoulderIndex].y)<0.1f &&
                Mathf.Abs(jointsPos[leftHandIndex].y-
                    jointsPos[leftShoulderIndex].y)<0.1f;

            Vector3 jointPos=jointsPos[gestureData.joint];
            CheckPoseComplete(ref gestureData, timestamp, jointPos, isInPose,
                    KinectInterop.Constants.PoseCompleteDuration);
            break;
        }
        break;

//动作停止
case Gestures.Stop:
    switch(gestureData.state)
    {
        case 0:    //姿势检测
            if(jointsTracked[rightHandIndex] && jointsTracked[rightHipIndex] &&
                (jointsPos[rightHandIndex].y-jointsPos[rightHipIndex].y)<0f &&
                jointsTracked[leftHandIndex] && jointsTracked[leftHipIndex] &&
                (jointsPos[leftHandIndex].y-jointsPos[leftHipIndex].y)<0f)
            {
                SetGestureJoint(ref gestureData, timestamp, rightHandIndex,
                    jointsPos[rightHandIndex]);
            }
            break;

        case 1:    //姿势完成
            bool isInPose=jointsTracked[rightHandIndex] &&
                jointsTracked[rightHipIndex] &&
                (jointsPos[rightHandIndex].y-jointsPos[rightHipIndex].y)<0f &&
                jointsTracked[leftHandIndex] && jointsTracked[leftHipIndex] &&
```

```
                (jointsPos[leftHandIndex].y—jointsPos[leftHipIndex].y)<0f;

            Vector3 jointPos=jointsPos[gestureData.joint];
            CheckPoseComplete(ref gestureData, timestamp, jointPos, isInPose,
                    KinectInterop.Constants.PoseCompleteDuration);
        break;
        }
        break;

//挥手
case Gestures.Wave:
    switch(gestureData.state)
    {
        case 0:    //动作第一阶段
            if(jointsTracked[rightHandIndex] && jointsTracked[rightElbowIndex] &&
                (jointsPos[rightHandIndex].y—jointsPos[rightElbowIndex].y)>0.1f &&
                (jointsPos[rightHandIndex].x—jointsPos[rightElbowIndex].x)>0.05f)
            {
                SetGestureJoint(ref gestureData, timestamp, rightHandIndex,
                        jointsPos[rightHandIndex]);
                gestureData.progress=0.3f;
            }
            else if(jointsTracked[leftHandIndex] && jointsTracked[leftElbowIndex] &&
                (jointsPos[leftHandIndex].y—jointsPos[leftElbowIndex].y)>0.1f &&
                (jointsPos[leftHandIndex].x—jointsPos[leftElbowIndex].x)<—0.05f)
            {
                SetGestureJoint(ref gestureData, timestamp, leftHandIndex,
                        jointsPos[leftHandIndex]);
                gestureData.progress=0.3f;
            }
            break;

        case 1:    //动作第二阶段
            if((timestamp—gestureData.timestamp)<1.5f)
            {
                bool isInPose=gestureData.joint==rightHandIndex?
                    jointsTracked[rightHandIndex] &&
                    jointsTracked[rightElbowIndex] &&
                    (jointsPos[rightHandIndex].y—
```

```
                    jointsPos[rightElbowIndex].y)>0.1f &&
                    (jointsPos[rightHandIndex].x－jointsPos[rightElbowIndex].x)<－0.05f:
                    jointsTracked[leftHandIndex] && jointsTracked[leftElbowIndex] &&
                    (jointsPos[leftHandIndex].y－jointsPos[leftElbowIndex].y)>0.1f &&
                    (jointsPos[leftHandIndex].x－jointsPos[leftElbowIndex].x)>0.05f;

                    if(isInPose)
                    {
                        gestureData.timestamp=timestamp;
                        gestureData.state++;
                        gestureData.progress=0.7f;
                    }
                }
                else
                {
                    //取消动作
                    SetGestureCancelled(ref gestureData);
                }
                break;

        case 2: //姿势完成
            if((timestamp－gestureData.timestamp)<1.5f)
            {
                bool isInPose=gestureData.joint==rightHandIndex?
                jointsTracked[rightHandIndex] && jointsTracked[rightElbowIndex] &&
                (jointsPos[rightHandIndex].y－jointsPos[rightElbowIndex].y)>0.1f &&
                (jointsPos[rightHandIndex].x－jointsPos[rightElbowIndex].x)>0.05f:
                jointsTracked[leftHandIndex] && jointsTracked[leftElbowIndex] &&
                (jointsPos[leftHandIndex].y－jointsPos[leftElbowIndex].y)>0.1f &&
                (jointsPos[leftHandIndex].x－jointsPos[leftElbowIndex].x)<－0.05f;

                if(isInPose)
                {
                    Vector3 jointPos=jointsPos[gestureData.joint];
                    CheckPoseComplete(ref gestureData, timestamp, jointPos, isInPose, 0f);
                }
            }
            else
            {
```

```
                    //cancel the gesture
                    SetGestureCancelled(ref gestureData);
                }
                break;
        }
        break;

//向左滑动
case Gestures.SwipeLeft:
    switch(gestureData.state)
    {
        case 0:    //动作姿势第一阶段
            if(jointsTracked[rightHandIndex] && jointsTracked[rightElbowIndex] &&
                (jointsPos[rightHandIndex].y－jointsPos[rightElbowIndex].y)＞－0.05f
                &&
                (jointsPos[rightHandIndex].x－jointsPos[rightElbowIndex].x)＞0f)
            {
                SetGestureJoint(ref gestureData, timestamp, rightHandIndex,
                        jointsPos[rightHandIndex]);
                gestureData.progress＝0.5f;
            }
            break;

        case 1:    //动作姿势第二阶段(完成动作)
            if((timestamp－gestureData.timestamp)＜1.5f)
            {
                bool isInPose＝gestureData.joint＝＝rightHandIndex?
                jointsTracked[rightHandIndex] && jointsTracked[rightElbowIndex] &&
                Mathf.Abs(jointsPos[rightHandIndex].y－
                    jointsPos[rightElbowIndex].y)＜0.1f &&
                Mathf.Abs(jointsPos[rightHandIndex].y－
                    gestureData.jointPos.y)＜0.08f &&
                (jointsPos[rightHandIndex].x－gestureData.jointPos.x)＜－0.15f:
                jointsTracked[leftHandIndex] && jointsTracked[leftElbowIndex] &&
                Mathf.Abs(jointsPos[leftHandIndex].y－
                    jointsPos[leftElbowIndex].y)＜0.1f &&
                Mathf.Abs(jointsPos[leftHandIndex].y－
                    gestureData.jointPos.y)＜0.08f &&
                (jointsPos[leftHandIndex].x－gestureData.jointPos.x)＜－0.15f;
```

```
                    if(isInPose)
                    {
                        Vector3 jointPos=jointsPos[gestureData.joint];
                        CheckPoseComplete(ref gestureData, timestamp, jointPos, isInPose, 0f);
                    }
                }
                else
                {
                    //取消当前动作
                    SetGestureCancelled(ref gestureData);
                }
                break;
            }
            break;

//向右滑动
case Gestures.SwipeRight:
    switch(gestureData.state)
    {
        case 0:    //动作姿势检测第一阶段
            if(jointsTracked[leftHandIndex] && jointsTracked[leftElbowIndex] &&
              (jointsPos[leftHandIndex].y－jointsPos[leftElbowIndex].y)＞－0.05f &&
              (jointsPos[leftHandIndex].x－jointsPos[leftElbowIndex].x)＜0f)
            {
                SetGestureJoint(ref gestureData, timestamp, leftHandIndex,
                        jointsPos[leftHandIndex]);
                gestureData.progress＝0.5f;
            }
            break;

        case 1:    //动作姿势检测第二阶段(完成)
            if((timestamp－gestureData.timestamp)＜1.5f)
            {
                bool isInPose＝gestureData.joint＝＝rightHandIndex?
                jointsTracked[rightHandIndex] && jointsTracked[rightElbowIndex] &&
                Mathf.Abs(jointsPos[rightHandIndex].y－
                    jointsPos[rightElbowIndex].y)＜0.1f &&
                Mathf.Abs(jointsPos[rightHandIndex].y－
                    gestureData.jointPos.y)＜0.08f &&
```

```
            (jointsPos[rightHandIndex].x－gestureData.jointPos.x)＞0.15f:
            jointsTracked[leftHandIndex] && jointsTracked[leftElbowIndex] &&
            Mathf.Abs(jointsPos[leftHandIndex].y－
                jointsPos[leftElbowIndex].y)＜0.1f &&
            Mathf.Abs(jointsPos[leftHandIndex].y－
                gestureData.jointPos.y)＜0.08f &&
            (jointsPos[leftHandIndex].x－gestureData.jointPos.x)＞0.15f;

        if(isInPose)
        {
            Vector3 jointPos＝jointsPos[gestureData.joint];
            CheckPoseComplete(ref gestureData, timestamp, jointPos, isInPose, 0f);
        }
    }
    else
    {
        //cancel the gesture
        SetGestureCancelled(ref gestureData);
    }
    break;
}
break;

//向上滑动
case Gestures.SwipeUp:
    switch(gestureData.state)
    {
        case 0:    //动作姿势检测第一阶段
        if(jointsTracked[rightHandIndex] && jointsTracked[rightElbowIndex] &&
            (jointsPos[rightHandIndex].y－jointsPos[rightElbowIndex].y)＜－0.05f &&
            (jointsPos[rightHandIndex].y－jointsPos[rightElbowIndex].y)＞－0.15f)
        {
            SetGestureJoint(ref gestureData, timestamp, rightHandIndex,
                    jointsPos[rightHandIndex]);
            gestureData.progress＝0.5f;
        }
        else if(jointsTracked[leftHandIndex] && jointsTracked[leftElbowIndex] &&
            (jointsPos[leftHandIndex].y－jointsPos[leftElbowIndex].y)＜－0.05f &&
            (jointsPos[leftHandIndex].y－jointsPos[leftElbowIndex].y)＞－0.15f)
```

```csharp
            {
                SetGestureJoint(ref gestureData, timestamp, leftHandIndex,
                            jointsPos[leftHandIndex]);
                gestureData.progress=0.5f;
            }
            break;

        case 1:    //动作姿势检测第二阶段(完成)
            if((timestamp-gestureData.timestamp)<1.5f)
            {
                bool isInPose=gestureData.joint==rightHandIndex?
                    jointsTracked[rightHandIndex] && jointsTracked[rightElbowIndex] &&
                    jointsTracked[leftShoulderIndex] &&
                    (jointsPos[rightHandIndex].y-jointsPos[leftShoulderIndex].y)>0.05f &&
                    Mathf.Abs(jointsPos[rightHandIndex].x-gestureData.jointPos.x)<0.08f:
                    jointsTracked [leftHandIndex] && jointsTracked [leftElbowIndex] &&
                    jointsTracked[rightShoulderIndex] &&
                    (jointsPos[leftHandIndex].y-jointsPos[rightShoulderIndex].y)>0.05f &&
                    Mathf.Abs(jointsPos[leftHandIndex].x-gestureData.jointPos.x)<0.08f;

                if(isInPose)
                {
                    Vector3 jointPos=jointsPos[gestureData.joint];
                    CheckPoseComplete(ref gestureData, timestamp, jointPos, isInPose, 0f);
                }
            }
            else
            {
                //cancel the gesture
                SetGestureCancelled(ref gestureData);
            }
            break;
    }
    break;

//向下滑动
case Gestures.SwipeDown:
    switch(gestureData.state)
    {
```

```csharp
case 0:    //动作姿势检测第一阶段
    if(jointsTracked[rightHandIndex] && jointsTracked[leftShoulderIndex] &&
       (jointsPos[rightHandIndex].y－jointsPos[leftShoulderIndex].y)>＝0.05f)
    {
        SetGestureJoint(ref gestureData, timestamp, rightHandIndex,
                    jointsPos[rightHandIndex]);
        gestureData.progress＝0.5f;
    }
    else if(jointsTracked[leftHandIndex] && jointsTracked[rightShoulderIndex] &&
       (jointsPos[leftHandIndex].y－jointsPos[rightShoulderIndex].y)>＝0.05f)
    {
    SetGestureJoint(ref gestureData, timestamp, leftHandIndex,
                jointsPos[leftHandIndex]);
    gestureData.progress＝0.5f;
    }
    break;

case 1:    //动作姿势检测第二阶段(完成)
    if((timestamp－gestureData.timestamp)<1.5f)
        {
            bool isInPose＝gestureData.joint＝＝rightHandIndex?
            jointsTracked[rightHandIndex] && jointsTracked[rightElbowIndex] &&
            (jointsPos[rightHandIndex].y－gestureData.jointPos.y)<－0.2f &&
            Mathf.Abs(jointsPos[rightHandIndex].x－gestureData.jointPos.x)<0.08f:
            jointsTracked[leftHandIndex] && jointsTracked[leftElbowIndex] &&
            (jointsPos[leftHandIndex].y－gestureData.jointPos.y)<－0.2f &&
            Mathf.Abs(jointsPos[leftHandIndex].x－gestureData.jointPos.x)<0.08f;

            if(isInPose)
            {
                Vector3 jointPos＝jointsPos[gestureData.joint];
                CheckPoseComplete(ref gestureData, timestamp, jointPos, isInPose, 0f);
            }
        }
        else
        {
            //cancel the gesture
            SetGestureCancelled(ref gestureData);
        }
```

```
            break;
      }
      break;

      //
      case Gestures.ZoomOut:
      switch(gestureData.state)
      {
            case 0:   //float distZoomOut=((Vector3)(jointsPos[rightHandIndex]-
                                  jointsPos[leftHandIndex])).magnitude;

                  if(jointsTracked[leftHandIndex] && jointsTracked[leftElbowIndex] &&
                  jointsTracked[rightHandIndex] && jointsTracked[rightElbowIndex] &&
                  (jointsPos[leftHandIndex].y-jointsPos[leftElbowIndex].y)>0f &&
                  (jointsPos[rightHandIndex].y-jointsPos[rightElbowIndex].y)>0f &&
                  distZoomOut<0.2f)
            {
                  SetGestureJoint(ref gestureData, timestamp, rightHandIndex,
                              jointsPos[rightHandIndex]);
                  gestureData.progress=0.3f;
            }
            break;

            case 1:   //if((timestamp-gestureData.timestamp)<1.0f)
                  {
                        bool isInPose=jointsTracked[leftHandIndex] &&
                                    jointsTracked[leftElbowIndex] &&
                              jointsTracked[rightHandIndex] && jointsTracked[rightElbowIndex] &&
                              ((jointsPos[leftHandIndex].y-jointsPos[leftElbowIndex].y)>0f||
                              (jointsPos[rightHandIndex].y-jointsPos[rightElbowIndex].y)>0f);

                        if(isInPose)
                        {
                              SetZoomFactor(userId, ref gestureData, 1.0f, ref jointsPos,
                                    ref jointsTracked);
                              gestureData.timestamp=timestamp;
                              gestureData.progress=0.7f;
                        }
                  }
```

```
                    else
                    {
                        //cancel the gesture
                        SetGestureCancelled(ref gestureData);
                    }
                    break;
            }
            break;

        //
        case Gestures.ZoomIn:
            switch(gestureData.state)
            {
                case 0:    //动作姿势检测第一阶段
                    float distZoomIn=((Vector3)jointsPos[rightHandIndex]-
                                    jointsPos[leftHandIndex]).magnitude;
                    if(jointsTracked[leftHandIndex] && jointsTracked[leftElbowIndex] &&
                        jointsTracked[rightHandIndex] && jointsTracked[rightElbowIndex] &&
                        (jointsPos[leftHandIndex].y-jointsPos[leftElbowIndex].y)>0f &&
                        (jointsPos[rightHandIndex].y-jointsPos[rightElbowIndex].y)>0f &&
                        distZoomIn>=0.7f)
                    {
                        SetGestureJoint(ref gestureData, timestamp, rightHandIndex,
                                    jointsPos[rightHandIndex]);
                        gestureData.tagFloat=distZoomIn;
                        gestureData.progress=0.3f;
                    }
                    break;

                case 1:    //动作姿势检测第二阶段(聚焦)
                    if((timestamp-gestureData.timestamp)<1.0f)
                    {
                        bool isInPose=jointsTracked[leftHandIndex] &&
                                    jointsTracked[leftElbowIndex] &&
                            jointsTracked[rightHandIndex] && jointsTracked[rightElbowIndex] &&
                            ((jointsPos[leftHandIndex].y-jointsPos[leftElbowIndex].y)>0f ||
                            (jointsPos[rightHandIndex].y-jointsPos[rightElbowIndex].y)>0f);

                        if(isInPose)
```

```
                {
                    SetZoomFactor(userId, ref gestureData, 0.0f, ref jointsPos,
                                    ref jointsTracked);
                    gestureData.timestamp = timestamp;
                    gestureData.progress = 0.7f;
                }
            }
            else
            {
                //cancel the gesture
                SetGestureCancelled(ref gestureData);
            }
            break;
    }
    break;


case Gestures.Wheel:
Vector3 vectorWheel = (Vector3)jointsPos[rightHandIndex] －
                    jointsPos[leftHandIndex];
float distWheel = vectorWheel.magnitude;

switch(gestureData.state)
{
    case 0:   //动作姿势检测第一阶段
        if(jointsTracked[leftHandIndex] && jointsTracked[leftElbowIndex] &&
            jointsTracked[rightHandIndex] && jointsTracked[rightElbowIndex] &&
            (jointsPos[leftHandIndex].y － jointsPos[leftElbowIndex].y)＞0f &&
            (jointsPos[rightHandIndex].y － jointsPos[rightElbowIndex].y)＞0f &&
            distWheel＞0.2f && distWheel＜0.7f)
        {
            SetGestureJoint(ref gestureData, timestamp, rightHandIndex,
                            jointsPos[rightHandIndex]);
            gestureData.tagVector = vectorWheel;
            gestureData.tagFloat = distWheel;
            gestureData.progress = 0.3f;
        }
        break;

    case 1:   //动作姿势检测第二阶段(聚焦)
```

```
                    if((timestamp-gestureData.timestamp)<1.5f)
                    {
                            bool isInPose=jointsTracked[leftHandIndex] &&
                                    jointsTracked[leftElbowIndex] &&
                        jointsTracked[rightHandIndex] && jointsTracked[rightElbowIndex] &&
                        ((jointsPos[leftHandIndex].y-jointsPos[leftElbowIndex].y)>0f ||
                        (jointsPos[rightHandIndex].y-jointsPos[rightElbowIndex].y)>0f &&
                        Mathf.Abs(distWheel-gestureData.tagFloat)<0.1f);

                            if(isInPose)
                            {
                                SetWheelRotation(userId, ref gestureData, gestureData.tagVector,
                                            vectorWheel);
                                gestureData.timestamp=timestamp;
                                gestureData.tagFloat=distWheel;
                                gestureData.progress=0.7f;
                            }
                    }
                    else
                    {
                        //取消动作
                            SetGestureCancelled(ref gestureData);
                    }
                    break;
            }
            break;

    //跳起
    case Gestures.Jump:
    switch(gestureData.state)
    {
        case 0:   //动作姿势检测第一阶段
                if(jointsTracked[hipCenterIndex] &&
                    (jointsPos[hipCenterIndex].y>0.8f) && (jointsPos[hipCenterIndex].y<1.3f))
                    {
                        SetGestureJoint(ref gestureData, timestamp, hipCenterIndex,
                                    jointsPos[hipCenterIndex]);
                        gestureData.progress=0.5f;
                    }
```

```
                break;

        case 1:    //动作姿势检测第二阶段(完成)
            if((timestamp－gestureData.timestamp)＜1.5f)
            {
                bool isInPose＝jointsTracked[hipCenterIndex] &&
                    (jointsPos[hipCenterIndex].y－gestureData.jointPos.y)＞0.15f &&
                    Mathf.Abs(jointsPos[hipCenterIndex].x－gestureData.jointPos.x)＜0.15f;

                if(isInPose)
                {
                    Vector3 jointPos＝jointsPos[gestureData.joint];
                    CheckPoseComplete(ref gestureData, timestamp, jointPos, isInPose, 0f);
                }
            }
            else
            {
                //取消动作
                SetGestureCancelled(ref gestureData);
            }
            break;
    }
    break;

//蹲
case Gestures.Squat:
    switch(gestureData.state)
    {
        case 0:    //动作姿势检测第一阶段
            if(jointsTracked[hipCenterIndex] &&
                (jointsPos[hipCenterIndex].y＜0.8f))
            {
                SetGestureJoint(ref gestureData, timestamp, hipCenterIndex,
                    jointsPos[hipCenterIndex]);
                gestureData.progress＝0.5f;
            }
            break;

        case 1:    //动作姿势检测第二阶段(完成)
```

```
                    if((timestamp－gestureData.timestamp)＜1.5f)
                    {
                            bool isInPose＝jointsTracked[hipCenterIndex] &&
                            (jointsPos[hipCenterIndex].y－gestureData.jointPos.y)＜－0.15f &&
                            Mathf.Abs(jointsPos[hipCenterIndex].x－gestureData.jointPos.x)＜0.15f;

                            if(isInPose)
                            {
                                    Vector3 jointPos＝jointsPos[gestureData.joint];
                                    CheckPoseComplete(ref gestureData, timestamp, jointPos, isInPose, 0f);
                            }
                    }
                    else
                    {
                            //取消动作
                                SetGestureCancelled(ref gestureData);
                    }
                    break;
            }
            break;

//推
case Gestures.Push:
switch(gestureData.state)
    {
            case 0:    //动作姿势检测第一阶段
                    if(jointsTracked[rightHandIndex] && jointsTracked[rightElbowIndex] &&
                    (jointsPos[rightHandIndex].y－jointsPos[rightElbowIndex].y)＞－0.05f &&
                    Mathf.Abs(jointsPos[rightHandIndex].x－jointsPos[rightElbowIndex].x)＜0.15f &&
                    (jointsPos[rightHandIndex].z－jointsPos[rightElbowIndex].z)＜－0.05f)
                    {
                    SetGestureJoint(ref gestureData, timestamp, rightHandIndex,
                                    jointsPos[rightHandIndex]);
                    gestureData.progress＝0.5f;
                    }
                    else if(jointsTracked[leftHandIndex] && jointsTracked[leftElbowIndex] &&
                    (jointsPos[leftHandIndex].y－jointsPos[leftElbowIndex].y)＞－0.05f &&
                    Mathf.Abs(jointsPos[leftHandIndex].x－jointsPos[leftElbowIndex].x)＜0.15f &&
                    (jointsPos[leftHandIndex].z－jointsPos[leftElbowIndex].z)＜－0.05f)
```

```
                {
                    SetGestureJoint(ref gestureData, timestamp, leftHandIndex,
                            jointsPos[leftHandIndex]);
                    gestureData.progress = 0.5f;
                }
            break;

        case 1:    //动作姿势检测第二阶段(完成)
            if((timestamp - gestureData.timestamp) < 1.5f)
            {
                bool isInPose = gestureData.joint == rightHandIndex?
                jointsTracked[rightHandIndex] && jointsTracked[rightElbowIndex] &&
                Mathf.Abs(jointsPos[rightHandIndex].x - gestureData.jointPos.x) < 0.15f &&
                Mathf.Abs(jointsPos[rightHandIndex].y - gestureData.jointPos.y) < 0.15f &&
                (jointsPos[rightHandIndex].z - gestureData.jointPos.z) < -0.15f:
                jointsTracked[leftHandIndex] && jointsTracked[leftElbowIndex] &&
                Mathf.Abs(jointsPos[leftHandIndex].x - gestureData.jointPos.x) < 0.15f &&
                Mathf.Abs(jointsPos[leftHandIndex].y - gestureData.jointPos.y) < 0.15f &&
                (jointsPos[leftHandIndex].z - gestureData.jointPos.z) < -0.15f;

                if(isInPose)
                {
                    Vector3 jointPos = jointsPos[gestureData.joint];
                    CheckPoseComplete(ref gestureData, timestamp, jointPos,
                            isInPose, 0f);
                }
            }
            else
            {
                //取消动作
                SetGestureCancelled(ref gestureData);
            }
            break;
        }
    break;

//拉
case Gestures.Pull:
    switch(gestureData.state)
```

```
            {
                case 0:    //动作姿势检测第一阶段
                    if(jointsTracked[rightHandIndex] && jointsTracked[rightElbowIndex]&&
                    (jointsPos[rightHandIndex].y−jointsPos[rightElbowIndex].y)>−0.05f&&
                    Mathf.Abs(jointsPos[rightHandIndex].x−jointsPos[rightElbowIndex].x)<0.15f&&
                    (jointsPos[rightHandIndex].z−jointsPos[rightElbowIndex].z)<−0.15f)
                    {
                        SetGestureJoint(ref gestureData, timestamp, rightHandIndex,
                                jointsPos[rightHandIndex]);
                        gestureData.progress=0.5f;
                    }
                    else if (jointsTracked[leftHandIndex] && jointsTracked[leftElbowIndex]&&
                        (jointsPos[leftHandIndex].y−jointsPos[leftElbowIndex].y)>−0.05f&&
                        Mathf.Abs(jointsPos[leftHandIndex].x−jointsPos[leftElbowIndex].x)<0.15f&&
                        (jointsPos[leftHandIndex].z−jointsPos[leftElbowIndex].z)<−0.15f)
                    {
                        SetGestureJoint(ref gestureData, timestamp, leftHandIndex,
                                jointsPos[leftHandIndex]);
                        gestureData.progress=0.5f;
                    }
                    break;

                case 1:    //动作姿势检测第二阶段(完成)
                    if((timestamp−gestureData.timestamp)<1.5f)
                    {
                        bool isInPose=gestureData.joint==rightHandIndex?
                        jointsTracked[rightHandIndex] && jointsTracked[rightElbowIndex] &&
                        Mathf.Abs(jointsPos[rightHandIndex].x−gestureData.jointPos.x)<0.15f &&
                        Mathf.Abs(jointsPos[rightHandIndex].y−gestureData.jointPos.y)<0.15f &&
                        (jointsPos[rightHandIndex].z−gestureData.jointPos.z)>0.15f:
                        jointsTracked[leftHandIndex] && jointsTracked[leftElbowIndex] &&
                        Mathf.Abs(jointsPos[leftHandIndex].x−gestureData.jointPos.x)<0.15f &&
                        Mathf.Abs(jointsPos[leftHandIndex].y−gestureData.jointPos.y)<0.15f &&
                        (jointsPos[leftHandIndex].z−gestureData.jointPos.z)>0.15f;

                        if(isInPose)
                        {
                            Vector3 jointPos=jointsPos[gestureData.joint];
                            CheckPoseComplete(ref gestureData, timestamp, jointPos, isInPose, 0f);
```

```
                    }
                }
                else
                {
                    //取消动作
                    SetGestureCancelled(ref gestureData);
                }
                break;
            }
            break;
    }
}
```

5. 手掌模拟鼠标控制脚本

在人机交互娱乐功能模块,一切操作都是由人体的动作来完成的,因此在该功能上是通过手掌模拟鼠标来控制界面的返回。具体实现如下:

```
public class InteractionManager：MonoBehaviour
{//手势事件类型
    public enum HandEventType：int
    {
        None＝0,
        Grip＝1,
        Release＝2
    }

    //手的光标
    public bool useHandCursor＝true;

    //手光标纹理
    public Texture gripHandTexture;
    public Texture releaseHandTexture;
    public Texture normalHandTexture;

    //光标移动平滑度
    public float smoothFactor＝3f;

    //鼠标光标
    public bool controlMouseCursor＝false;
```

```csharp
//鼠标拖动
public bool controlMouseDrag = false;

//转为全屏坐标
public bool convertMouseToFullScreen = false;

//用于显示调试信息
public GameObject debugText;

private Int64 primaryUserId = 0;

private bool isLeftHandPrimary = false;
private bool isRightHandPrimary = false;

private bool isLeftHandPress = false;
private bool isRightHandPress = false;

private Vector3 cursorScreenPos = Vector3.zero;
private bool dragInProgress = false;

private KinectInterop.HandState leftHandState = KinectInterop.HandState.Unknown;
private KinectInterop.HandState rightHandState = KinectInterop.HandState.Unknown;

private HandEventType leftHandEvent = HandEventType.None;
private HandEventType lastLeftHandEvent = HandEventType.Release;

private Vector3 leftHandPos = Vector3.zero;
private Vector3 leftHandScreenPos = Vector3.zero;
private Vector3 leftIboxLeftBotBack = Vector3.zero;
private Vector3 leftIboxRightTopFront = Vector3.zero;
private bool isLeftIboxValid = false;
private bool isLeftHandInteracting = false;
private float leftHandInteractingSince = 0f;

private Vector3 lastLeftHandPos = Vector3.zero;
private float lastLeftHandTime = 0f;
private bool isLeftHandClick = false;
private float leftHandClickProgress = 0f;
```

```csharp
private HandEventType rightHandEvent = HandEventType.None;
private HandEventType lastRightHandEvent = HandEventType.Release;

private Vector3 rightHandPos = Vector3.zero;
private Vector3 rightHandScreenPos = Vector3.zero;
private Vector3 rightIboxLeftBotBack = Vector3.zero;
private Vector3 rightIboxRightTopFront = Vector3.zero;
private bool isRightIboxValid = false;
private bool isRightHandInteracting = false;
private float rightHandInteractingSince = 0f;

private Vector3 lastRightHandPos = Vector3.zero;
private float lastRightHandTime = 0f;
private bool isRightHandClick = false;
private float rightHandClickProgress = 0f;

//用于交互的数据库与Kinect初始化
private bool interactionInited = false;

//实例
private static InteractionManager instance;
//获取实例
public static InteractionManager Instance
{
    get
    {
        return instance;
    }
}

//功能:判断库是否初始化
public bool IsInteractionInited()
{
    return interactionInited;
}

//功能:获取用户Id
public Int64 GetUserId()
```

```
        {
            return primaryUserId;
        }


        //功能:获取当前左手事件
        public HandEventType GetLeftHandEvent()
        {
            return leftHandEvent;
        }


        //功能:获取最后检测到的左手事件
        public HandEventType GetLastLeftHandEvent()
        {
            return lastLeftHandEvent;
        }


        //功能:获取左手在屏幕上的坐标
        public Vector3 GetLeftHandScreenPos()
        {
            return leftHandScreenPos;
        }


        //功能:判断左手的关键
        public bool IsLeftHandPrimary()
        {
            return isLeftHandPrimary;
        }


        //功能:判断左手是否按下
        public bool IsLeftHandPress()
        {
            return isLeftHandPress;
        }


        //功能:检测左手是否点击
        public bool IsLeftHandClickDetected()
        {
            if(isLeftHandClick)
            {
```

```csharp
            isLeftHandClick=false;
            leftHandClickProgress=0f;
            lastLeftHandPos=Vector3.zero;
            lastLeftHandTime=Time.realtimeSinceStartup;
            return true;
        }
        return false;
}

//功能:左手点击事件处理
public float GetLeftHandClickProgress()
{
        return leftHandClickProgress;
}

//功能:获取右手事件
public HandEventType GetRightHandEvent()
{
        return rightHandEvent;
}

//功能:获取最后一个右手事件
public HandEventType GetLastRightHandEvent()
{
        return lastRightHandEvent;
}

//功能:获取右手在屏幕上的坐标
public Vector3 GetRightHandScreenPos()
{
        return rightHandScreenPos;
}

//功能:判断右手的主要事件
public bool IsRightHandPrimary()
{
        return isRightHandPrimary;
}
```

```csharp
//功能:判断右手是否按下
public bool IsRightHandPress()
{
    return isRightHandPress;
}

//功能:检测右手点击事件
public bool IsRightHandClickDetected()
{
    if(isRightHandClick)
    {
        isRightHandClick = false;
        rightHandClickProgress = 0f;
        lastRightHandPos = Vector3.zero;
        lastRightHandTime = Time.realtimeSinceStartup;
        return true;
    }
    return false;
}

//功能:右手点击事件处理
public float GetRightHandClickProgress()
{
    return rightHandClickProgress;
}

//功能:获取光标位置
public Vector3 GetCursorPosition()
{
    return cursorScreenPos;
}

//----------------------------------------------------------------//
void Start()
{//实例初始化
    instance = this;
//使用交互功能
    interactionInited = true;
}
```

```
void OnApplicationQuit()
{
    //关闭交互功能
    if(interactionInited)
    {
        interactionInited = false;
        instance = null;
    }
}

void Update ()
{
    KinectManager kinectManager = KinectManager.Instance;

    //更新 Kinect 的交互
    if(kinectManager && kinectManager.IsInitialized())
    {
        primaryUserId = kinectManager.GetPrimaryUserId();

        if(primaryUserId != 0)
        {
            HandEventType handEvent = HandEventType.None;

            //获取左手状态
            leftHandState = kinectManager.GetLeftHandState(primaryUserId);

            //检测左手是否使用
            isleftIboxValid = kinectManager.GetLeftHandInteractionBox(primaryUserID,
                    ref leftIboxLeftBotBack, ref leftIboxRightTopFront,
                    isleftIboxValid);

            if(isleftIboxValid && //bLeftHandPrimaryNow &&
                kinectManager.GetJointTrackingState(primaryUserID, (int)KinectInterop.
                    JointType.HandLeft)!= KinectInterop.TrackingState.NotTracked)
            {
                leftHandPos = kinectManager.GetJointPosition(primaryUserID,
                    (int)KinectInterop.JointType.HandLeft);
```

```
leftHandScreenPos.x=Mathf.Clamp01((leftHandPos.x-
                    leftIboxLeftBotBack.x)/(leftIboxRightTopFront.x-
                    leftIboxLeftBotBack.x));
leftHandScreenPos.y=Mathf.Clamp01((leftHandPos.y-
                    leftIboxLeftBotBack.y)/(leftIboxRightTopFront.y-
                    leftIboxLeftBotBack.y));
leftHandScreenPos.z=Mathf.Clamp01((leftIboxLeftBotBack.z-
                    leftHandPos.z)/(leftIboxLeftBotBack.z-
                    leftIboxRightTopFront.z));

bool wasLeftHandInteracting=isLeftHandInteracting;
isLeftHandInteracting=(leftHandPos.x>=(leftIboxLeftBotBack.x-1.0f)) &&
    (leftHandPos.x<=(leftIboxRightTopFront.x+0.5f)) &&
    (leftHandPos.y>=(leftIboxLeftBotBack.y-0.1f)) &&
    (leftHandPos.y<=(leftIboxRightTopFront.y+0.7f)) &&
    (leftIboxLeftBotBack.z>=leftHandPos.z) &&
    (leftIboxRightTopFront.z*0.8f<=leftHandPos.z);
//bLeftHandPrimaryNow=isLeftHandInteracting;
if(!wasLeftHandInteracting && isLeftHandInteracting)
{
        leftHandInteractingSince=Time.realtimeSinceStartup;
}

//检测左手是否按下
isLeftHandPress=(leftIboxRightTopFront.z>=leftHandPos.z);
//检测左手是否点击
 float fClickDist=(leftHandPos-lastLeftHandPos).magnitude;
 if(isLeftHandInteracting && (fClickDist<
        KinectInterop.Constants.ClickMaxDistance))
{
        if((Time.realtimeSinceStartup-lastLeftHandTime)>=
                KinectInterop.Constants.ClickStayDuration)
            {
                if(!isLeftHandClick)
                  {
                        isLeftHandClick=true;
                        leftHandClickProgress=1f;

                        if(controlMouseCursor)
```

```
                    {
                            MouseControl.MouseClick();

                            isLeftHandClick = false;
                            leftHandClickProgress = 0f;
                            lastLeftHandPos = Vector3.zero;
                            lastLeftHandTime = Time.realtimeSinceStartup;
                    }
                }
            }
            else
            {
                leftHandClickProgress = (Time.realtimeSinceStartup - lastLeftHandTime)
                            / KinectInterop.Constants.ClickStayDuration;
            }
        }
        else
        {
            isLeftHandClick = false;
            leftHandClickProgress = 0f;
            lastLeftHandPos = leftHandPos;
            lastLeftHandTime = Time.realtimeSinceStartup;
        }
    }
    else
    {
        isLeftHandInteracting = false;
        isLeftHandPress = false;
    }

//获取右手状态
rightHandState = kinectManager.GetRightHandState(primaryUserId);

//检测右手是否使用
isRightIboxValid = kinectManager.GetRightHandInteractionBox(primaryUserId,
        ref rightIboxLeftBotBack, ref rightIboxRightTopFront,
        isRightIboxValid);

if(isRightIboxValid && //bRightHandPrimaryNow &&
```

```
            kinectManager.GetJointTrackingState(primaryUserId, (int)KinectInterop.JointType.
                HandRight)!=KinectInterop.TrackingState.NotTracked)
    {
            rightHandPos=kinectManager.GetJointPosition(primaryUserId,
                    (int)KinectInterop.JointType.HandRight);

            rightHandScreenPos.x=Mathf.Clamp01((rightHandPos.x－rightIboxLeftBotBack.x)/
                    (rightIboxRightTopFront.x－rightIboxLeftBotBack.x));
            rightHandScreenPos.y=Mathf.Clamp01((rightHandPos.y－rightIboxLeftBotBack.y)/
                    (rightIboxRightTopFront.y－rightIboxLeftBotBack.y));
            rightHandScreenPos.z=Mathf.Clamp01((rightIboxLeftBotBack.z－rightHandPos.z)/
                    (rightIboxLeftBotBack.z－rightIboxRightTopFront.z));

            bool wasRightHandInteracting=isRightHandInteracting;
            isRightHandInteracting=(rightHandPos.x>=(rightIboxLeftBotBack.x－0.5f)) &&
                (rightHandPos.x<=(rightIboxRightTopFront.x＋1.0f)) &&
                (rightHandPos.y>=(rightIboxLeftBotBack.y－0.1f)) &&
                (rightHandPos.y<=(rightIboxRightTopFront.y＋0.7f)) &&
                (rightIboxLeftBotBack.z>=rightHandPos.z) &&
                (rightIboxRightTopFront.z*0.8f<=rightHandPos.z);
            //bRightHandPrimaryNow=isRightHandInteracting;

            if(!wasRightHandInteracting && isRightHandInteracting)
            {
                    rightHandInteractingSince=Time.realtimeSinceStartup;
            }

            if(isLeftHandInteracting && isRightHandInteracting)
            {
                if(rightHandInteractingSince<=leftHandInteractingSince)
                        isLeftHandInteracting=false;
                    else
                        isRightHandInteracting=false;
            }

        //检测右手是否按下
        isRightHandPress=(rightIboxRightTopFront.z>=rightHandPos.z);

        //检测右手是否点击
```

```csharp
float fClickDist=(rightHandPos－lastRightHandPos).magnitude;
if(isRightHandInteracting && (fClickDist<KinectInterop.Constants.ClickMaxDistance))
{
    if((Time.realtimeSinceStartup－lastRightHandTime)>=
        KinectInterop.Constants.ClickStayDuration)
    {
        if(!isRightHandClick)
        {
            isRightHandClick=true;
            rightHandClickProgress=1f;

            if(controlMouseCursor)
            {
                MouseControl.MouseClick();
                isRightHandClick=false;
                rightHandClickProgress=0f;
                lastRightHandPos=Vector3.zero;
                lastRightHandTime=Time.realtimeSinceStartup;
            }
        }
    }
    else
    {
        rightHandClickProgress=(Time.realtimeSinceStartup－lastRightHandTime)/
                    KinectInterop.Constants.ClickStayDuration;
    }
}
else
{
    isRightHandClick=false;
    rightHandClickProgress=0f;
    lastRightHandPos=rightHandPos;
    lastRightHandTime=Time.realtimeSinceStartup;
}
}
else
{
    isRightHandInteracting=false;
    isRightHandPress=false;
```

```
}

//处理左手事件
handEvent=HandStateToEvent(leftHandState, lastLeftHandEvent);

    if((isLeftHandInteracting!=isLeftHandPrimary)||(isRightHandInteracting!=
                        isRightHandPrimary))
{
    if(controlMouseCursor && dragInProgress)
    {
        MouseControl.MouseRelease();
        dragInProgress=false;
    }

        lastLeftHandEvent=HandEventType.Release;
        lastRightHandEvent=HandEventType.Release;
}
if(controlMouseCursor && (handEvent!=lastLeftHandEvent))
{
    if(controlMouseDrag &&!dragInProgress && (handEvent==HandEventType.Grip))
    {
        dragInProgress=true;
        MouseControl.MouseDrag();
    }
        else if(dragInProgress && (handEvent==HandEventType.Release))
    {
        MouseControl.MouseRelease();
        dragInProgress=false;
    }
}

leftHandEvent=handEvent;
if(handEvent!=HandEventType.None)
{
    lastLeftHandEvent=handEvent;
}

//如果左手是主要事件,确定光标位置
if(isLeftHandInteracting)
```

```
    {
        isLeftHandPrimary=true;
        if((leftHandClickProgress<0.8f) &&!isLeftHandPress)
        {
            cursorScreenPos=Vector3.Lerp(cursorScreenPos, leftHandScreenPos,
                              smoothFactor*Time.deltaTime);
        }
        else
        {
            leftHandScreenPos=cursorScreenPos;
        }

        if(controlMouseCursor &&!useHandCursor)
        {
            MouseControl.MouseMove(cursorScreenPos, convertMouseToFullScreen);
        }
    }
    else
    {
        isLeftHandPrimary=false;
    }
    //处理右手事件
    handEvent=HandStateToEvent(rightHandState, lastRightHandEvent);

    if(controlMouseCursor && (handEvent!=lastRightHandEvent))
    {
        if(controlMouseDrag &&!dragInProgress && (handEvent==HandEventType.Grip))
        {
            dragInProgress=true;
            MouseControl.MouseDrag();
        }
        else if(dragInProgress && (handEvent==HandEventType.Release))
        {
            MouseControl.MouseRelease();
            dragInProgress=false;
        }
    }

    rightHandEvent=handEvent;
```

```
        if(handEvent!=HandEventType.None)
        {
            lastRightHandEvent=handEvent;
        }

        //如果右手是主要事件,设置光标位置
        if(isRightHandInteracting)
        {
            isRightHandPrimary=true;

            if((rightHandClickProgress<0.8f) &&!isRightHandPress)
            {
                cursorScreenPos=Vector3.Lerp(cursorScreenPos, rightHandScreenPos,
                                smoothFactor*Time.deltaTime);
            }
            else
            {
                rightHandScreenPos=cursorScreenPos;
            }

            if(controlMouseCursor &&!useHandCursor)
            {
                MouseControl.MouseMove(cursorScreenPos, convertMouseToFullScreen);
            }
        }
        else
        {
            isRightHandPrimary=false;
        }
    }
    else
    {
        leftHandState=KinectInterop.HandState.NotTracked;
        rightHandState=KinectInterop.HandState.NotTracked;

        isLeftHandPrimary=false;
        isRightHandPrimary=false;

        isLeftHandPress=false;
```

```csharp
            isRightHandPress = false;

            leftHandEvent = HandEventType.None;
            rightHandEvent = HandEventType.None;

            lastLeftHandEvent = HandEventType.Release;
            lastRightHandEvent = HandEventType.Release;

            if(controlMouseCursor && dragInProgress)
            {
                MouseControl.MouseRelease();
                dragInProgress = false;
            }
        }
    }
}

//功能:将手的状态转为手的事件
private HandEventType HandStateToEvent(KinectInterop.HandState handState,
    HandEventType lastEventType)
{
    switch(handState)
    {
        case KinectInterop.HandState.Open:
            return HandEventType.Release;

        case KinectInterop.HandState.Closed:
        case KinectInterop.HandState.Lasso:
            return HandEventType.Grip;

        case KinectInterop.HandState.Unknown:
            return lastEventType;
    }
    return HandEventType.None;
}

void OnGUI()
{
    if(!interactionInited)
```

```csharp
            return;

        //显示调试信息
        if(debugText)
        {
            string sGuiText = string.Empty;

            if(isRightHandPrimary)
            {
                sGuiText = "Cursor: " + cursorScreenPos.ToString();

                if(lastRightHandEvent == HandEventType.Grip)
                {
                    sGuiText += "RightGrip";
                }
                else if(lastRightHandEvent == HandEventType.Release)
                {
                    sGuiText += "RightRelease";
                }

                if(isRightHandClick)
                {
                    sGuiText += "RightClick";
                }
                if(isRightHandPress)
                {
                    sGuiText += "RightPress";
                }
            }
        }

        if(isLeftHandPrimary)
        {
            sGuiText = "Cursor: " + cursorScreenPos.ToString();

            if(lastLeftHandEvent == HandEventType.Grip)
            {
                sGuiText += "LeftGrip";
            }
            else if(lastLeftHandEvent == HandEventType.Release)
```

```
            {
                sGuiText+="LeftRelease";
            }

            if(isLeftHandClick)
            {
                sGuiText+="LeftClick";
            }

            if(isLeftHandPress)
            {
                sGuiText+="LeftPress";
            }
        }
        debugText.GetComponent<GUIText>().text=sGuiText;
}

//显示光标状态和坐标
if(useHandCursor)
{
    Texture texture=null;

    if(isLeftHandPrimary)
    {
        if(lastLeftHandEvent==HandEventType.Grip)
            texture=gripHandTexture;
        else if(lastLeftHandEvent==HandEventType.Release)
            texture=releaseHandTexture;
    }
    else if(isRightHandPrimary)
    {
        if(lastRightHandEvent==HandEventType.Grip)
            texture=gripHandTexture;
        else if(lastRightHandEvent==HandEventType.Release)
            texture=releaseHandTexture;
    }

    if(texture==null)
    {
```

```
            texture=normalHandTexture;
        }

    if(useHandCursor)
    {
        if(isLeftHandPrimary || isRightHandPrimary)
        {
            Rect rectTexture=new Rect(cursorScreenPos.x*Screen.width-texture.width/2,
                        (1f-cursorScreenPos.y)*Screen.height-texture.height/2,
                        texture.width, texture.height);
            GUI.DrawTexture(rectTexture, texture);
            if(controlMouseCursor)
            {
                MouseControl.MouseMove(cursorScreenPos, convertMouseToFullScreen);
            }
        }
    }
    }
}
```

四、太极拳学习-反馈功能模块实现

使用 Kinect 作为动作捕捉的传感器，技术成熟，有完善的 SDK 及技术文档。由于其他设备动作捕捉数据与 Kinect 捕捉的关节数据在 unity 中进行三维的点对点匹配数据转换及容错率很低，所以使用 Kinect 捕捉到关节点后转换为二维屏幕坐标，与屏幕上的动作图关节进行匹配，可以精确地反应动作的准确性。

1. 转换 Kinect 三维坐标到屏幕脚本

```
public class calePostion：MonoBehaviour
{
    public float inTopPos;
    public float inRightPos;
    public float textHeight=0.0f;
    public GameObject inputPosObj;
    private Vector3 postions;
        void Update ()
        {
    postions.x=((inputPosObj.transform.position.x+inRightPos)/(inRightPos*2))*Screen.width;
```

```
            postions.y=(((inputPosObj.transform.position.y+inTopPos)/(inTopPos*2))*Screen.height)
                +textHeight;
            transform.position=postions;
        }
    }
```

2. Kinect 关节检测点匹配脚本

具体代码如下：

```
public class KinectOverlayer：MonoBehaviour
{
    //要进行匹配的关节点
    public KinectInterop.JointType spinebaseJoint=KinectInterop.JointType.SpineBase;
    public KinectInterop.JointType handLeftJoint=KinectInterop.JointType.HandLeft;
    public KinectInterop.JointType handRightJoint=KinectInterop.JointType.HandRight;
    public KinectInterop.JointType kneeLeftJoint=KinectInterop.JointType.KneeLeft;
    public KinectInterop.JointType kneeRightJoint=KinectInterop.JointType.KneeRight;
    //关节点对像
    public GameObject prefab;
    public GameObject lHprefab;
    public GameObject rHprefab;
    public GameObject lKprefab;
    public GameObject rKprefab;
    public GameObject handPrefab;
    //平滑度
    public float smoothFactor=5f;
    //调试文本
    public GUIText debugText;
    //距离主相机的距离
    private float distanceToCamera=10f;
    private bool showlogoOnce=true;

    void Start()
    {
    }
    void Update ()
    {
        KinectManager manager=KinectManager.Instance;
        if(manager && manager.IsInitialized())
        {//获取关节点索引值
            int iJointIndex=(int)spinebaseJoint;
```

```csharp
int jJointIndex=(int)handLeftJoint;
int kJointIndex=(int)handRightJoint;
int lJointIndex=(int)kneeLeftJoint;
int mJointIndex=(int)kneeRightJoint;

if(manager.IsUserDetected())
{//获取用户 id
    long userId=manager.GetPrimaryUserId();
//初始化关节点对象
    GameObject sbpo=GameObject.Find(userId.ToString()+"spinebase");
    GameObject lHpo=GameObject.Find(userId.ToString()+"leHand");
    GameObject rHpo=GameObject.Find(userId.ToString()+"riHand");
    GameObject lKpo=GameObject.Find(userId.ToString()+"leKnee");
    GameObject rKpo=GameObject.Find(userId.ToString()+"riKnee");
//获取脊柱底部的坐标
    if(!sbpo)
    {
        sbpo=GameObject.Instantiate(lHprefab) as GameObject;
        sbpo.name=userId.ToString()+"spinebase";
        GameObject sptex=GameObject.Instantiate(handPrefab) as GameObject;
        sptex.name=userId.ToString()+"sbtex";
        sptex.transform.parent=GameObject.Find("Canvas").transform;
        sptex.GetComponent<calePostion>().inputPosObj=sbpo;
    }
//检测左臀部关节点是否存在,如果不存在创建一个关节点
    if(!lHpo)
    {
        lHpo=GameObject.Instantiate(lHprefab) as GameObject;
        lHpo.name=userId.ToString()+"leHand";
        GameObject lHtex=GameObject.Instantiate(handPrefab) as GameObject;
        lHtex.name=userId.ToString()+"lHtex";
        lHtex.transform.parent=GameObject.Find("Canvas").transform;
        lHtex.GetComponent<calePostion>().inputPosObj=lHpo;
    }
//检测右臀部关节点是否存在,如果不存在创建一个关节点
    if(!rHpo)
    {
        rHpo=GameObject.Instantiate(rHprefab) as GameObject;
        rHpo.name=userId.ToString()+"riHand";
```

```
        GameObject rHtex=GameObject.Instantiate(handPrefab) as GameObject;
            rHtex.name=userId.ToString()+"rHtex";
            rHtex.transform.parent=GameObject.Find("Canvas").transform;
            rHtex.GetComponent<calePostion>().inputPosObj=rHpo;
        }
//检测左膝关节点是否存在,如果不存在创建一个关节点
        if(!lKpo)
        {
            lKpo=GameObject.Instantiate(rHprefab) as GameObject;
            lKpo.name=userId.ToString()+"leKnee";
        GameObject lKtex=GameObject.Instantiate(handPrefab) as GameObject;
            lKtex.name=userId.ToString()+"lKtex";
            lKtex.transform.parent=GameObject.Find("Canvas").transform;
            lKtex.GetComponent<calePostion>().inputPosObj=lKpo;
        }
//检测右膝关节点是否存在,如果不存在创建一个关节点
        if(!rKpo)
        {
            rKpo=GameObject.Instantiate(rHprefab) as GameObject;
            rKpo.name=userId.ToString()+"riKnee";
        GameObject rKtex=GameObject.Instantiate(handPrefab) as GameObject;
            rKtex.name=userId.ToString()+"rKtex";
            rKtex.transform.parent=GameObject.Find("Canvas").transform;
            rKtex.GetComponent< calePostion>().inputPosObj=rKpo;
        }
//判断关节点是否被跟踪
        if(manager.IsJointTracked(userId, iJointIndex))
        {//获取脊柱关节点的空间坐标
            Vector3 sbJoint=manager.GetJointKinectPosition(userId, iJointIndex);
        if(sbJoint!=Vector3.zero)
            {
            //将空间三维坐标转为空间二维坐标
            Vector2 sbDepth=manager.MapSpacePointToDepthCoords(sbJoint);
            ushort sbValue=manager.GetDepthForPixel((int)sbDepth.x, (int)sbDepth.y);
            if(sbValue>0)
            {
            //将深度图像坐标转为彩色图像坐标
            Vector2 sbColor=manager.MapDepthPointToColorCoords(sbDepth, sbValue);
            //获取 x,y 轴的坐标值
```

```
            float xlNorm=(float)sbColor.x / manager.GetColorImageWidth();
            float ylNorm=1.0f -(float)sbColor.y / manager.GetColorImageHeight();
                    if(sbpo)
                        {
                            Vector3 sbOverlay=Camera.main.ViewportToWorldPoint(new
                                        Vector3(xlNorm, ylNorm, distanceToCamera));
                            sbpo.transform.position=Vector3.Lerp(sbpo.transform.position,
                                        sbOverlay, smoothFactor*Time.deltaTime);
                        }
                }
        }
//判断关节点是否被跟踪
    if(manager.IsJointTracked(userId, jJointIndex))
        {//获取左手关节点的空间坐标
            Vector3 lHandJoint=manager.GetJointKinectPosition(userId, jJointIndex);
            if(lHandJoint!=Vector3.zero)
        {//将空间三维坐标转为深度图像二维坐标
            Vector2 lHandDepth=manager.MapSpacePointToDepthCoords
                        (lHandJoint);
            ushort lHandValue=manager.GetDepthForPixel((int)lHandDepth.x,
                        (int)lHandDepth.y);

            if(lHandValue>0)
                {
            //将深度图像坐标转为彩色图像坐标
                Vector2 lHandColor=manager.MapDepthPointToColorCoords(lHandDepth,
                            lHandValue);
            //获取 x,y 轴的坐标值
            float xlNorm=(float)lHandColor.x / manager.GetColorImageWidth();
            float ylNorm=1.0f -(float)lHandColor.y / manager.GetColorImageHeight();
            if(lHpo)
                {
                    Vector3 lHandOverlay=Camera.main.ViewportToWorldPoint(new Vector3
                                (xlNorm, ylNorm, distanceToCamera));
                    lHpo.transform.position=Vector3.Lerp(lHpo.transform.position,
                                lHandOverlay, smoothFactor*Time.deltaTime);
                }
        }
}
```

```
            }
        }


                    //判断关节点是否被跟踪
                        if(manager.IsJointTracked(userId, kJointIndex))
                        {//获取右手关节点的空间坐标
                            Vector3 rHandJoint=manager.GetJointKinectPosition(userId, kJointIndex);
                                if(rHandJoint!=Vector3.zero)
                                {
                    //将空间三维坐标转为深度图像二维坐标
                            Vector2 rHandDepth=manager.MapSpacePointToDepthCoords(rHandJoint);
                            ushort rHandValue=manager.GetDepthForPixel((int)rHandDepth.x,
                                            (int)rHandDepth.y);
                            if(rHandValue>0)
                                {
                    //将深度图像坐标转为彩色图像坐标
                            Vector2 rHandColor=manager.MapDepthPointToColorCoords
                                            (rHandDepth, rHandValue);
                    //获取 x,y 轴的坐标值
                            float xrNorm=(float)rHandColor.x / manager.GetColorImageWidth();
                            float yrNorm=1.0f -(float)rHandColor.y / manager.GetColorImageHeight();
                            if(rHpo)
                            {
                            Vector3 rHandOverlay=Camera.main.ViewportToWorldPoint
                                            (new Vector3(xrNorm, yrNorm, distanceToCamera));
                            rHpo.transform.position=Vector3.Lerp(rHpo.transform.position,
                                            rHandOverlay, smoothFactor*Time.deltaTime);
                            }
                        }
                    }
                }
            }


                    //判断关节点是否被跟踪
                    if(manager.IsJointTracked(userId, lJointIndex))
                        {//初始化关节点的坐标
                            Vector3 lkneeJoint=manager.GetJointKinectPosition(userId, lJointIndex);
                            if(lkneeJoint!=Vector3.zero)
                                {
                    //将空间三维坐标转为深度图像二维坐标
```

```
            Vector2 lkneeDepth=manager.MapSpacePointToDepthCoords(lkneeJoint);
            ushort lkneeValue=manager.GetDepthForPixel((int)lkneeDepth.x,
                        (int)lkneeDepth.y);
                if(lkneeValue>0)
                {
//将深度图像坐标转为彩色图像坐标
                Vector2 lkneeColor=manager.MapDepthPointToColorCoords
                            (lkneeDepth, lkneeValue);
//获取 x,y 轴的坐标值
            float xrNorm=(float)lkneeColor.x / manager.GetColorImageWidth();
            float yrNorm=1.0f -(float)lkneeColor.y / manager.GetColorImageHeight();
                if(lKpo)
                {

Vector3 lkneeOverlay=Camera.main.ViewportToWorldPoint
                        (new Vector3(xrNorm, yrNorm, distanceToCamera));
            lKpo.transform.position = Vector3.Lerp (lKpo.transform.position, lkneeOverlay,
                            smoothFactor*Time.deltaTime);
                }
            }
        }
    }

            //判断关节点是否被跟踪
            if(manager.IsJointTracked(userId, mJointIndex))
                {//初始化关节点的坐标
                Vector3 rkneeJoint=manager.GetJointKinectPosition(userId, mJointIndex);
                if(rkneeJoint!=Vector3.zero)
                {
//将空间三维坐标转为深度图像二维坐标
                Vector2 rkneeDepth=manager.MapSpacePointToDepthCoords(rkneeJoint);
                ushort rkneeValue=manager.GetDepthForPixel((int)rkneeDepth.x,
                            (int)rkneeDepth.y);
                if(rkneeValue>0)
                {
//将深度图像坐标转为彩色图像坐标
Vector2 rkneeColor=manager.MapDepthPointToColorCoords
                        (rkneeDepth, rkneeValue);
//获取 x,y 轴的坐标值
            float xrNorm=(float)rkneeColor.x / manager.GetColorImageWidth();
```

```
            float yrNorm= 1.0f -(float)rkneeColor.y / manager.GetColorImageHeight();
                if(lKpo)
                {

                Vector3 rkneeOverlay= Camera.main.ViewportToWorldPoint
                            (new Vector3(xrNorm, yrNorm, distanceToCamera));
                rKpo.transform.position= Vector3.Lerp(rKpo.transform.position, rkneeOverlay,
                            smoothFactor*Time.deltaTime);
                }
            }
          }
         }
        }
       }
      }
    }
}
```

3. 判断是否与标准动作点重合脚本

具体定义如下：

```
public class triggerPoint：MonoBehaviour
    {
    void OnTriggerEnter2D(Collider2D other)
    {
        Globe.totalPoint++;
        Debug.Log(Globe.totalPoint);
    }

    void OnTriggerExit2D(Collider2D other)
    {
        Globe.totalPoint-;
    }
}
```

参 考 文 献

蔡瑞妍.基于Kinect的多点触控系统的设计与实现[D].大连:大连大学,2012.
成红艳.大规模古代士兵群体运动建模与仿真研究[D].西安:西安工程大学,2012.
崔玉超.陈氏太极拳发展阶段研究[D].郑州:郑州大学,2014.
崔周,杨旭.非物质文化遗产视角下的太极拳发展[J].贵州民族学院学报(哲学社会科学版),2012
    (1):77-81.
丁立芳.陈氏太极拳经典动作拳理的生物力学分析[D].石家庄:河北师范大学,2015.
宫可想.手部运动仿真技术的研究[D].北京:首都师范大学,2005.
谷枫.杨式太极拳练习者搂膝拗步下肢动作的生物力学分析[D].北京:北京体育大学,2004.
顾杰,王万宾,郭振兴,等.太极拳中膝关节弯曲的力学[J].中华武术·研究,2015,4(11):36-52.
何昆林.基于Kinect的三维人体快速建模与蒙皮动画研究[D].广州:华南理工大学,2014.
胡雁宾.优秀太极拳运动员二十四式太极拳主要动作的生物力学分析[D].北京:北京体育大学,
    2003.
姜南.杨式太极拳"野马分鬃"动作肩胸与骨盆旋移运动的生物力学分析[D].北京:北京体育大学,
    2010.
柯福军.三维人体建模理论研究及着装仿真初探[D].杭州:浙江大学,2004.
乐小燕,郑海滨.Kinect与Unity结合的人体骨骼控制方法[J].信息与电脑(理论版),2013(4):2-4.
李想.骨骼皮肤绑定技术的研究及实现[D].杭州:浙江大学,2006.
李晓丹,肖明,曾莉.人体动作捕捉技术综述以及一种新的动作捕捉方案陈述[J].中国西部科技,
    2011,10(15):35-37.
李亚昆.三维动画及运动仿真技术的研究[D].大连:大连理工大学,2004.
李宇放.基于Android平台的增强现实太极拳教学软件研究与开发[D].长春:吉林大学,2014.
李岳.分析陈式太极拳动作名称术语[J].民族传统体育,2013,3(27):141-144.
林伟峰.太极拳"云手"的运动学分析[D].福州:福建中医药大学,2013.
刘畅.三种骨骼动画蒙皮算法比较研究[D].广州:华南理工大学,2014.
刘雷.人体运动仿真建模方法研究[J].计算机仿真,2009,26(1):166-168.
马建晓,贺毅辉,夏凯,等.虚拟人运动建模中的逆向运动学方法研究[J].计算机技术与发展,2011,
    21(9):88-91.
彭莹.吴式太极拳弓步动作运动生物力学研究[D].北京:首都体育学院,2012.
钱锋,梅雪,林锦国.基于矩形骨架的人体动作识别[J].微计算机信息,2012,28(4):100-102.
申宏芬.战场环境三维视景仿真平台设计与实现[D].济南:山东大学,2013.
宋薇.基于物理模型的人体运动建模与仿真[D].武汉:武汉理工大学,2012.
陶许波.三维模型骨骼搭建方式的研究与讨论[J].科技展望,2015(3):160.

万齐亮.基于学习的逆向运动学人体运动合成[D].武汉:华中科技大学,2011.

汪丽.面向动作分析的虚拟人体建模研究[D].济南:山东大学,2006.

王若冰,姜敬敏.2003—2013年太极拳发展研究评述[J].搏击·武术科学,2014,11(11):12-14.

王少伟.基于3DS MaxScript三维角色动画与库插件的设计与开发[D].上海:上海师范大学,2012.

王晓燕,杨建营.太极拳的现代化分化发展[J].武汉体育学院学报,2014,48(4):49-55.

王院成.陈式太极拳:历史、现状与展望[J].焦作师范高等专科学校学报,2013,29(4):5-8.

吴晓军,刘伟军,王天然.基于八叉树的三维网格模型体素化方法[J].工程图学学报,2005(4):1-7.

夏时洪.人体运动仿真综述[J].计算机研究与发展,2010,47(8):1354-1361.

许之星.太极拳的多元发展策略[D].重庆:西南大学,2011.

杨震.基于3DS Max的人体软组织器官建模与仿真研究[D].西安:第四军医大学,2015.

姚翠莉,袁瑶等.Kinect在Unity平台上的开发实例[J].计算机光盘软件与应用,2014(12):3-7.

于涛.基于动作捕捉的太极拳数字化保护研究[D].广州:中山大学,2013.

余涛.Kinect应用开发实战[M].北京:机械工业出版社,2013:44-57.

张居峰.实体建模技术及其应用研究[D].西安:西安电子科技大学,2014.

张志勇.从太极拳技术演变的历史谈太极拳的起源与发展[J].体育学刊,2013,20(1):113-119.

赵朝阳,张徐亮.基于Kinect的人体行为分析系统[J].北京服装学院学报,2012(3):189-195.

赵蕾.从太极拳的演变论竞技太极拳的发展[D].郑州:河南大学,2007.

郅正.二十四式简化太极拳典型动作对人体脊柱和足底压力影响的初探[D].北京:北京体育大学,2005.

朱晓东,冯霞.太极拳发展研究综述[J].搏击·武术科学,2009,6(1):33-34.

Unity T. Unity 4.X从入门到精通[M].北京:中国铁道出版社,2013:89-259.

Will G. Unity Game Development Essentials[M]. Packt Publishing,2009:32-48.

Wren C,Azarbayejani A,Darrell T,*et al*. Real-time tracking of the humanbody[J]. IEEE Transactions on Pattern Analysis and Machine Intelligence,1997,19(7):780-785.